The Publicity Process

EDITED BY

James W. Schwartz

WITH CHAPTERS BY

Edmund G. Blinn
Richard L. Disney
Rodney Fox
Carl Hamilton
Robert C. Johnson
William F. Kunerth
Dwight L. Teeter
Donald E. Wells

James W. Schwartz is head of the Department of Technical Journalism, Iowa State University, Ames, Iowa. Contributing authors Edmund G. Blinn, Richard L. Disney, Rodney Fox, Robert C. Johnson, William F. Kunerth, and Donald E. Wells are members of the technical journalism staff. Carl Hamilton is director of university relations, Iowa State University, and Dwight L. Teeter is a member of the School of Journalism staff, The University of Wisconsin, Madison, Wisconsin.

The photographs on the title page and chapter openings are by Robert C. Johnson. The photographs in Chapter 6 are from 1000 Ideas for Better News Pictures *by Hugh Sidey and Rodney Fox, The Iowa State University Press, 1956.*

© 1966 The Iowa State University Press
All rights reserved. Composed and printed by The Iowa State University Press, Press Building, Ames, Iowa

First edition, 1966

Library of Congress Catalog Card Number: 66–26696

★ Contents

986   4

★ The Publicity Process

★ *Words may have meaning and impact or may merely lead to confusion. Skills in effective communication are essential to the publicity process.*

★ 1 ★ Effective Communication
Leads to Success

As you learn to use publicity techniques and public relations concepts with increasing skill and perception, you will find they can become a determining factor in winning success for your ideas, ambitions, or commodities—and for you, too. You may, for example, wish to promote or defend your political, social, or religious ideas, support or oppose a particular project, sell goods or services, try to establish something new, or defeat something you think is wrong. Whatever your purpose, the more you know about how to influence, direct, change, or manipulate public opinion the more likely it is that your efforts will be successful.

USE MASS MEDIA INTELLIGENTLY

One essential way to influence public opinion, hopefully in the direction you want it to take, is to provide accurate, adequate information that people can use in forming their decisions. Perhaps the most efficient and speediest avenue for conveying quantities of information to large groups of people is what we know as the mass media "network"—newspapers, radio-television, and magazines. Obviously, those persons who understand the needs of mass media and know a great deal about how the media operate will be in an especially favorable position to use effectively whatever knowledge they have acquired about the ways of publicity and public relations.

Because ours is a competitive world, you must assume that for every idea or cause you want to promote, for every product or service you want to sell, there will be people on the "other side." They will oppose your ideas, try to frustrate your causes, and offer products and services in competition with yours. If the opposition turns out to be more skilled than you in supplying information to the public through the mass media, they command a potent weapon that could well defeat you and your ambitions. To stay in the competition, you or somebody on "your side" had better be prepared to use public information and persuasion techniques with skill and force. It doesn't really matter whether the devices used and policies followed are called public relations, publicity, propaganda, advertising, or something else. All are forms of an organized effort to persuade people in a particular direction. This is not to say that all such organized efforts are successful. There have been too many spectacular failures for anyone to support that contention. But there is little doubt that intelligent use of the techniques of mass persuasion can be a powerful factor in determining the outcome of any competitive struggle.

IS MASS PERSUASION "BAD"?

Over the years, there has been widespread criticism of mass information and persuasion efforts, much of it justified. But don't let such criticism beguile you into believing that all mass persuasion methods are harmful to mankind. Actually, whether the techniques being used to achieve certain goals are "good" or "bad" is a complicated ethical question. If against the background of your religious, political, economic, and other beliefs, prejudices, and knowledge, the purposes of a specific public persuasion effort seem desirable, then you call those purposes good. If, on the other hand, the purposes seem undesirable, you call them bad. And so it is with all of society. Its many groups will hold a variety of viewpoints about the good or evil that may result from a specific persuasion effort.

In spite of the criticisms, however, organized attempts at mass persuasion are not going to fade away. As a matter of fact, they will continue to be an essential part of the way our society is going to work during the foreseeable future. That this should be true is entirely in keeping with an important democratic principle: *the open marketplace of ideas.* That concept argues that all facts, ideas, and opinions should be displayed in a common marketplace where citizens of a democracy can consider them and "buy" those that appeal. Although citizens may sometimes buy some inferior or wrong ideas in this ideological supermarket, it is contended that society eventually will select wisely that which is good because man is a rational being. The argument is both simple and direct, but it is basic to the theory of democracy.

PUBLICITY IN THE DEMOCRATIC PROCESS

The efforts of the publicity and public relations experts can be characterized as attempts to bring their ideas effectively into the open marketplace. Professional publicists will do their best, of course, to develop their ideas into attractive displays and to present them in the best possible light and with maximally attractive color. But their basic job consists nonetheless of bringing facts and ideas to the marketplace where they may be considered as part of the democratic process. As long as all ideas are equally free to be considered, the democratic process will be served by the professional persuaders. If great availability of money makes possible the more attractive and extensive display of some ideas, it can be argued that shrewd application of intelligence and skill can make less adequately financed displays of ideas contend successfully with their more affluent competitors.

As you acquire knowledge about the potentials and limitations of mass persuasion; about ways to work with newspapers, radio-television, and magazines; and about the techniques used by professionals, you can increase your effectiveness as a participant in the challenging job of displaying your ideas and the ideas of your organization in the marketplace. By so doing you will serve the causes in which you believe and at the same time have an active part in making the democratic process work.

In addition, by learning about the methods the professionals use in dressing up their displays in this marketplace, you will be better prepared as a rational member of a democratic society to select the most desirable and beneficial ideas. You also will be better prepared to take leadership in helping others to make wise choices from among the displayed ideas. Which ideas are selected and which are rejected by the individual shopper eventually determines the direction of public opinion, that all-important element in human affairs.

NEARLY EVERYONE USES PUBLIC RELATIONS

So vast are the efforts being made to influence public opinion in America today that ours has been called a public relations society. Many millions of dollars are spent annually by government, industry, labor, political parties, religious organizations, universities and institutions, special interest groups, charitable associations, and all sorts of other organizations to catch the attention of the public mind and influence it. At least 100,000 persons are engaged professionally in public relations activities alone, and many thousands more work in other communication jobs at the business of shaping public opinion.

As numerous as the full-time professional persuaders may be, however, they are outnumbered many times over by individuals who use publicity techniques on a part-time basis. The latter are members of that vast army of people in all walks of life who supply countless items of news to the media every day of the year; who arrange interviews, talks, and demonstrations for radio and television; who contribute pictures to newspapers and magazines; who create posters, window displays, and banners; who write and place advertising; and who in scores of other ways use publicity methods to sell their ideas and programs.

YOUR ROLE IN PUBLIC RELATIONS

Since it is not likely that you intend to work as a full-time persuader in public relations or advertising, your interest should be in knowing as much as you can about how the professionals work so as to improve your part-time efforts to promote whatever is important to you. You may, for example, work for government as an extension specialist, a conservation official, a recreation officer, or in some other capacity. In such jobs much of your success in persuading the public to accept your ideas will depend on your ability to get your story adequately told in the mass media. Or, as a landscape architect, you may become a specialist in urban planning and will need to know all you can about how to convince citizens that they should spend money for parks, playgrounds, and other improvements of a like nature. Or you may work for a commercial firm and need to know, on a part-time basis, how to promote the sale of your product or the goodwill of your community toward your company. If you go into education, you will be interested in promoting the welfare and public image of your school and some of its programs. Principals, teachers, and coaches have a special need for developing skills in practicing the arts of public relations. Whether yours is a public institution or a private firm, you will be deeply concerned with building a favorable image of the organization for which you work.

Quite aside from attending to the day-to-day requirements of your job, you are likely to become active in promoting the welfare of your political party, your church, your favorite charity. Or you may want to fight a condition that you regard as a blight on the community. You may, for example, want better parks, slum clearance, school improvement, more adequate fire and police protection, equal rights for all men, or any one of a hundred other undertakings that seem worthwhile to you and beneficial to society in general. In planning and carrying out any such campaign for change, one of your most important concerns will be the state of public opinion.

WHAT DO WE MEAN BY "PUBLIC OPINION"?

Just what is the nature of public opinion—that elusive entity that is supposed to be subject to influence and change? To answer that question fully would require that you read many books, selected from the hundreds that deal with the problem or with phases of it. By all means read as many of these books as you can; but even though you read them all, your insight into the nature of public opinion still will be imperfect. The reason is that authorities do not altogether agree about details. When you talk about the public, you talk about people. And people are extraordinarily complex creatures about whose behavior patterns and characteristics we know very little. The concept of opinion, too, is extremely complex, though it may seem simple enough to you. It is no wonder, then, that complete agreement as to the precise meaning of the term *public opinion* never has been reached by the authorities in journalism, psychology, sociology, public relations, advertising, political science, and related fields.

TERMS YOU'LL NEED TO KNOW

Still, before you and the authors of this book can communicate meaningfully about public opinion and the methods of influencing it, there must be a reasonable degree of mutual understanding as to what is meant by key terms. Without indulging in detailed discussions about the nuances of meaning debated by authorities in the field, here are informal definitions to indicate meanings of important terms as used in this book:

1. A *public* is a fairly large group of persons with a common interest or interests and with at least some degree of formal or informal organization. Just how many persons are required to make up a "fairly large" group is not specified, but the number probably involves a significant proportion of a community. All the people who live in a city, because they have common interests in such matters as police and fire protection and because they are organized, constitute a *public*. Within the city,

however, there are many *other publics*, such as a Republican public, a Roman Catholic public, a Masonic public, and so on. An individual may belong to several publics at the same time, including some local publics and other publics in the larger society of which his city is but a part.

2. A public differs from a *crowd*, which is just a group of people with only coincidental common interests and without any real organization. All the persons who happen to be sitting or walking in a park constitute a crowd. And all the persons watching a football game constitute a crowd rather than a public, in spite of their common interest in the sport and some slight degree of organization. Members of the Mickey Mantle fan clubs throughout the United States, on the other hand, would constitute a public rather than a crowd.

3. Both a public and a crowd differ from a *mob* which is a group dominated by irrational behavior.

4. An *opinion* is a conclusion held at a given time concerning a controversial matter. To say that a man holds an opinion is to say that he concedes there is at least one other conclusion that may be reached concerning the matter in question.

5. An opinion differs from a *belief*. One who holds a belief will not concede that any other conclusion properly can be reached.

6. Both an opinion and a belief differ from a *fact*, which is a statement that can be verified by impersonal means.

7. *Public opinion* is the expression of conclusions at a given point in time by a sizable and somewhat organized group or groups of persons. By means of interaction within groups and between groups a consensus is reached on an issue or a problem. That consensus emerges as public opinion—the device by which men formulate and express their common interests.

You may have been puzzled while reading the earlier parts of this chapter because such terms as *public relations, mass persuasion,* and *publicity* were apparently being used interchangeably. Adding to the possibilities for confusion is the similarity in meaning for such words as *propaganda, education,* and even *advertising.* As is true of the term *public opinion,* authorities never have reached full agreement on the specific meanings of these words. Again, here are informal definitions indicating how the terms are used in this text:

1. *Public relations* means a skilled, intelligent approach to the job of influencing public opinion in favor of a specific viewpoint, company, institution, cause, commodity, service, or something else. Public relations uses publicity, propaganda, advertising, and education as basic tools; but its program is much broader than merely getting information into publications and on radio-television. Public relations organizations typically create elaborate programs which involve such activities as speakers bureaus, charities and other good works, company picnics, bowling leagues, lobbying at legislative sessions, and so on. A public relations organization is interested in the public at large and in many lesser publics as well. A university public relations department, for example, is interested in publics made up of students, faculty, other employees, parents, taxpayers and/or donors, alumni, legislators, the community in which the school is situated, and many others. A corporation public relations department is interested in publics consisting of employees, stockholders, customers, dealers, legislators, the community in which a plant is situated, and others. Whether a public relations director or organization is interested in a company or corporation, school, church, or charity, one important function is to counteract as much as possible unfavorable rumors, or the adverse effects of unfortunate publicity resulting from disasters, scandals, or misfortunes. When adversity strikes a company or institution, the best action a public relations expert normally can take is to provide the press with full and accurate information about the unfortunate situation. To do otherwise is to invite an even greater amount of unfavorable publicity when the full story comes to light, as it almost certainly will.

2. *Publicity* is information prepared for widespread dis-

semination, usually by the mass media. Most publicity releases are scrupulously accurate. Publicity usually contributes at least something toward informing the public and it frequently presents highly significant and important news essential to the democratic process. Publicity is widely used by those who are engaged in public relations work. Because publicity is expected to play a part in building a favorable image of a company, an institution, or a cause, it typically contains news and information favorable to its sponsor but does not include or at least plays down unfavorable news. Since publicity characteristically favors one side, organization, or point of view over another or others, technically it must be considered propaganda.

3. *Propaganda* attempts to influence public opinion either favorably or unfavorably with respect to an idea or ideas, a company, an institution, a commodity, or something else. While the popular notion about propaganda is that it is universally bad, it more accurately might be considered either good or bad, depending upon the agreement or disagreement with its aims by the person making the decision. Sometimes propaganda efforts are concealed or disguised, but more often they are not.

4. Propaganda differs from *education.* Education attempts to furnish facts and a variety of viewpoints. Propaganda attempts to tell people what to think. Education provides people with material to think about and tries to stimulate thinking. But education and propaganda have so much in common that often it is almost impossible to determine whether a given persuasive effort amounts to one or the other. Much that the professional information specialist, publicist, public relations worker, propagandist, advertiser—call him what you choose— does is to furnish facts and ideas that can be used in the education process. Much of his output, therefore, can be classified as education.

5. Ethical *advertising* also is accurate and without falsehoods, although it presents only an argument in favor of the commodities, ideas, or services it promotes. Technically, advertising is propaganda for which space or

time in mass media or elsewhere has been purchased. It is used extensively in public relations activities. Responsibly done, advertising can contribute to the education and democratic processes.

SUMMARY

What do you need to learn if you are to find out how to promote and protect what is important to you? Whether you regard yourself as a part-time public relations worker, publicist, or even propagandist, don't think of yourself as an amateur. You shouldn't, because how well you achieve your goals will help to determine your success in the world. That fact should make you consider yourself a part-time professional.

The most basic task before you is to learn as much as you can about news values, what news is, how to write news stories, and what is expected of a news source. It is through well-timed news presented in the mass media that you have your best chance of getting your information and ideas before large groups.

You need to know something, too, about ethical problems involved in mass communication, about laws affecting publication, about the practices of advertising, about the history and traditions of the press. And if you are to be responsible in this vital task of influencing public opinion, you will be eager to learn about certain responsibilities you share with professional journalists and about the effects your efforts may have on society and democracy. Succeeding chapters will attempt to provide you with this information.

SUGGESTED READING

ABELSON, HERBERT I. *Persuasion.* New York: Springer, 1959.
CANFIELD, BERTRAND R. *Public Relations.* Homewood, Ill.: Irwin, 1964.
CUTLIP, SCOTT M., AND CENTER, ALLEN H. *Effective Public Relations.* New York: Prentice-Hall, 1964.
GILBERT, DOUGLAS L. *Public Relations in Natural Resources Management.* Minneapolis, Minn.: Burgess, 1964.

GORDON, GEORGE N., FALK, IRVING, AND HODNAP, WILLIAM. *The Idea Invaders.* New York: Hastings, 1963.

MARSTON, JOHN E. *The Nature of Public Relations.* New York: McGraw, 1963.

SAMSTAG, NICHOLAS *Persuasion for Profit.* Norman, Okla.: Univ. of Okla., 1957.

SCHOENFELD, CLARENCE A. *Publicity Media and Methods.* New York: Macmillan, 1963.

★ *These tools for writing are not all you need to produce your story. Knowledge of basic forms will make your news item more meaningful.*

★ 2 ★ You Need To Know
Two News Story Forms

MANY BEGINNING JOURNALISTS have the mistaken idea that there is something mysterious about the building of a news story. They don't realize that such a story follows a pattern they have been using all their lives. Consider the following breathless announcement by a 14-year-old:

"Jimmie Elingson got hit by a car this noon. He got a broken leg and a cut on the head. It was at Locust and 16th street. They took him away in an ambulance. The car driver didn't see Jimmie because he jumped out between two cars."

Fourteen-year-old Tom gave this bulletin-like, I-saw-it-with-my-own-eyes report to his fellow students as he rushed into class after lunch. In a manner of speaking, Tom was "writing" a news story, and he was doing a pretty good job of it. He was communicating basic information concisely. He was wasting no words on details or digressions.

Later, with the story "lead" out of the way, Tom would elaborate:

"You know Jimmie; he's in the seventh grade. He lives over at Gray and School streets. His dad's a lawyer. He's got a little sister and an older brother. The car that hit him was a green Ford with a 77 license. The man driving it was

alone. Jimmie yelled some. Both wheels of the car went right over him. A man from the filling station covered him up with a blanket. The police came . . . and then the ambulance. The man that hit Jimmie said his name was Larry Kinney and that he worked for an oil company. He said he just didn't see Jimmie until it was too late. He felt bad. He said he had a little boy, too."

Thus Tom, an eyewitness, "covered" the story adequately. Later—perhaps that evening—his listeners would read the newspaper or listen to radio or television to see what the police had to say, whether charges had been filed, and whether Jimmie might have been hurt more seriously than Tom had known.

YOUR PART IN THE NEWS STORY

If all news were as simple as that event, there would be little need for this chapter on how to write a news story. But it isn't. As the dramatic story of civilization unfolds from day to day and year to year, myriads of both simple and highly complex news situations are identified and reported by the mass media. You are a part of that ongoing story. Wherever you may go or whatever you may do, you will be making news yourself, or serving as a news source, or reporting news, or consuming news, or adapting the basic news story idea to any number of personal assignments.

As you will find, the well-written news story is a model of concise communication that is useful to anyone. The agronomist, the home economist, the scientist, the teacher, the coach, the engineer, the preacher, the doctor, or anyone else who has acquired and polished a skill in news writing all enjoy a distinct advantage over the person who has not. His "story"—whether it involves trying to teach or make a sale or explain a new discovery—will come through faster and more clearly if he has mastered the discipline required of a good reporter. He will get to the point quickly. He will not waste words. When he is through he will stop.

And chances are that his audience still will be with him.

Knowing the art of writing a news story, you will both write and speak more effectively in all areas. And learning to write accurately and objectively—as the news man must—will give you a new respect for fact, for truth.

JOURNALISM HAS A "STYLE"

Most persons have a background in English composition courses—and perhaps they also harbor an uneasy feeling that "journalism is different." Actually the journalist is as keenly respectful of good diction and clarity of expression as the English instructor; he is equally as pained by spelling errors and bad grammar.

To meet his particular requirements, however, the journalist will adopt some special writing or style characteristics. For example, if you are writing a straight news story—that is, reporting some event that has occurred or is anticipated—you probably will use shorter, less complicated sentences and shorter paragraphs than those you normally use in other writing. You also should be especially aware of the need for objectivity, accuracy, and brevity.

But journalism is not concerned solely with the spot news story. There are the interpretative account that usually carries the writer's name as a by-line, the opinion editorial, the depth report, the feature or color story, and others. One might be written in first person; another might have all the characteristics of the traditional short story except that it will be factual rather than fictional; still another might use the verbatim question-and-answer technique. Each offers its own opportunity for detail, color, and perhaps even suspense.

The point here is that no single mark distinguishes journalism from other forms of writing. You need not approach it as through there were some mystery about it. There isn't. But there are some "rules" and skills that will be emphasized and that will, if remembered and practiced, serve you well in a variety of ways.

YOU'LL USE TWO BASIC STORY FORMS

Although the information you receive from newspapers, magazines, radio, and television is as broad as the thoughts and activities of man himself, two basic story forms will serve for almost any reporting assignment.

1. The *straight* (or spot) news story, reporting events that have occurred or are about to occur.

2. The *feature* story, reporting ideas, discussions, interpretations, background, or human interest matters rather than strictly past or coming events.

READERS RELY ON THE STRAIGHT NEWS STORY

Typically, the straight news story reports political developments, labor and management relations, court actions, accidents, crime and other wrongdoing, deaths, public meetings and events, weather details, and the like. Such information is needed by citizens if they are to form intelligent decisions about their government. They also need facts of this sort in order to conduct business or to carry out their day-to-day affairs.

But the amount of spot news which exists is staggering, and the time a person has is limited. This means that the reader-listener places two conflicting demands upon his newspaper or news broadcaster: He wants to be *fully* informed, at least about certain events, and he also wants to be *concisely* informed. In other words, he wants the greatest possible amount of information in the shortest possible time or space.

A basic story form has developed over the years that attempts to meet that demand. This straight news story structure, called the *inverted pyramid*, tells the most important facts first and the least important ones last. As a result, any person who wants basic facts quickly can get them by absorbing the first paragraph or two, while one who wants more details can read or listen to the entire account.

THE LEAD INTRODUCES YOUR STORY

The most important element of the straight news story, then, is the beginning, or *lead*. It may be one paragraph long or even longer, but not uncommonly it will be a single sentence that summarizes the entire story. For example:

> A month-long drought was broken in the southwest quarter of the state yesterday when 3 inches of moisture fell during the day-long rain.

Because it sums up the important facts, this is known as a *summary lead*. It answers the primary questions the reader will ask of his news source. That is, it tells him *What* (drought broken), *Where* (in southwest quarter of the state), *When* (yesterday), and *How* (day-long rain). If the questions *Who* and *Why* had been significant to the story, these also would have been answered.

The summary lead does all this in the briefest possible fashion. The information reported in the foregoing example will satisfy many readers. But for a farmer or a grain dealer, this will not be enough. They will want to know what the rain means to crops at this stage of development, whether there were erosion losses, and other related facts. They will read on into the story. On the other hand, a city dweller may be satisfied with little more than passing attention to the lead paragraph, then will turn to some item on which he wants more details. And so it goes with the entire audience. In newspapers and broadcasting you must remember constantly that you are writing for the *general public* whose members have many diverse interests.

The summary lead can introduce almost any straight news story, big or little. Perhaps the most important single news story since World War II was the assassination in 1963 of President John F. Kennedy. Here was a typical lead on that staggering news event:

> President Kennedy and Gov. John Connally of Texas were gunned down by a hidden sniper as they drove out of downtown Dallas today in what had been a triumphal motorcade.

(AP's third-lead Kennedy—1:25 P.M.)

Millions of words were written and spoken in covering that event. Yet this one sentence told Who, What, When, Where, and How. The Why isn't known to this day.

In spite of the direct simplicity of the one sentence lead, however, there is nothing sacred about it. Some leads will take two sentences. Others, to be really complete, may require two, three, or even more paragraphs. Actually, there may be no clearly recognizable break as one moves from the lead into the body of the story—nothing that says, "There, we are through with the lead; now we will get down to the details." In most cases, however, a transition will be apparent. It occurs where elaboration of the lead facts begins.

Whether we discover that the lead we are writing is turning out to be one sentence or two paragraphs long, however, we cannot shirk the duty of fashioning a statement that summarizes the story quickly and clearly. It is the lead that captures the reader-viewer-listener's attention and entices him into the story.

In preparing to write a summary lead, ask yourself this question: "If I could use only 10 words (or even just 5) to tell my story, which 10 would I choose, and which would come first?" If you had been faced with the assignment of reporting the Kennedy assassination, for example, the first of your 10-word quota might well have come right out of those used on the actual story cited previously:

> President Kennedy . . . (was)
> gunned down . . . today.

Certainly that would be far more direct and emphatic than a lead which backed into the most important facts, as this one does:

> Today, as he was riding with Governor John Connally of Texas through the crowd-lined streets of Dallas, Texas, President Kennedy was shot.

As you sort out the facts you intend to use as a beginning for your story, therefore, think in terms of the Who, the What, the When, the Where, the Why, and the How. Almost always one or a combination of those elements is clearly the most important or the most significant fact. Frequently it is What happened (or will happen) to Whom under what circumstances? In any case, search for the standout information, *use it as a lead beginning,* and try to keep your lead as short as possible. You may write a

Who lead: Historian Alex Lightfoot will deliver a memorial lecture here today.

What lead: A new variety of soybeans was released by the state experiment station today.

When lead: Monday, Dec. 6, will be the first day that persons may apply for next year's auto licenses.

Where lead: Lake Pickett will be the site of the Fourth of July picnic sponsored by the local Chamber of Commerce.

Why lead: Because of sharp increases in university enrollment, a regular schedule of night classes is being introduced.

How lead: Plenty of sleep and an adequate diet were suggested today as the best way of avoiding the flu bug that is plaguing the campus.

Additional examples of summary leads could have been included to illustrate the infinite variety possible within this basic lead style. A more fertile approach, however, is for you to study newspapers or listen to news broadcasts to sharpen your eye and ear by identifying examples on your own. Most straight news stories begin with summary leads.

ORGANIZE YOUR NEWS STORY

The inverted pyramid story structure has advantages not only for the reader but also for the editor and the writer. You already know how convenient it is to find the most important facts packed into the first few paragraphs of a story. These may give the reader all the information he wants. But if he wants more details and has time to read them, they are there, too, in the latter part of the story.

The inverted pyramid also saves editors time. This is important, for newspapers and news broadcasts are fast-moving operations. Deadlines arrive within hours or minutes. How is time saved? Space (in a newspaper) and time (on radio-television) are at a premium, and to make news fit the available space or time, editors and makeup men frequently must shorten some stories. You know from experience how slow this job can be. When a report follows the inverted pyramid pattern, however, an editor can quickly cut off its final paragraph or paragraphs and feel secure in the knowledge that he is not discarding some essential fact.

The advantage of the inverted pyramid for the writer has to do with ease of story organization, for once the writer has familiarized himself with this story structure, he will find that almost any news event can be told efficiently and effectively with it. It is likewise a form that is easily learned because it represents the natural way to report an important story—the vital facts first, then those of progressively less significance as the account moves on toward its conclusion. If we were to diagram an inverted pyramid story structure, it would look this way:

SUMMARY LEAD

ELABORATION OF LEAD

DETAILS BECOME

LESS AND LESS

IMPORTANT

AS STORY

UNFOLDS

•

Do you see now why it is called the inverted pyramid?

It should be emphasized that a diagram can represent only an approximation of a typical news story's organization. Once the writer has completed his summary lead, he has to use his own best judgment about what comes next. His goal should be to tell the story as clearly and concisely as he can, moving smoothly from fact to fact in an orderly and logical manner.

That arrangement might be based on chronology (as in a play-by-play account of a football game), on priority (as in a speech report—the speaker's most important remarks may have come last in the speech but are first in the news report), or on sequence (as in any cause-and-effect situation). But however you may shape the body of your story, remember that the story as a whole demands *important facts first*.

Here is an example of a publicity release that begins with a summary lead and is developed in inverted pyramid body style:

From: American Society of Agricultural Engineers
Saint Joseph, Michigan 49085
The Julian J. Jackson Agency
11 S. LaSalle St.,
Chicago, Ill. 60603

For immediate release

The agricultural engineer's growing importance in our over-all economy and his broadening interests in a new age in agriculture will be explored at the 59th annual meeting of the American Society of Agricultural Engineers June 26–29 on the campus of the University of Massachusetts, Amherst, Mass.

The world food crisis, housing, water treatment and use, food processing and distribution, and educational specialization will be among the subjects discussed in addition to specific agricultural problems involving engineering.

A panel session on food freeze-drying will deal with the latest research developments in this technique, including applications for meats and Romano cheese. Methods for reducing air-borne contamination in freeze-drying and other food processing operations also will be explored.

In a symposium on water treatment and use, the sanitary hazards of farmstead and rural water system and plumbing connections and the problem of pesticides in farmstead water supplies will be considered.

An innovation at this year's ASAE annual meeting will be a special session on rural family housing. Papers presented at this session will suggest answers to housing problems that also affect other than farm families; for example, housing for the elderly, reduction of sound levels in family houses, economy housing for home and abroad, and home furnishings for gracious living.

More than 200 scientific papers will be presented at the meeting, including many reports on new machinery and techniques to speed full automation of food production on the farm from planting to warehouse or processing plant.

WRITE AS OBJECTIVELY AS POSSIBLE

The lead and story styles discussed thus far are so widely used in news reporting that learning how to use them at least passably well should be your first concern. But reporting involves one other less tangible concept. That is the principle of objectivity. Complete objectivity is no more possible in journalism than it is in any other human endeavor. We all tend to see things from our own point of view or in the light of our personal needs and desires. A soaking rain, for example, may appear as a disaster to the contractor who finds his freshly dug basement ruined by cave-ins. But to the farmer the same rain may mean the difference between crop failure and bumper yields. A story reporting this rain would be written differently in the contractor's trade paper than it would in a farm journal because each publication serves a different audience.

Regardless of where a story appears, it should be written as objectively as possible. This means the reporter attempts to be fair and impartial in selecting facts for emphasis and carefully attributes all statements of opinion to some authority or principal involved. Learning to report objectively is important. Learning to detect a lack of objectivity—as a consumer of news—is also important.

Let us take a simple example, using the accident story at the beginning of this chapter. Seventh-grader Jimmie Elingson is hit by a car. A reporter appears on the scene. The boy is crying, obviously in great pain. A broken leg hurts. There is blood on the pavement. The reporter could return to his office and write that "Jimmie Elingson was seriously injured this afternoon when hit by a car at the corner of Locust and 16th street."

But was he "seriously" injured? To Jimmie's mother (and to Jimmie) a broken leg and a cut on the head are no doubt serious. To the doctor, however, the injuries could be pretty routine. If the reporter is to be objective, he should not attempt to interpret the "seriousness" of the matter. He should simply report the broken bone and the cut on the head. If, on checking at the hospital, the reporter found that the injuries were indeed serious and some member of

the hospital staff would say so, then the story would go
something like this:

> Jimmie Elingson, 13, son of
> Mr. and Mrs. Bert Elingson, 123
> Gray, is reported in serious con-
> dition at St. Anthony's Hospital
> as the result of an accident at
> the corner of Locust and 16th
> street this afternoon.
> Dr. James McArthur said the
> boy suffered internal injuries
> when he stepped from between
> two cars and was hit by an auto
> driven by Larry Kinney of 1319
> Jefferson St., Moberly, Mo.

The principle observed here is known as *attribution*.
The "seriousness" is attributed to some authority, because
it is an expression of a judgment or viewpoint. A story saying that "Dr. Jonathan Cluber gave an interesting talk at
the West Side PTA meeting on the subject of school drop-
outs" will cause the alert editor to run his pencil through the
word "interesting." The talk may have interested you; it
may have been an utter bore to everyone else in the room.

So much for the basic form of the straight news story.
We are not finished, however. As do many newsmen, we
may talk of a second basic story form and call it the *feature
story*.

THE FEATURE DEMANDS CAREFUL HANDLING

It is true that journalists use the term *feature* in several
ways. They sometimes use it to describe almost anything
that goes into the newspaper except the straight news story
or news picture. Crossword puzzles, cartoons, and advice-
to-the-lovelorn columns, for instance, are features in this
sense. In another setting, a news chief may ask a subordi-
nate, "What'll we feature today?" In effect, he is asking,
"What can we use for today's main story?"—the story that

will go at the top of page one or will take the most important position in a broadcast. The discussion that follows, however, will concern itself with a third meaning—the meaning that a reporter grasps when his chief orders, "Let's do a feature story on the new fire station," or, "Find a feature angle and do something on the state fair."

How does such a *feature story* differ from the *straight news story*? We have learned that a writer, as he works his way through a straight news story, is trying to give a report of important facts, as quickly and efficiently as he can and with a priority order in mind. The writer of a feature story, on the other hand, has something else in view. He may have relatively small concern about how many facts he can jam into a reader's mind—or how fast. Indeed, in contrast to the inverted pyramid story, some feature stories are written so that the most important fact of all—the "punch line," so to speak—comes last.

All of this means that feature stories can seldom be trimmed safely by an editor who arbitrarily strikes away the last sentences or paragraphs, as he would be able to do with the inverted pyramid story. Essential facts may be lost if he does so. The editing of a feature story, therefore, must be a skillful *internal operation* rather than a bit of mechanical surgery that begins with the tip of the story's tail and moves upward through its body.

Feature stories are most commonly found in magazines and in the magazine supplements of Sunday newspapers. But they are regular and important fare as well in daily and weekly newspapers and in broadcasting. The story form is ideally suited for background reports on the news, interpretative pieces, human interest accounts, broadcast documentaries, and opinion and personality interviews. It even adapts well to those bright little oddity stories in newspapers and news broadcasts that oftentimes are based on spot news but really are more a commentary on the human condition than they are a straight news report.

FEATURE LEADS AROUSE INTEREST

Like straight news accounts, feature stories must have leads. These come in as many shapes and sizes as there are people to write them, but the better leads tend to be short and to arouse the audience's self-interest or human interest impulses. An example might grow out of the discovery that the governor would be sworn into office on his birthday:

> Hugh Johnson will get a new chair for his forty-sixth birthday. It will be behind the governor's desk at the state capital where he will be sworn in on January 4—46 years to the day following his birth on an Adair County farm.
>
> The governor's mother, reached at her home on the same farm where Gov. Johnson was born, said that this event was "beyond her greatest hopes" and that she couldn't think of a "nicer birthday present for either a son or his mother."

From this point on the story could be developed into a biographical sketch recounting other important developments that had occurred on the governor's previous birthdays and his age in relation to others who had held the office. The alert reporter might also check the age of the governor's chair to discover whether it was as old as or older than the governor himself.

Obviously, the lead on this story does not attempt to summarize the who, what, when, where, why, and how of gubernatorial ceremonies. Instead, the writer has chosen an unusual human interest angle and attempted to arouse with it the reader's or listener's curiosity and to lead him into the story. The account itself makes no attempt to single out the most important items for early treatment although it may have singled out the most interesting.

Here are additional examples of leads on feature stories:

> They say lightning never strikes twice in the same place, but it does! Lightning kills more than 400 farmers and destroys thousands of farm build-

ings every year. And most of those deaths and losses can be prevented.

The young homemaker in America today appears to be a breed of woman unlike any before in history.

Judi Browne, national baton twirling champion, says learning to twist and twirl at the same time "just comes naturally—if you've got rhythm."

That old jalopy in Leonard Wood's garage at 1418 West Street is ready to roll again.

When the Fine Arts Committee opens its first annual Art Fair next Monday, the work of nine Bayville residents will be among the 173 original canvases on display.

And here is an example of a complete feature story:

CLARINDA—Having families of six children, working at two full-time jobs, and living 40 miles from college facilities haven't stopped two Imogene men from continuing their education.

Bill Ditmars, 38, and James Skahill, 42, make the 80-mile round trip from Imogene each Monday, Wednesday, and Friday to attend two classes at Clarinda Community College.

They both work nights at Union Carbide in Red Oak. Both have other businesses in Imogene (Ditmars in the bottle gas business and Skahill operating a grocery-hardware store), and both have six children anxious for free moments with dad.

"We really see more of our families than you might think," they pointed out. "When we have a free evening, we really make good use of the time. While some people may go bowling on a free night, we plan to stay home and enjoy our families."

On the three days they have classes, the two men are away from home nearly 18 hours. They leave Imogene before 10 A.M. to make their 11 o'clock class at CCC. With their afternoon class finished about 3 P.M., they are off to Red Oak to work a full eight-hour night shift at Union Carbide. And by the time they get home, it is usually 3–3:30 in the morning.

ADVANTAGES OF THE FEATURE

Feature stories normally do not depend upon spot news developments, although they may well be based on news breaks. Therefore they have, relatively speaking, a timeless quality that is not enjoyed by the straight news story. The latter must be published as soon as possible after the event occurs or, in the case of anticipated events, properly timed prior to the incident. Failing this, the news can become stale in a matter of hours, or it may be published so far ahead of the event that it lacks interest for the consumer. Feature stories, on the other hand, often can be held for publication until space or time becomes available—providing, of course, that the subject matter remains relevant. The story about the Imogene men, for example, could be published at any time within a period of several months. The story does not depend for its existence upon the occurrence or anticipation of any particular news event.

The self-interest or human interest appeal so typical of

feature stories can be of great value to the teacher, the salesman, or anyone who places importance on face-to-face communication. The salesman may use it to capture the client's
attention when a straight hard sell might get him pitched
out the door. Good speakers frequently use such an appeal
to gain quick attention. The scientist may have special need
to use the appeal of self-interest or human interest as he
attempts to inform laymen about a subject in which their
interest is slight. Business uses it in advertising. Teachers
use it constantly, or attempt to. Developing the skill to
write a dynamic human interest lead should be just as important as learning how to summarize the five W's and an
H for the straight news story.

Just as there are no hard and fast rules for developing
the straight news story, there likewise are none for organizing the feature story. It can build to a climax, develop in a
first-second-third order, take advantage of the way an interview progressed, or assume any one of many other structural forms. As you read your newspaper or listen to your
favorite news broadcaster, identify the feature stories and
analyze (1) how the leads were written and (2) how the
stories were organized. You will find this a diverting game,
and you will be learning at the same time.

The information upon which you base your stories for
the media is collected in a variety of ways—from speeches,
through interviews, by observation, and through research.
Somewhat different approaches are needed by the reporter
covering an event like a football game simply by observing
it and by the reporter covering a speech for which a text
may or may not be available. But by learning the two general reporting forms emphasized here—the straight news
story and the feature story—you will be acquiring a basic
skill that can be readily adapted to the requirements of the
mass media—newspapers, broadcasting, magazines. (Because of the special considerations that must be given to researching, writing, and marketing magazine articles, all of
Chapter 8 is devoted to that subject.)

USING LANGUAGE EFFECTIVELY

Thus far in this chapter we have been talking about
leads and story arrangement. Now we should talk about

language and how it can be used most effectively. Because this is such a broad subject, we can suggest here only a few relatively simple guidelines.

Know Your Audience

Identifying the audience you intend to reach is the first and most important step in deciding which words to use and how to arrange them (for a discussion of the communication process, see Chapter 10). In a professional journal or specialized magazine reaching an already well-informed and highly educated audience, it is possible to use longer sentences and a more specialized language or jargon than would be wise in the typical news story. But that does not mean that writing a news story is a simple process for simple-minded people. On the contrary it is, although a straightforward task, one which is very exacting. An enormously wide range of subject matter—the whole spectrum of the day's news—must be presented in a way that will appeal to and be understood by a cross section of the local population.

Choose Words Your Readers Know

Use simple, direct language in ways that will draw the clearest possible picture in the shortest possible space or time. The reporter who is conscious of his audience will use words, phrases, sentences, and concepts that are familiar to his consumers and do not greatly exceed their level of education. When it is possible to do so, for example, he uses the simple rather than the difficult word. In conversation, people say "buy" more often than they do "purchase." They also will prefer "need" to "requirement." In spite of this, however, the right word, the one that says precisely what you want it to say, is more important than using the simple or easy word. If a "big" word is called for, use it.

Build Active Sentences, Paragraphs

Strive for variety in both sentence length and structure. There is no ideal sentence length, of course, and a series of sentences of equal length is a sure path to monotony. Mix them up. Make some short, some medium in length, and a few on the long side. Generally speaking, average sentence length in news stories tends to be less than the average in most magazines, books, and other written material. Widely read newspapers, news magazines, and other publications have an average sentence length of from 16 to 20 words. Magazines that appeal to a more sophisticated and, presumably, better-educated audience may go substantially above that average. Regardless of audience, however, most writing can be improved by shortening sentences and varying sentence length. That 16- to 20-word average is a good figure to keep in mind.

For vigor and emphasis, you should make most of your sentences declarative in form. Cast them in the active voice rather than the passive. "The dog bit the cat" is a stronger statement than "The cat was bitten by the dog." Not only are direct sentences forceful but they also are less likely to suffer from the burden of vague and needless words.

Don't let your paragraphs get out of hand. The guide for paragraph length is much the same as that for sentences. Build them around a topic sentence and concentrate on only one major idea. Remember, too, that when a paragraph exceeds four typewritten lines, it is getting pretty long for newspaper use or for easy reading by a radio-television announcer.

Quotations Add Interest, Drama

Put "conversation" into your story. Most people feel that talking is easier than reading. So they feel that "talk" in print is easier reading than other print and are more comfortable with direct quotations and indirect quotations than with straight exposition. Conversation helps in another way, too. Letting your audience know that "this is what the story source said" adds both a human quality and authority. Because the reporter seldom finds it practical to get accurate and extensive direct quotations unless he is getting his information from a printed text or a tape recording, he uses such direct quotations sparingly. He tends to be rather liberal, however, with paraphrases and indirect quotations.

Direct quotations may be handled in several ways. You may use a complete, verbatim quotation:

> "Americans who oppose foreign aid on the ground that it is unpatriotic to spend American

> dollars on un-American causes
> are playing with fire," Rep. Carl
> Smith (R) charged here last
> night.

You may eliminate irrelevant parts of the speaker's statement, indicating omission:

> "Americans who oppose foreign aid . . . are playing with
> fire," Rep. Carl Smith (R)
> charged here last night.

You may even choose to quote only a cogent word or phrase and paraphrase the rest of his statement:

> Opponents of foreign aid are
> "playing with fire," Rep. Carl
> Smith (R) charged here last
> night.
> Smith also said he was a
> "possible" candidate for the Republican nomination for governor next year.

("Possible" is quoted to emphasize Smith's status.)

If you quote someone and his remarks extend over one paragraph, handle it this way:

> "Every American citizen has
> a sworn obligation to uphold
> the foreign policies set by the
> administration in power," Rep.
> Carl Smith (R) declared here
> last night. "That is the first and
> foremost requirement in today's
> complex world.
> "To oppose a united front
> against our Communist enemy
> is to strike a fatal blow in the
> midsection of our foreign policy."

Although the attributive phrases appear at the end of sentences in the foregoing examples, they don't have to do so. For the sake of variety and rhythm they can and should

appear just as frequently in the middle of quoted or para-
phrased sentences or even, at times, at the beginning:

> "Debate over foreign policy,"
> Representative Smith asserted,
> "should end at our shores."
> The Congressman empha-
> sized that he was not recom-
> mending that free discussion be
> stifled, only that it is essential
> that "we speak as one voice
> abroad."

In paraphrasing (not using direct quotations but putting the speaker's comments in your own words) accuracy
of meaning is vital. Be sure your summary faithfully reflects what someone has said. Furthermore, be sure of the
accuracy of the attributives you use—such phrases as *he
said, he observed, he commented, he added, he stated, he
pointed out, he emphasized, he declared.* A variety of attributives is desirable as long as they accurately reflect what
the speaker was doing, but remember that "he said" is still
the best one of all.

EDITORS LIKE CORRECTLY PREPARED COPY

As you write your publicity story, observing the following suggestions for mechanical presentation will assure a
favorable reception when you submit it to the newspapers
and broadcasting stations you select as outlets:

1. All news copy—for whatever use—should be double-
   spaced on one side only of 8½ x 11-inch white paper
   and should begin 2 or 3 inches down from the top of
   the first page. Set your typewriter for a 60-space line.
   Typed copy will have a better chance of being used,
   and correctly, than will handwritten copy. But if it
   has to be handwritten follow the same rules.

2. Do not erase on typed copy. Simple XXXX out the section you want deleted and go on. If you misspell a
   word, XXXX it out and spell it correctly unless the error

is simply a transposition of characters. Correct errors of that sort this way: toꝺy.

3. In the upper left corner of the first page, put your name and telephone number. Just beneath your name include a few words indicating the subject matter covered in the story: Chamber of Commerce Meeting . . . Football practice begins . . . Night school opens Sept. 9. If date of publication is important to the news value of the story, type DO NOT RELEASE BEFORE . . . and the date. Otherwise, type FOR IMMEDIATE RELEASE.

4. If your story runs more than one page, center the word "more" at the bottom of Page 1 and continue your account about 2 inches down from the top of Page 2. In the upper left corner of the second and succeeding pages, write "Page 2—Chamber meeting." At the close of the story, center the word "End" or "-30-" below the final paragraph.

5. Never put more than one story on a sheet of paper, even if the story is only one paragraph long.

6. Do not attempt to write headlines for your news stories. You have no idea of the headline size and style the editor will want, and broadcasters do not normally use headlines. Neither is it wise to demand that a story carry a particular headline or that it appear on a certain page in the newspaper. The editor will do the best he can and his judgment will be better than yours.

7. On stories being prepared for either broadcast or newspaper use, do not try to guess when the material will appear by referring to dates as "tomorrow" or "yesterday" or "Wednesday." Instead, report the event as being held (or to be held) on Wednesday, Dec. 15. The editor or news broadcaster will change that to suit his timing, whereas if you have labeled it "tomorrow"— even though your copy is dated—he still may be uncertain.

8. Write as much of your copy as you can and use the telephone as little as possible. Phones, next to type-

writers, are the most used pieces of equipment in a newsroom. But expecting newsmen to take long items or many items over the telephone only invites errors and disappointment. Write it out—and *get it in early.*

9. You may feel that a picture would help your story or that your news event might well be worth a picture. Call the editor and ask him. Perhaps you can take a picture or have one taken that will be suitable. If you ask some member of the news staff to serve as photographer, do this one thing above all else: Say specifically *when* the picture can be taken and then arrange matters so that it can be taken promptly when the photographer arrives. Making a newsman wait through an hour-long business meeting, in which there is no news, to take a picture of the newly elected officers will not improve your public relations with the media.

10. Check all names, dates, places, and other vital facts for accuracy.

SUMMARY

Preparation of material according to the suggestions given in this chapter will not automatically guarantee publication, but it will help. Busy editors and broadcasters are always on the lookout for news, but usually don't have time to rewrite badly written copy or check out fuzzy information. If the copy you submit appears technically professional and is dependable, you will find the news media more than willing to cooperate with you and your organization— both now and in the future.

SUGGESTED READING

ALSOP, JOSEPH AND STEWART. *The Reporter's Trade.* New York: (Reynal & Co.) Morrow, 1958.

AULT, PHILLIP H., AND EMERY, EDWIN. *Reporting the News.* New York: Dodd, 1959.

CAMPBELL, LAURENCE, AND WOLSELEY, ROLAND. *How To Report and Write the News.* Englewood Cliffs, N.J.: Prentice-Hall, 1961.

CHARNLEY, MITCHELL V. *Reporting.* New York: Holt, 1959.

FOX, RODNEY. *Agricultural and Technical Journalism.* Englewood Cliffs, N.J.: Prentice-Hall, 1952.

STRUNK, WILLIAM, JR., AND WHITE, E. B. *The Elements of Style.* New York: Macmillan, 1959.

WARD, WILLIAM B. *Reporting Agriculture.* Ithaca, N.Y.: (Comstock) Cornell, 1959.

★ *What makes front-page headlines? A "nose for news" is the mark of a crack reporter.*

★3★ Develop Your News Sense

LEARNING THE FUNDAMENTALS of news story writing is important, but the successful publicist or public relations specialist soon finds that good writing alone will not sell his material to the mass media. What editors are looking for, in addition to competent writing, is that elusive commodity we call "news."

The professional journalist knows that his customers want news and are willing to pay for it. Every day, people buy newspapers and magazines by the millions of copies and tune their radio and television sets to favorite news broadcasts. They seem to have an insatiable appetite for news and information. They want facts about hundreds of matters that may affect them and their existence, either directly or indirectly. In plain words, they want to know what is going on—and what it means.

RECOGNIZE NEWS PEOPLE WANT

A number of writers have reasoned that people want news because it offers a reward. They say further that the reward is of two kinds—*immediate* and *delayed*.[1] Immedi-

---

[1] For a discussion of the "immediate and delayed reward" concept see Wilbur Schramm, "The Nature of News," *Journalism Quarterly*, Sept. 1949, Vol. 26, No. 3, p. 259.

ate-reward news is the sort that appeals to the emotions. It might be the young couple killed in an auto accident on the way to their wedding, or the little boy found wandering in the woods unharmed, or the championship golf match, or the bank cashier who embezzled a half-million dollars from his employer. The public identifies closely with such events because the occurrences relate meaningfully to personal experience. The identification is a vicarious one, to be sure, but it is there all the same. In psychological terms, the public empathizes with immediate-reward news.

Delayed-reward news, on the other hand, involves information that will have a long-term or future effect. In this category would be reports of governmental policy, economic trends, changes in educational methods, scientific discovery, and the like. Undoubtedly there is some immediate reward in such news, but its full impact on the public will be experienced later. Because the real significance of delayed-reward news can be missed at the outset, the consuming public tends to pay less attention to it than to stories that have a direct emotional effect.

At times, of course, there is no real line of separation between the two types of news. A single news story might very well have both immediate- and delayed-reward implications. As a matter of fact, some persons argue that all news involves immediate reward, and some news has elements of both. In any event the reward theory at least helps to explain why the public bothers with news at all.

A primary purpose of the mass media is that of conveying these sought-after facts to a waiting public as quickly, accurately, and completely as possible. But because competition for the available time and space is great, the well-written publicity story that is based on real news is much more likely to be accepted and used than is the equally well-written story that is short on news or amounts to little more than empty puffery.

As a general rule, in fact, even the poorly written story that is packed with news has a better chance of being published than does the well-written account that lacks this essential ingredient. The former story may have to be rewritten and that takes time. But the editor knows it offers something potentially valuable to his audience and that justifies spending a reasonable amount of rewrite time shaping the story to fit his requirements.

YOU CAN MEASURE NEWS VALUES

If the news ingredient is so important, how does one recognize it? For some this is comparatively easy. They seem to have that "nose for news" that is the mark of a crack reporter. For others, the task is more difficult. The story is told of the music critic who was assigned to review the premiere of an opera one evening for his newspaper. When he arrived at the theater the critic learned that the performance had been cancelled because the star had taken poison. No opera, he reasoned, no story, so he returned home without writing a word and without notifying his newspaper. The unhappy consequence was that the newspaper was scooped by every one of its competitors—and its naive critic learned a hard lesson in what, besides musical performances, makes news.

Whether that story is true is not really important. The point is that, while news *patterns* may change rather drastically over the years, the *yardsticks* that editors apply in measuring news values remain relatively standard. Almost all books on professional reporting devote a section to this question, and most of them agree that news possesses certain qualities. These include:
1. Importance or significance.
2. Unusualness or uniqueness.
3. Recency or timeliness.
4. Proximity.
5. Human interest.

Importance or Significance

Although these terms are not synonymous, there is enough overlap in the way they apply to particular news situations to warrant discussing them together. The death of an obscure person, for example, will be important to those close to him and may have lasting significance for them as well. But the event will be of no particular importance or significance to the world at large. The death of a national leader, on the other hand, will be enormously important and significant to millions. It will be important to all those who were subject to his far-flung influence and significant because it raises questions about the continuation of policies and programs for which he was responsible.

When the route of a new superhighway is announced, the news is crucially important to those persons living along its projected path. Overshadowing the announcement's short-run importance, however, will be the long-run significance to the many communities that are destined to thrive or wither because of the economic effects of the new thoroughfare. Similarly, passage of federal civil rights legislation was an event of great importance at the moment the required number of votes were cast. But the bill's significance is measured in the effect its provisions are having and will have on the country's conduct and institutions.

What applies on a large scale also is true of lesser situations. When the Community Chest drive reaches its dollar quota, the successful conclusion to the campaign is important to the community's pride and self-respect. The significance, on the other hand, lies in how that money is spent, who is to benefit, and whether the community gets its money's worth.

The point being stressed here is that editors are alert to both of these qualities when they evaluate news events. The greater a story's relative importance and significance for the editor's audience, the more likely it is that he will find the space or the time to publish the details.

Unusualness or Uniqueness

It is almost axiomatic that editors are not particularly interested in the commonplace. But if that is so why do news media carry accounts of auto accidents, weather conditions, conventions, crime, public celebrations, strikes, marriages, fund drives, demonstrations, fires, social affairs, sports events, and all manner of other everyday occurrences? Are these not usual rather than unusual? Not really. Unquestionably, they are an expected part of the passing scene, but each one affects a different person or set of persons, occurs under different conditions, changes with time, contributes new information, and so on. In that sense each is unique unto itself.

As an example, let us consider what perhaps is the most familiar of all ongoing stories—the weather. Not only do newspaper readers expect an account of the weather they experienced yesterday, they also want a prediction of what is to come. These same people tune their radio sets to almost any station to hear up-to-the-minute reports on what the weather is now and what it is expected to be through the next 24 hours or so. They may even subscribe to magazines or buy almanacs that predict the weather for the next six months or year. At times the weather takes a sudden turn—a drenching downpour, a devastating windstorm, a crippling snowfall, a damaging hailstorm, a prolonged drought, a howling tornado. Everyone knows these things happen sometimes but when they do they are so uncommon for the affected region that what was being handled as a routine story becomes an event of major consequence and is featured accordingly.

What pertinence does this question of unusualness have to the publicity process? Perhaps another example or two will help to illustrate its application. A state fair occurs routinely every year, normally in the fall, and can be expected to receive a moderate amount of publicity in the press announcing the various crowd-pulling events. But suppose the fair managers are fortunate enough to obtain the country's two major presidential candidates as speakers. That "master stroke" alone would greatly amplify the amount of publicity carried by the state's news media—before, during, and after the candidates' appearances.

Similarly, thousands of communities stage benefits of all descriptions every year, and the sponsors expect news media to cooperate in promoting these events with a reasonable amount of publicity. But the publicity chairman who hits upon the unusual or novel attention-getting feature for his community's affair will be the one who maximizes its publicity potential. He must be careful not to resort to the ridiculous, or he can kill the news value of the event just as surely as intelligent application of the unusual can increase it. There is no denying that the gimmick and the stunt will capture at least a limited amount of short-run publicity.

But that sort of unusualness soon wears thin. Over the long haul, there is no adequate substitute for substance—either in the publicity project itself or in the stories reporting it.

Recency or Timeliness

Each of these two terms embraces the same general concept but in somewhat different ways. That is, a story ought to have the quality of freshness, of newness, if it is to qualify as news. As anyone in the profession knows, the here-today-gone-tomorrow character of news means that it tends to go stale in a hurry and therefore must be published as soon after it occurs as possible. Charles Dickens illustrated the point well in this passage from *A Tale of Two Cities:* The "waves of four months had rolled over the trial for treason, and carried it, as to the public interest and memory, far out to sea. . . ."

Some information, however, is of such a specialized and enduring nature that immediate publication is not necessary or perhaps even desirable. Its news value will be greatest if it is published at an especially appropriate time. Let us examine these two principles more closely.

A five-day-old fire would be considered recent and publishable in a weekly newspaper, but probably would be rejected as outdated information by a daily newspaper staff. Similarly, yesterday's political speech qualifies as recent information for a morning daily but might well be discarded by newsmen in a radio or television station, where the emphasis is on what is happening today or even on what occurred during the last hour. A monthly magazine, on the other hand, may base its content on recent developments but will concentrate on the significance and the application rather than on the news itself.

Still, recency, does not always require that events occur within the immediate past. Though years or even centuries had gone by since the original event took place, uncovering new facts or reinterpreting old ones would satisfy the recency principle. Discovery in 1954 of the Dead Sea Scrolls, for example, proved to be news of the highest order, as did their subsequent translation. Unearthing the ruins of an ancient city periodically rates extensive coverage by news media throughout the world. In England, Stonehenge monument has stood on Salisbury Plain since prehistoric times, but every new interpretation of its origin and meaning continues to be newsworthy. In each of these instances, the news had its genesis thousands of years earlier, but present-day developments give it the quality of recency.

Timeliness, on the other hand, refers to information that is especially appropriate at the moment of publication. For example, there is little point in reporting new corn borer control methods in the dead of winter, since the farmer has many other more important concerns during that season of the year. But he will find information of that sort highly pertinent and newsworthy if it is published when he can put it to immediate use. The same reasoning suggests that it does not make a great deal of sense to seek publicity for a project or an event too far ahead of the time the audience is supposed to become involved. They will not be the least interested in it. In other words, timing becomes extremely important. Remember always that your publicity is competing with all the other messages being aimed at the group you want to reach. If they are like the rest of us, they will be inclined to select those messages that seem most immediately vital to them and to reject or pay only slight attention to the rest.

Applying the principles of recency and timeliness to publicity situations is not difficult. If an extended campaign involving several stories is planned, discuss timing wth representatives of the various media and remember to treat all competing media fairly. If only a one-time announcement is involved, schedule it for release at a time that will assure the widest possible distribution and get it into the hands of those being asked to publish it well ahead of the release date. Finally, if an event of some sort is being staged, deliver your follow-up stories to the media without delay.

Proximity

In analyzing the quality of proximity, both physical and psychological nearness must be considered. It is obvious to anyone who thinks about the matter at all that, generally speaking, local news will attract more interest from the home-town audience than will news from afar. After all, we are naturally more interested in the people, objects, events, and issues surrounding us than we are in the remote and far away. We have a strong sense of personal involvement in the former but less in the latter. In other words, local affairs are likely to possess both physical and psychological proximity.

People, objects, events, and issues can be clustered around us psychologically even though they are far away geographically. A war may be raging thousands of miles from our shores; but if our countrymen are involved in it, that conflict moves ever so much closer to us psychologically. And if a close relative is in the battle zone, our deep concern for his welfare may make that remote struggle more important to us than anything purely local could be. Likewise, the tax story from Washington or the state legislature's decision to require written tests of all motorists applying for a driver's license would have psychological proximity for us because we would be directly affected.

The publicity process is subject to these same "rules." The perceptive publicity man knows that his work begins at home—that he should search out and take full advantage of what professional newsmen call the local angles. Suppose you were faced with planning a publicity campaign. You might find it helpful to picture the total area you want to reach as a gigantic wheel. At the hub is the local audience— the people most likely to have the greatest interest in what you have to say. That hub could involve a single community, a county, several counties, or even an entire state.

Once you identify what this local (or hub) audience is, that is where you will concentrate your heaviest publicity effort, and you will rely primarily on the news media whose circulations are diffused chiefly among the people who make up this audience. In the case of a single community, that will mean the newspapers and broadcasting stations located in that community or near enough to regard it as part of the primary coverage area. If the audience you want to reach is spread throughout an entire state, you will want your publicity to appear in the newspapers, broadcasting stations, and other appropriate media serving that state. This latter situation presents some rather complex coverage problems, and you will be well advised to seek professional advice and help in planning and carrying out your publicity campaign.

As your potential audience begins to thin out along the spokes toward the theoretical rim of the wheel, you will invest progressively less time and effort on publicity. The reasoning is quite simple. The farther away you get from the hub, the less audience interest and participation there is likely to be. Beyond the rim, it is useless to spend any time at all on publicity. You will simply be wasting energy that could be directed much more profitably toward designing and scheduling publicity messages aimed at the primary (local) audience.

To restate the proximity principle: Look for ways to localize your messages, to "bring home" the substance of your publicity in both the geographical and psychological sense.

Human Interest

Stories that evoke an emotional response are said to have human interest appeal. They may cause your audience to laugh or cry, betray anger or delight, experience a sense of pity or pride, or express any of the numberless other emotions that are a part of man's mysterious psychological makeup.

When stories have this human interest quality, you can be reasonably sure they will attract more than routine attention from your audience. As a matter of fact, studies indicate that the relatively unimportant story that is high in human interest appeal will invariably outdraw the more important story that lacks this alluring quality. For example, a personality story about the aging prospector who is firmly convinced that some day he will make his big gold strike will get much higher readership in almost any American newspaper than will a story about the success of the European Common Market. Whether this is desirable is certainly a debatable question, but the fact remains that it is the prevailing pattern.

How, then, does one go about developing human interest appeal in his publicity stories? Generally speaking, stories will automatically have this quality if they involve:

1. People, especially children.
2. Animals, particularly when so-called human traits of animals are emphasized.
3. Conflict or competition, including contests of all descriptions.
4. Adventure, meaning any 'expedition' into the unknown.
5. Success, especially the discovery and rags-to-riches varieties.
6. Love, whether romantic, brotherly, parental, or whatever.

Although this is by no means an exhaustive listing, it should suffice to illustrate the point. Once you grasp the idea, the possibilities for using human interest elements for publicity purposes suggest themselves: Stories (and pictures) emphasizing the need for community beautification, the enterprise of the man who developed a new marketing system, the background of the boy who won the essay contest, the way a handicapped person is making the most of his capabilities, how Johnny will profit from improved educational facilities, how a winning team planned its strategy, how a volunteer worker helped aging people identify and develop satisfying interests, and so on. The only practical limits to the possibilities are the extent of your imagination and the dictates of good taste.

DEFINITION OF "NEWS" ELUSIVE

As you broaden your understanding of the qualities discussed in the preceding pages, you also will be improving your ability to recognize what news is and to analyze news values. We have intentionally avoided burdening you with the many definitions of news that writers have attempted, chiefly because any such exercise necessarily is forced to occupy itself with generalities.

The nature of the problem is well illustrated in a court decision that observed cautiously: News is that "indefinable quality of information which arouses public attention." In other words, news is anything that we did not already know. Or, putting it another way, news is what one *says* it is.

More important than abstract definitions as you plan publicity programs is recognition of two principles: (1) News always is relative, and (2) news patterns undergo constant change.

The Relative Nature of News

It is natural for anyone in charge of a publicity campaign to want his stories to get as favorable a play as possible. He would like his material to appear on newspaper front pages and early in broadcast news programs. But the knowledgeable publicity man realizes that is not always possible. Every news story must be judged against all the others that are competing for space and time. The decisions as to where and how they will be played are made by those who have the responsibility of publishing the news media. You may not always agree with their judgments, but you can be sure the decisions are not made capriciously. A sincere effort is made to judge all content—where and how or whether it is to appear—on the basis of relative worth.

What that often means is that news qualifying for front page treatment today might very well do no better than an inside page tomorrow. The example of President Kennedy's assassination furnishes an excellent illustration of how relative news can be. When the first terse bulletin of that tragedy moved on the news wires, afternoon newspapers either had been distributed or were in the midst of that process. As the somber details poured into newsrooms, front pages—and many inside pages as well—were completely remade. What previously had been front page news was moved elsewhere, and other news that had been carried in earlier editions was dropped out altogether. Everything was subordinated to this crucially important story.

The broadcasting industry's response was equally dramatic. At first, regular programs were interrupted as successive bulletins chattered into newsrooms. Gradually, the unfolding particulars commanded more and more broadcast time, until the networks eventually mobilized their reporting forces to the point where all regular programming was cancelled. From then on until funeral and burial services had drawn to their melancholy conclusion, the networks concentrated almost exclusively on reporting the Kennedy story in all of its shocking ramifications. Only occasionally was time devoted to brief accounts of other news.

Obviously, few events call for such drastic revision of mass media content. But the daily process of news evaluation, less frantic though it may be, is nevertheless identical in nature. The publicity man who realizes that this process is typical and necessary will be in a good position to understand it and to act accordingly. He is just as free as the professional newsman to change his timing—to reassess his publicity plan—in the light of news developments.

Changing News Patterns

As is true of all things, news is far from being static in character. Anyone who believes it is has not observed the changes of even the past few years. For one thing, audiences now demand a great deal more than the bare fact news event that was so typical of news media content only a short time ago. They want to know what the news means—what its significance might be. In other words, they are demanding more depth and breadth in their news reports.

But there are other important changes as well. The public now is avidly following news—and asking for still more of it—that was covered only nominally if at all in years past. In addition to the traditional news categories— disasters, politics, crime, governmental activities, international crises, wars, and the like—whole new areas of reporting are developing. Among them are education, health, economics, automation, space exploration, science, religion, race relations, law, recreation, conservation, and many others.

These changing news patterns have clear significance for anyone concerned with the publicity process. By becoming a discerning student of the media and of their practices and by analyzing the needs and wants of the public, he can steadily improve his effectiveness as a communicator.

The questions of what makes news and how it is to be evaluated are perpetual ones. In this age of communication, how they are being answered is of consequence to you as a social being and as one who is inevitably involved in the communication process.

SUGGESTED READING

AULT, PHILLIP H., AND EMERY, EDWIN. *Reporting the News.* New York: Dodd, 1959.

CHARNLEY, MITCHEL V. *Reporting.* New York: Holt, 1959.

HOHENBERG, JOHN. *The Professional Journalist.* New York: Holt, 1960.

MACDOUGALL, CURTIS D. *Interpretative Reporting.* New York: MacMillan, 1963.

RIVERS, WILLIAM L. *The Mass Media: Reporting, Writing, Editing.* New York: Harper, 1964.

★ *The public is impatient with errors and inaccurate information. Facts that cannot be verified should not be used.*

★ 4 ★ Be Accurate, Be Fair

WHEN THE LOCAL NEWSPAPER QUOTES the mayor as telling his constituents that they "need a fiend in city hall," a good many readers will chuckle with amusement over the error. Others, particularly the mayor's relatives and friends, will be understandably irritated and even resentful. Some will go so far as to accuse the reporter or another staff member of deliberately substituting "fiend" for "friend." They will insist that the offending word was not a mistake at all. And what about the mayor? He might be so angered over the misquotation and what he claims are other distortions of his message that he sues the newspaper for libel.

WHY MISTAKES HAPPEN

The foregoing illustration may be unique, but the situation it represents is a familiar one. You have found errors of a like nature in newspapers or in other mass media, and there probably have been times when you thought a particular account was biased in one direction or another. But what you may not have realized is that those who are responsible for the tone and content of mass media are at least as deeply concerned over these questions as the public often claims to be. Professional journalists regard the twin problems of achieving *accuracy* and *balanced reporting* as among the most important ones they face. They know the public can be intolerant of an endless string of errors. And they are mindful, too, of the many accusations of slanted reporting that are leveled at the press.

Anyone familiar with publishing procedures would know that the "fiend" error was wholly unintentional—an unfortunate misprint for which those responsible would be genuinely sorry. He knows, too, that the conscientious journalist makes a sincere attempt to reflect as it actually was whatever situation or event he must report. In other words, he tries to be objective. But the knowledgeable person also realizes the broader significances of the publishing process: That errors, sometimes major ones capable of doing a great deal of harm, are bound to occur; and that there is no such thing as a wholly objective report.

This does not mean that inaccuracies are excusable. Far from it. The very nature of his profession makes the journalist acutely aware that the mass communication system requires people to work under heavy pressure to meet deadlines—to collect, verify, and process huge quantities of facts at great speed and to compress this information into less space or time than they would like. Under such drastic circumstances he knows that on the smallest newspaper, the shortest news broadcast, or the most modest of magazines the opportunities for error can multiply enormously.

YOUR ROLE IN QUEST FOR ACCURACY

As a consequence, the journalist might be dismayed but not surprised by error. Certainly he is not complacent about it. He believes that he and everyone else connected with collecting and reporting information have an obligation to take all possible precautions to prevent inaccuracies. To him, that means responsibility rests upon reporters, editors, writers, proofreaders, and others who make their livelihood in the mass communication industry. But responsibility does not end there. It also rests upon those who supply information to the media, whether they are being interviewed as news sources or are voluntarily contributing material to the press. Perhaps the journalist's responsibility is the greater because he handles the material last, but neither can in good conscience relax his vigilance.

On those occasions when you serve as an interview source or write for publication, your guiding rule for carrying out your share of the responsibility for accuracy should be this: Make no assumptions about facts. Never assume, for example, that you know how to spell a name; that you know without question the date, time, and place of an event; that you are quoting someone correctly; that because you were told something it must be so; that you are citing a statistic or any other fact accurately. Either look it up in a reliable reference work, ask the person or persons directly involved, or do whatever is necessary to establish beyond a reasonable doubt the accuracy of the information. There is no real substitute for being certain, and the only sure way to be certain is to verify, verify, verify. Facts that cannot be verified should not be used.

If you are being interviewed on a sensitive matter or one that involves many intricate details, a verification possibility may be open to you that usually is not available when you contribute material to the press. Ask your interviewer if you might review the completed story or tape for accuracy before publication or broadcast. Normally, he will be happy to oblige. He might, in fact, suggest it himself. But this will be the case only if you review the material promptly and adhere to your original pledge—that is, to *check for accuracy,* not for manner of expression.

Not all representatives of the press will grant you this review privilege. When this happens, you might deal with the problem in several ways: (1) Refuse further interviews if the published material proves to be inaccurate through no fault of yours, (2) make the review privilege a condition to any interview, and (3) require that questions be submitted in writing so you may answer in a like manner. None of these alternatives, however, is nearly as satisfactory as the freely conducted interview based on mutual confidence and respect. Whatever you can do to develop press relationships of this character will be to your advantage over the long run. Most press relations problems melt away automatically when that atmosphere prevails.

Once the material passes through your hands for the last time, there is little you can do to insure its accuracy. You are uneasily aware that an editor's alteration, a typesetter's lapse, an announcer's slip of the tongue, or whatever can produce a published version marred by inaccuracy. But there is another way of looking at it. The many checkpoints the material must clear before it finally is approved for publication can serve as additional guarantees of accuracy. Editors and their assistants are trained to spot the inconsistency, the doubtful assertion, the questionable fact. As a consequence they can, and often do, head off embarrassment for the information source by correcting or rechecking with him what he may have overlooked.

THE MYTH OF "PURE OBJECTIVITY"

Much of what has been said thus far about the difficulty of achieving accuracy also applies to what is called objectivity. A great deal of nonsense has been written about the need for purely objective reporting in the press. For years a controversy has raged among journalists over whether reports should be interpretative, objective, or both. Most of the debate is beside the point because purely objective reporting does not exist. All true reporting is interpretation of a sort, and the more one digs for information the more interpretations he uncovers.

For centuries philosophers have known that people are the prisoners of their experience. They perceive selectively, remember selectively, report selectively. When they observe an objective fact (the rising sun), the information immediately becomes subjective to them (beautiful, colorful, routine, disgusting, frightening, or any one of hundreds of other value judgments).

The journalist is no different from others in this respect, nor should anyone expect him to be. Although heavy stress ought to be and is placed on an *objective approach* to the reporting process, the journalist still must select the facts he will use and discard the others, decide which facts to emphasize, and which ones to play down, and determine what writing form will best lend itself to the information he intends to report. Similarly, the editor is unable to use all that comes to his desk. He must therefore decide what stories to publish, which ones to condense and which ones to expand, which stories are to receive major and minor emphasis, what manner of headline to use, how the story is to be illustrated, and so on. All of this involves human judgment. The process amounts to a never-ending series of subjective decisions based on uncertain criteria the journalist has developed through experience—criteria that he believes will serve him and his purposes best.

THE FAIR-MINDED APPROACH TO REPORTING

What the debate about objective reporting eventually boils down to is a firmly held judgment on all sides that the press should practice a high standard of *fairness*. Certainly no one would quarrel with that as an ideal. The trouble is that seldom can any two persons agree on what is fair and what is not. The journalist soon learns and accepts this as a distressing and often frustrating fact, but it does not (or should not) deter him from adhering to what he regards as a *fair-minded approach* to the reporting process. Someone has suggested this calls for a sublime mixture of both objectivity and subjectivity. In more pragmatic terms, however, the fair-minded approach means:
1. Offering all sides of controversy an opportunity to be heard.
2. Striving to report situations in perspective.
3. Discarding loaded words and labels in favor of facts.
4. Submerging personal biases and prejudices.
5. Paying careful attention to the context of events and situations.
6. Avoiding a participant's role in events.
7. Guarding against depicting the account with overly colorful expression.
8. Providing background information wherever it is needed.
9. Reserving personal opinion for the page, section, or broadcast openly devoted to that purpose.
   Where printed media such as newspapers and mag-

azines are concerned, the level of fairness practiced depends largely upon the ethical standards of those responsible for what appears in the media—the reporters, editors, and publishers. Ultimately, public opinion also has its effect on what they may do. Broadcast media, on the other hand, are governed by an additional set of rules imposed by the Federal Communications Commission, the agency that licenses radio and television stations. Stated simply, the FCC requires that:

1. When time is given or sold to a candidate for political office, all other bona fide candidates for that office must be offered equal time on the same basis.
2. When controversial matters involving the public welfare are broadcast, the station or network must provide opportunity for all sides to be heard.

REPORTING OPINION AND JUDGMENT

You are certainly aware that the press publishes a great deal of opinion in many different forms—advertising, so-called comic strips or pages, editorial cartoons, letters to the editor, syndicated columns, political commentaries, editorial page expression, lovelorn columns, and so on. Presumably, the public understands this and accepts the material for whatever it is worth. But the press also publishes vast quantities of opinion as legitimate news and feature material. Examples are the remarks of politicians and of candidates for public office, the pleas for cooperation from charitable institutions and organizations, the evaluation of the season's prospects by the football coach, the propaganda issued by the myriads of committees formed to support or oppose whatever may be currently at issue, the by-lined interpretations of the changing scene by journalistic specialists or other qualified persons, the efforts at persuasion by spokesmen for various governmental agencies, and the recommendations for applying scientific discoveries to the processes of everyday endeavor.

All of this involves expression of opinion and judgment. But it also qualifies as news—information that people want and need. Not only is the press obligated to carry out this phase of its overall reporting function as fully as circumstances will permit but the objective approach requires also that the press make clear to the public *who and what agency is responsible for the observation being reported.* To restate and enlarge upon the principle emphasized in Chapter 2: All such opinions and judgments should be credited to the source, clearly and unmistakably. Some examples will help to clarify the point:

WRONG	RIGHT
This will be an extremely important meeting that everyone should plan to attend.	The Chamber of Commerce president urged interested persons to attend what he described as "an extremely important meeting."
Building a dam may create a lake, but it also will lower the value of adjoining farmland.	John Smith, chairman of the Natural Resources Council, asserted that "building a dam may create a lake, but it also will lower the value of adjoining farmland."
Vote a straight party ticket.	Representative Burns urged his listeners to vote a straight party ticket.
It's going to be the biggest and best fair in Center County history.	Blaine Evans, fair manager, predicted that this year's event will be "the biggest and best in Center County history."
The funds will be used for a good cause. The high school band is badly in need of new uniforms.	Mrs. Richard Wheaton, PTA president, explained the funds would be used to buy "badly needed uniforms for the high school band."

The foregoing examples illustrate the attribution principle for single statements. Here is a short, but complete, story illustrating the difference between the subjective (non-attributed) and the objective (attributed) approaches:

SUBJECTIVE	OBJECTIVE
A large crowd was on hand Tuesday night to hear Rep. John Jessup speak at the Democratic rally for the Fourth Precinct. His remarks were enthusiastically received.	A crowd of approximately 350 persons attended a meeting Tuesday night to hear Rep. John Jessup speak at the Democratic rally for the Fourth Precinct.
The meeting was larger than any held in this community this year and indicated the growing strength of the Democratic party in this area.	John Heald, Democratic county chairman, said that the meeting was the most enthusiastic held this fall and indicated growing strength of the Democratic party in this area.
Republicans have been at fault in not being more concerned with the inadequate medical facilities of Johnson county.	Representative Jessup charged that the Republican party had been negligent in not providing more adequate medical facilities in Johnson county.

In any such situation, the opinions or judgments must be credited to the proper source. If they are not, the reader or listener is perfectly justified in assuming that the statements are expressions of the person who wrote the story. Where facts are not in dispute (the time of a meeting, the location of an event, the details of a program, the date of an election, and so on), there is no need to attribute the material to a source.

REPORTERS DIG FOR FACTS

There will be times when the working journalist comes to you for your opinions, or you may want to volunteer them for publication by calling in a reporter or scheduling a news conference. So far, so good. But don't be surprised or disturbed if the journalists you talk to also seek out the views of others on that particular subject. That is their job, and to be fair they ought to solicit all available information. If your remarks are reported accurately and in context—that is, fairly—you should have no complaint. The democratic process assumes the public must have access to the widest possible range of opinion if it is to make intelligent choices from the available alternatives. By functioning as a market-place for ideas and opinions, the press and all those who contribute to this marketplace are supplying fundamental encouragement to the growth and development of the demo-cratic ideal.

This latter consideration is one of the overriding reasons why mass media bear a heavy responsibility to pres-ent accurate and fair reports, insofar as that is humanly possible. The great problem, as has been indicated, is that most persons do not appreciate the difficulty of carrying out that responsibility, nor do they have a sufficient respect for its necessity.

READERS DEMAND ACCURACY

More than we may realize, modern man depends upon mass media to satisfy a variety of wants and needs. Studies indicate the average adult spends from four to six hours each day with the mass communication devices at his dis-posal—newspapers, magazines, radio, television, books, movies. He relies upon them for countless pieces of infor-mation and for clues upon which he bases rather fun-damental decisions, both consequential and inconsequential. He checks the weather forecast, for example, to decide whether to go golfing, plan a picnic with his family, cancel his out-of-town trip, stay inside for the day, or carry an umbrella. He studies the financial pages to see how his in-vestments are faring and to decide what his next moves will be. He seeks the report of the city council meeting to find out how his tax money is being spent and to discover whether projects he opposes or favors are being con-templated. For many of these same reasons he keeps up with the latest publications serving his profession or busi-ness, the local school board news, the court report, state-house developments, Washington news, the international scene, and so on. *He wants to know.*

The only agency equipped to supply this information on a regular, continuing, and efficient basis is the press. Moreover, the average person realizes that in spite of its occasional inaccuracies and other shortcomings the press has an impressive overall record of reliability. He demonstrates his confidence every day by accepting as fair and accurate the great bulk of the information he finds in the press.

Another reason for the industry's great emphasis on fair and accurate reporting is a frankly selfish one—its own economic well-being. Although you undoubtedly can find numerous examples to the contrary, it is generally true that persistent inaccuracies and unprincipled exaggerations or distortions can contribute to a declining public confidence in the press. For a specific firm that can mean a drop in circulation or audience, less advertising, reduced income, and even the difference between a profit and a loss.

LIBEL—AN EVER PRESENT DANGER

In addition there is always the possibility that careless and sloppy reporting can bring on a costly libel suit. The Associated Press pamphlet entitled *The Dangers of Libel* singles out carelessness as the major cause of such suits. So much of the content of mass media deals with subject matter that is potentially libelous—crime and wrongdoing of all descriptions—that fairness and accuracy become more than simple virtues; they are prime necessities. Inaccurately or unfairly reported facts of this nature may hurt innocent persons. When that happens, even though the mistake or unfairness was not intentional, the consequences can be serious for the offending publication. It is not uncommon for persons who feel they have been defamed in the press to file libel suits asking thousands, sometimes even millions, of dollars in damages. Journalists are uncomfortably aware that the amounts of money awarded in successful libel actions have been climbing steadily for years. And their discomfort is not eased by the knowledge that a wrong name, initial, address, or similar lapse can trigger a libel suit if the error results in damage to someone's good name.

LEARN TO RECOGNIZE LIBEL

Although it is not likely that you will ever be involved in a libel action, understanding at least the fundamentals of libel law can broaden your appreciation for the rights and responsibilities of both the press and the news source. Under the law, both can be held liable for a published injury to a person's or a firm's reputation. In other words, the injured party may sue separately or jointly anyone who had a part in publishing the libel: the reporter, the editors, the publishing medium itself, and if he wishes, the source of that damaging piece of information when the source knew he was speaking for publication. For example, if Citizen A unjustly describes Citizen B as "a liar and a fraud," knowing that the remark is to be published in the local newspaper, Citizen B may sue the newspaper, Citizen A, or both.

Generally speaking, the press is legally responsible for any libels it may publish, whether they occur in advertising, letters to the editor, photographs, drawings, news stories, headlines, feature articles, reprinted material, contributed articles, editorials, or wherever. The reasoning is simply that the agency that gives circulation to the libel must also accept the responsibility for any damage it might do.

How do you recognize a libel? There are three elements that must be present before a libel can exist. They are:

1. *Defamation.* The words used must somehow injure a reputation or sully a good name. Many words are defamatory in themselves (crook, cheater, prostitute, Communist, racketeer, and hundreds more that indicate dishonesty, immorality, or impropriety). Others become defamatory because of special circumstances (the story falsely reporting that a clergyman attended what was widely known to have been a wild party). In short, any false statement which subjects the injured party to public ridicule, hatred, scorn, or contempt, or adversely affects him in his job or professional capacity is defamatory.

2. *Publication.* Where mass media are concerned, publication exists the moment the presses roll or the broadcast goes on the air. At that moment, distribution begins and publication has been accomplished. From a strictly legal point of view, however, publication exists the moment a third party hears or sees the defamatory statement.

3. *Identification.* The offending statement must refer to an ascertainable person or persons. The identification, however, need not be by name. It can be accomplished by means of a personality sketch, an address, a photograph, a drawing, by describing an occupation, or citing physical characteristics. Identification exists when any circumstances or details make it possible for the public to single out some specific person or persons as the object of the offending statement.

TRUTH IS BEST DEFENSE

If any of these three elements is absent, there is no libel. Where all three are present, however, the injured party can bring suit for damage to his reputation. Whether he will be successful depends upon how the jury sees the evidence. And it is at this point that the chips go down. The best possible defense to any libel suit is *truth with good motives, when it can be established.* Unfortunately, it is one thing to know the truth (that John Doe is a crook) and quite another to prove it in court (that John Doe really is a crook).

The principle also applies when the press is quoting news sources. It is not enough for the press to plead that it has quoted someone accurately, although that is important, too. There must also be proof that what the person said is true. Proving the truth is especially hard when facts have been exaggerated (reporting that a man accused of petty thievery, a misdemeanor, is being charged with a felony, a penitentiary offense), when guilt by association is involved (his parents were criminals so he must be one also), or when innuendo is inherent in the wording (as a lawyer, he carefully avoids the appearance of soliciting business). Proving the truth is a somewhat easier proposition when the material in question is fair and accurate in all respects.

QUALIFIED PRIVILEGE, FAIR COMMENT ARE DEFENSES

Two other common defenses in a libel action are *qualified privilege* and *fair comment and criticism.* The doctrine of qualified privilege is a rule of law making it possible for the press to report official proceedings of the judicial, legislative, and executive branches of government without fear that successful libel suits will grow out of those reports. The requirements for establishing privilege as a defense are three: That the reports be fair and accurate, that the material be published in the public interest, and that the facts be obtained from official records or proceedings of the three branches of government.

The privilege principle applies to reports of city council proceedings, school board proceedings, the official actions of county commissioners or supervisors, court proceedings, grand jury reports, state and national legislative proceedings, and countless public records kept by governmental officers and agencies at all levels from the small municipality to Washington, D.C. Even though such records and proceedings may contain statements that damage someone's reputation or his business, he cannot successfully sue the press for reporting such statements—if the reports are fair and accurate. Statements made by speakers at conventions and at other public but nongovernmental meetings generally are not privileged, and the press reports any defamatory remarks at its own risk.

The principle of fair comment and criticism is derived from the right that both the public and the press have to comment on matters of public interest and concern. That would include the government and its officers as well as anyone or anything seeking public approval. The rule applies so long as the comment does not advocate violent overthrow of the government or exceed the limits of what is regarded as fair. As far as press criticism is concerned, a comment is considered fair if it is based on fact, or what is honestly believed to be fact, and is confined to that which is being offered for public approval. The usual targets of such criticisms are political candidates, public officers, actors, authors, artists, musicians, athletes, and so on, although public buildings and public organizations are legitimate subjects as well. If the comment and criticism are fair, there is no libel, however severe the wording may be.

Two other aspects of law deserve mention, only the

first of which is concerned with this chapter's major theme—fair and accurate reporting. They are *the right of privacy* and *the law of lottery.*

PROTECTION AGAINST UNWANTED PUBLICITY

The right of privacy refers to the individual's right to be let alone—to go through life unnoticed. Most of us would be desperately unhappy if that actually turned out to be our fate. But the law's purpose is not to hamper the legitimate publicity that most people want and even seek. Its goal instead is to provide protection against *unreasonable publicity* on the one hand and against commercial exploitation of an individual's name or likeness on the other.

Some invasions of privacy occur when persons are unfairly identified with objectionable or embarrassing feature articles, feature pictures, or radio-television dramatizations. Examples might be: Using a photograph of a person who was physically disfigured or dramatizing a spectacular crime and identifying one of the principals, even though he had led an exemplary life since paying his debt to society. In all likelihood, these would be regarded by the courts in most states as instances of unreasonable publicity.

Most privacy suits, however, arise because someone's name or picture has been used to advertise or promote a product without his permission. The safest and surest way to keep that from happening is to obtain a written release from the individual granting permission to use his name and likeness for advertising purposes and to pay him whatever sum of money is agreed upon for that permission. It is a precaution that should be taken whether the individual happens to be your next-door neighbor or a professional model. (See example in Chapter 6, p. 91.)

The privacy right does not apply to coverage of news and of matters commanding great public interest. Again and again the courts have ruled that anyone who is involved voluntarily or involuntarily in a legitimate news event loses his right to privacy in connection with that event. Insofar as the courts are concerned, the public's interest in news events outweighs the individual's private interests. It is also true that persons who seek public attention or acclaim, or who have become public personages as a consequence of their accomplishments or even their peculiarities, thereby give up claims to privacy that the less well-known person has. The only limitation on such reporting and on the coverage of news events in general is that it be reasonable. Unhappily, the guidelines here are fuzzy, but court interpretations generally have been more liberal than restrictive.

PUBLICIZING A LOTTERY? BEWARE!

The situation is quite the reverse where lottery laws are concerned. Long ago, lotteries were declared to be contrary to public policy in this country, and courts have given ground grudgingly since then on what manner of schemes will be permitted. In most states, lotteries are illegal and promoters of them are subject to a fine and/or imprisonment. In those states where lotteries have been legalized, they are subject to strict regulation, with stern penalties prescribed for those who violate the regulations. In addition, federal laws prohibit the broadcasting of lottery information, deny mailing privileges for the circulation of such information, and provide penalties for those who promote such schemes in violation of federal restraints.

By common definition, a lottery is any scheme where *prizes* may be won by *chance* for a *consideration*. All three elements must be present for a lottery to exist. If skill is needed to win, there is no lottery. Similarly, there is no lottery if participants may compete without giving up money, substantial time or effort, or anything else of value. Because prizes are always offered in promotions of this sort, this is seldom at issue. But there is a great deal of confusion over the chance and consideration questions. Part of the confusion stems from differing state court interpretations, part of it from the differences between federal court rulings and those in the several states, and part of it from the fact that court decisions change with the times. The person who wants to know whether a particular scheme is a lottery may (1) check it with the local postmaster or the Post Office Department in Washington, D.C., (2) familiarize himself with the latest court decisions in his state, (3) get an opinion from his lawyer, or (4) discuss the scheme with an advertising representative of the local newspaper or broadcasting station.

The lottery question usually arises when local merchants or organizations are looking for quick ways to increase business or raise money. They may decide to stage a raffle, a bingo party, a bean-in-the-jar guess contest, sponsor a "lucky cash register receipt" drawing, or participate in any one of scores of other lottery schemes. Normally, they will also want to advertise the affair in the local newspaper or over the community's broadcasting stations. No matter how good the cause, though, neither newspapers nor broadcasting stations will accept such material until it has been modified to the point where it no longer is a lottery. That means eliminating either the chance or the consideration requirement.

SUMMARY

Now that you have been introduced to several important aspects of press law, you may be wondering whether the mayor so unfortunately described as a "fiend" in the example at the outset of this chapter would succeed in a libel suit against the newspaper. The answer is that he probably would not. Readers of the paper would undoubtedly understand that the mistake was unintentional. Consequently, the mayor's reputation would not have suffered any real damage. But the wound to his pride would remain unhealed—all because an irritating error slipped through the net.

Joseph Pulitzer, the famed editor of the old New York *World*, is supposed to have said that the three cardinal rules for good journalism are: Accuracy! Accuracy! Accuracy! He was right. And he might have added that a fair-minded approach to the reporting process helps enormously to assure both factual and contextual accuracy.

SUGGESTED READING

ASSOCIATED PRESS. *The Dangers of Libel: A Summary for Newsmen.* New York: Associated Press, 1964.

ASHLEY, PAUL P. *Say It Safely.* Seattle, Wash.: Univ. of Wash., 1959.

HALE, WILLIAM G. *The Law of the Press.* St. Paul, Minn.: West, 1948.

KONVITZ, MILTON R. *First Amendment Freedoms.* Ithaca, N.Y.: Cornell, 1963.

STEIGLEMAN, WALTER A. *The Newspaperman and the Law.* Dubuque, Iowa: Wm. C. Brown Co., 1950.

SWINDLER, WILLIAM F. *Problems of Law in Journalism.* New York: Macmillan, 1955.

THAYER, FRANK. *Legal Control of the Press*, 4th ed. Brooklyn, New York: Foundation Press, 1962.

WITTENBERG, PHILIP. *Dangerous Words.* New York: Columbia, 1947.

★ *People rely heavily on radio and television for entertainment and as dependable news sources. Know how to use these media effectively.*

★5 ★ Publicity on the Air

NEXT TIME YOU FLICK ON THAT TRANSISTOR RADIO or settle down for an evening of television, consider how completely this infant industry has penetrated the American pattern of living. Since the first station began regular broadcasting in 1920, the percentage of American homes with at least one operating radio set (most have more than one) has rocketed from virtually zero to more than 99. To those millions upon millions of home sets must be added the millions more in automobiles, cafes, bars, hotels, offices, dairy barns, schools, barber shops, hospitals, shirt pockets, and any other spot where listening is not forbidden or impossible. The industry's proud boast that "Radio Is Everywhere" has become a near reality.

Television's story is equally astonishing. At the close of World War II, a mere handful of American homes had television sets and only six stations were on the air. Twenty years later, more than 90 per cent of the homes in this country had at least one operating receiver, and the percentage figure inches steadily toward the 100 mark with each passing year. In millions of American homes, people go to bed each night to television and wake up the next morning to radio. Broadcasting has become an almost constant, although not always welcome, companion. People everywhere rely heavily upon it for entertainment and diversion, and studies indicate they also regard it as a dependable source of news information.

KNOW YOUR STATION AND ITS AUDIENCE

Any communication medium capable of reaching such large audiences represents an important outlet for any story that may interest or have significance for the public. As is always the case where publicity campaigns are concerned, your information will receive a much more welcome reception at the station if you present it in readily usable form. What form that information takes depends upon the nature of the story you have to tell. It may amount to one or several short news items you contribute to the news department; you may take part in a live or taped interview, a panel discussion, or a question-and-answer program; or you may be asked to present a talk or demonstration.

Whether your contribution turns out to be only one or a combination of these possibilities, the logical way to approach the publicity question is to study individual station program schedules carefully. When you have done that, decide what programs lend themselves best to the story you have to tell. Then either prepare the material accordingly or discuss your publicity problem with the appropriate people at the station—or do both. If what you want to promote is important or interesting enough to the station's audience (and not openly commercial in character), the station will be happy to cooperate—through its news, farm and home service, or sports departments, or through its program director.

LOCALIZE FOR GREATER APPEAL

In planning any publicity campaign on radio and television, you must think in terms of *local*, not network, programs. The networks, concerned as they are with a national audience, seldom can spare the time for purely local events, but individual stations can. Just as weekly and small daily newspapers emphasize *local news*, so also do radio and television stations feature *local people and events* in their program schedules. As a matter of fact, the agency that licenses broadcasting stations, the Federal Communications Commission, requires that individual stations originate a reasonable amount of local public service programming. What is local depends somewhat upon how far the station's signal travels. Because both FM and television signals are what is known as "line of sight" transmission—that is, the signal travels in a straight line to the horizon—coverage is limited to a relatively small geographical area. Regular radio (AM broadcasting), however, may vary in its coverage from a radius of only 15 to 20 miles to an entire region of one or more states. Each station will define its local audience differently. Your task is to determine which stations serve the audience you want to reach.

ELECTRONIC v. PRINTED MEDIA

As you prepare publicity material for broadcast use, there is one major difference between electronic media and printed media that you must keep constantly in mind: Radio and television messages are for the ear, or for the ear and eye together, while printed messages are for the eye alone. That may seem simple enough, but you will find that it is not easy to shift smoothly from one medium to another unless you understand the significance of this difference.

In printed media, for example, the reader can study and review a passage several times if he is not sure of its meaning. He can even put the printed matter down and go back to it another time. In radio and television, however, the listener-viewer does not ordinarily have that review option. He hears the information once, or hears and sees it for a few fleeting seconds, and then it is gone. If he does not catch the meaning almost immediately, he may never know what the message intended. The point here, of course, is that extra care must be taken to prepare broadcast information simply, clearly, and logically so the audience "gets the message" without undue difficulty.

Naturally, all media strive for effective communication. But the uniquely transient character of the broadcast message puts special burdens on the person who wants to communicate via radio and television. If your listener-viewer has to puzzle even momentarily over what you are trying to tell him, or if you tangle his thought processes in a complex maze of marathon sentences or incompatible word-and-picture messages, you are not using the medium effectively.

WRITING RULES FOR BROADCAST PUBLICITY

Much of your publicity material normally will be in the form of news stories contributed to radio and television stations. The fundamental writing rules you have already learned are just as valid for broadcasting as they are for magazines or newspapers. That is, it is important to write with accuracy, clarity, and vigor for all media. The two basic story forms discussed in Chapter 2 will adapt as well to broadcasting as they do to newspapers.

Keep It Brief

But there are additional considerations when you write news stories for broadcast use. One of these is *brevity*. Comparatively speaking, broadcasting provides much less time for news programs in a given day than a daily newspaper does columns of space. Depending upon how important a station manager feels the news function is, news reports may range from little more than skeletal headline summaries to tightly written and edited programs of ten minutes to even an hour in length.

Whatever the station's policy, though, most of the stories it uses on news programs will be short—perhaps no more than one-half to one minute long. That is about 8 to 15 typewritten lines. Unless an event of unusual importance or significance occurs, even the two or three top stories of the day will rate no more than a few hundred words each on the station's major news programs. Obviously, if your publicity material is to be used it must be short and to the point.

Timing Is Important

Another consideration is *speed*. Broadcasting is equipped to flash news to a waiting public faster than any other medium, and prides itself on doing just that. Moreover, the public expects the industry to perform this important notification service. If your story is to compete with the hundreds of others that come pouring into the news desk, you must get it to the station *while it still is news.* Since events can go stale in a matter of hours in broadcasting, the effort should be to report happenings to the stations immediately after they occur in time for the next scheduled news program. Coming events, of course, should be submitted to the news department well in advance of their occurrence so the broadcaster can time releases most advantageously from his as well as from your point of view.

Write the Way You Talk

Because your news items are to be read aloud, it is important to write them so the announcer can handle them easily and naturally. The trick is to write in a *conversational* style and tone without lapsing into slang or folksiness. One way is to fashion simple, declarative sentences. After all, that is pretty much how people talk. And that sentence form also avoids the hanging attributive you will often find in newspaper writing but that is so unnatural for radio and television. For example, a newspaper lead might begin this way:

> "Center County will have a new public recreation area in operation by this time next year," John Jones, county conservation chairman, said today. "The project will cost $1,489,-680."

But that is not the way people usually phrase sentences when they talk with one another, and broadcast news involves a great deal of talk. Instead of tacking the attributive phrase onto the *end* of a sentence, as in the newspaper version, people are much more likely to use it at or near the *beginning.* For radio and television, therefore, the lead might be written this way:

> Center County residents should be enjoying a
> new public recreation area by this time next year.
> That prediction comes from county conservation
> chairman John Jones, who says the project will cost
> almost one and a half million dollars.

Besides avoiding the hanging attributive, the broadcast version of that lead embodies several other principles that are worth remembering. For one thing, it does not begin with a name. Even when the person is so exceptionally well known that you feel the name should be used early in the opening sentence, it is much wiser to begin with an identifying phrase (State Fish and Game Director Lee White) than it is to begin with the name itself. Such phrases amount to verbal signposts that help your listener-viewer by suggesting what is to come.

You will also note that quotation marks have been eliminated in the broadcast version. The quotation marks themselves cannot really be read aloud anyway, only implied by means of inflection or significant pause or by making awkward reference to the fact that the audience is hearing a quotation. It is best to phrase the sentence so the audience will know from your words that this is what the man said.

A third point is that the broadcast lead is written in present tense (comes, says) rather than past tense (came, said). The primary reason is that present-tense writing avoids the monotonous repetition of the word "today" from story to story. The technique should not be overdone, of course, and it would be unethical to use present tense to disguise an outdated story. But where that approach is logical and applicable, use it.

Finally, the rather complex dollar figure in the newspaper lead has been rounded off and written out. Handled in this manner, figures are easier for the listener-viewer to grasp and for the announcer to read.

Also Keep in Mind . . .

Some additional tips that may be helpful when you prepare publicity for radio and television are these:

1. If there is doubt about a word's pronunciation, use the phonetic spelling in parentheses. Example: Des Moines (Dee Moyne).

2. Typewrite your copy on one side only of 8½ x 11-inch white paper, double- or triple-space it leaving adequate margins, and have no more than one news item per page. If story requires more than one page make sure first page ends with a complete sentence, indicate "more," and continue on slugged second page.

3. Do not separate or hyphenate words at the end of a line. It is much easier for the announcer when all words are kept intact.

4. Avoid abbreviations, unless they are familiar to everyone (CIO, YMCA, etc.). Otherwise, spell them out—secretary, treasurer, the names of states, and so on.

5. Be on the alert for alliterations and tongue-twisting phrasings. The best way to spot potential stumbling blocks is to read your copy aloud.

6. A surplus of sibilant sounds shatters sensibilities. (Just try reading that sentence aloud if you doubt it!) Reword to avoid the persistent "s" sound.

7. Use personal pronouns (e.g., he, she, they, etc.) with care. If there is any question about the antecedent, it is better to repeat the name.

8. Where dates or specific times are involved, it might be well to repeat that information at the end of your story.

9. Keep your sentences relatively short. Announcers have to breathe regularly, and they normally like to do so at the end rather than in the middle of a sentence.

10. Be sure the context of your story reveals the meaning of the words you use. For example, cite, site, and sight all sound alike; but they have quite different meanings, as do many other sound-alike words in the language.

11. It is seldom wise to begin a radio-television news story with a question, and the same principle holds true for other media as well. Questions imply there are to be answers from the audience, but mass communication is essentially one-way.

12. When you are writing broadcast news, the need for brevity does not mean essential facts can be omitted. Make sure you answer as many of the Who, What,

When, Where, Why, and How questions as are pertinent to the story.

13. Audience participation is a useful interest-getting and educational device. When it is logical to do so, tell your audience where additional details may be obtained or what they can do specifically to carry out your suggestions or recommendations.

14. If you have been granted a specific amount of radio or television time, rehearse your material until you are sure it will come within five seconds of the time allotted.

15. When the event or project you are promoting is large enough for on-the-scene coverage by radio or television stations, your job becomes one of seeing to their needs. Talk with station personnel and find out what facilities will be required, then make whatever arrangements are necessary.

EXAMPLES FROM THE NAB

Radio and television stations provide millions of dollars worth of time and facilities each year for many worthwhile community programs, but there are not enough hours in a day to satisfy every request received. To enhance your own chances of getting public service time, make certain that your message is of importance and of widespread interest and that it is presented in the best possible form. Following are some sample releases prepared by the National Association of Broadcasters.[1]

Public Service Announcement for Radio

From:	AMERICAN EDUCATION
Frank W. Edwards	WEEK—RHODE ISLAND
Publicity Chairman	For use Monday,
Woonsocket Teachers Association	February 21,
Randolph Mason High School	through Friday,
Woonsocket, Rhode Island	February 25, _____
FAilure 9-0600	

[1] National Association of Broadcasters, *If You Want Air Time: A Handbook for Publicity Chairmen*, Washington, D.C., NAB, 1961.

AMERICAN EDUCATION WEEK IN RHODE ISLAND
February 21—February 28

Time: 30 seconds
Words: 74

ANNOUNCER: Drive by a school. Watch the faces of the hundreds of students as they come and go. These are the faces of the men and women who one day will govern this nation. During American Education Week, the teachers of Rhode Island invite you to watch this vital form of freedom in action. Visit your local school and observe the techniques of instruction that prepare our children for tomorrow. This is American Education Week.

Announcement on the Same Subject for Television

From:
Frank W. Edwards
Publicity Chairman
Woonsocket Teachers Association
Randolph Mason High School
Woonsocket, Rhode Island
FAilure 9-0600

AMERICAN EDUCATION
WEEK—RHODE ISLAND
For use Monday,
February 21,
through Friday,
February 25, _____

AMERICAN EDUCATION WEEK IN RHODE ISLAND
February 21—February 28

Time: 30 seconds
Words: 63

VIDEO

Slide No. _____
(School with many students walking alongside it)

Slide No. _____
(Lincoln Memorial with two children looking at statue)

Slide No. _____
(American Education Week. Visit Your Schools)

AUDIO

ANNOUNCER: Our nation's schools are home to millions of children for 17 years of their lives.

America looks to these future citizens for the maintenance of the free world, and these students look to the great men of the world for guidance to keep it free.

During American Education Week, visit your local school. Rhode Island teachers urge you to participate in this observance.

Note: The blank following "Slide No." is for the station to insert its own identifying number of your slide.

Public Service Announcement for Radio

From: GIRL SCOUT WEEK
Rose Hill Council   Starting Date: 3/12/___
Girl Scouts of the U.S.A.   Ending Date: 3/18/___
Miss Dorothy Smoothly
Publicity Chairman
259 East 36th Street
Pawtucket 2, Wisconsin
OVerlook 5-9432

GIRL SCOUT WEEK
March 12 to March 18, _____

Time: 20 seconds
Words: 47

This is Girl Scout Week. This week, the Girl Scouts celebrate their 49th birthday. Throughout the years, this fine organization has helped prepare young girls to be useful and active citizens in their home and world communities. Join in supporting the Girl Scouts. Help them BE PREPARED.

Announcement on the Same Subject for Television

From: GIRL SCOUT WEEK
Rose Hill Council   Starting Date: 3/12/___
Girls Scouts of the U.S.A.   Ending Date: 3/18/___
Miss Dorothy Smoothly
Publicity Chairman
259 East 36th Street
Pawtucket 2, Wisconsin
OVerlook 5-9432

GIRL SCOUT WEEK
March 12 to March 18, _____

Time: 20 seconds
Words: 35

VIDEO	AUDIO
Slide No. _____ (Girl Scout Badge)	ANNOUNCER: This is Girl Scout Week. This week the Girl Scouts are celebrating their 49th birthday. . . .
Slide No. _____ (Group of Girl Scouts)	This organization has helped prepare girls to be active and useful citizens. Support the Girl Scouts. Help them BE PREPARED.

News Release for Radio or Television

From:
Handley Music Club
W. A. Mozart
Publicity Chairman
1357 Lydian Street
Handley 6, California

For release:
Thursday, January 19, _____

Theresa Ann Blankenship has won the five-hundred-dollar first prize scholarship award in the Handley Music Club Essay Contest. Her entry was judged best in the 14th annual competition on the subject: "America Needs Music."

Miss Blankenship lives at 21 Spruce Street in Handley. She is a 17-year-old junior at Handley High School.

Results of the judging were announced at an awards dinner last night at the Wellington Hotel.

Runners-up were Edwin R. Newman, 15, of 245 Harvard Street, Handley, and Patricia Neff, 16, of 11 Nichols Avenue, Freemont. Each received a two-hundred-fifty-dollar scholarship.

The awards were presented by Mrs. Allan Saints, president of the Handley Music Club. Assisting her were Mrs. Albert Trenton, Milton Quinn, and Donald Monroe.

Note: The station may be able to use the entire item. If not, the main news is the first two paragraphs. If any names are difficult to pronounce, give the phonetic spelling. For example: Blankenship (Blan-kinn-ship).

News Release for Radio or Television

From:
The Rotary Club
John C. Corbert
Publicity Chairman
1632 Warren Street
Monmouth 4, Missouri
SToneacre 6-4280

For release:
Thursday, January 19, _____

Arthur C. Best is the new president of the Rotary Club of Monmouth.

He will take office on Friday, January 27.

Mr. Best, who resides at 435 Cluber Drive, has been active in Rotary affairs for the past six years. He was elected at a luncheon meeting today to succeed George W. Miles whose term has expired.

Henry P. Castle was elected vice-president, a post Mr. Best held for two years.

Other officers are Gordon H. Chandel, secretary, and Robert J. Lapham, treasurer.

ILLUSTRATING THE TELEVISION STORY

When you prepare publicity specifically for television, you will have an added dimension over radio to consider: *visualizing the story.* Television stations want both still and motion pictures—IF they are technically good, IF they add meaning to the story, and IF (in the case of film) the editing is tight enough so the rule of brevity is not bent out of shape. Fuzzy, indistinct, and poorly exposed pictures simply will not do, nor will pictures that are only vaguely related to the central purpose of the story. Where still pictures are concerned, stations ordinarily prefer 5 x 7-inch or 8 x 10-inch black and white matte (dull finish) prints on a horizontal format, although most can use color slides as well. The latter probably will be transmitted in black and white. The written story accompanying a film or set of pictures (or any visual device, for that matter) must be timed to coincide perfectly with picture or scene changes, must supply whatever details are not made clear from the pictures themselves, and must not dwell upon what already can be seen by the audience.

Effective photography requires a high degree of competence and skill. If you are uncertain about your abilities or don't have access to photographic equipment, hire a professional for the assignment. Or, better still, discuss with station personnel the possibility of having one of their staff photographers do the job. If that can be arranged, you are virtually guaranteed that the photography, editing, and reporting will meet the station's requirements.

It is not always true that photography will do the best job of illustrating the television story. Other possibilities are graphs, charts, drawings, maps, models, and similar devices. It is always a good plan, though, to discuss your visual ideas with appropriate station personnel before going to the trouble of preparing costly materials that might not be used. Above all, be sure in your own mind that any visual device you are considering really will add meaning or dimension to the story. Otherwise, it is likely to be excess baggage or, worse still, a distraction.

IF YOU'RE ASKED TO APPEAR . . .

What you wish to publicize may be so important to the radio or television audience that you will be invited to appear on one or more regular or special programs. Whenever that happens you will have the advice and cooperation of specialists at the station—a big help to anyone not professionally trained in the use of mass media. They will work out programming details with you, arrange for any necessary rehearsals, tell you in a general way what to expect, and explain whatever technical aspects of broadcasting they feel you will need to know.

Some stations have prepared printed pamphlets for amateur performers outlining such matters as what to wear, how to tell which camera is transmitting, what floor director signals indicate, what some of the studio jargon means, and so on. But even though you can count on a greater or lesser amount of this personalized counsel, the following general observations can help you to plan and carry out an effective performance on radio or television.

GOOD INTERVIEWS REQUIRE PLANNING

Whether the time allotted for an interview is 3 or 30 minutes, prepare yourself as thoroughly as you can on the subject to be covered. When you go on the air, work from notes or memory, not from a script. Avoid simple "yes" or "no" answers, even when the questions allow it. The interview will be more successful if you expand your remarks sufficiently to answer the questions satisfactorily. But don't ramble. Good interviews stay on the subject and move logically from point to point.

Don't try to convey a great deal of information in any one interview. Limit yourself to emphasizing a few basic principles—the information you want your audience to remember. Whether you are being interviewed on radio or television, don't shift around unnecessarily, tap pencils, rustle papers, or drum your fingertips on tabletops or chair arms. Such distractions can only divert the audience from your message. When you are on television, look at your interviewer most of the time. After all, you are in a conversation with him, not with the camera.

If you have an opportunity to do so, preview with your interviewer the fundamental ideas you wish to stress. Although neither of you wants a cut-and-dried performance, such a preview helps you both to organize your thoughts and offers the chance for you to converse freely in a sort of warm-up for the program to come. Once the interview is under way (or any other program involving two or more participants for that matter), keep the pleasantries and small talk to a minimum and get on with carrying out the purpose of the interview.

THE RADIO VOICE MUST BE EXPRESSIVE

Think of yourself as talking to just one person, not a vast, unseen audience. Actually, that is what a radio talk really is—a one-way discourse from you to the listener. Chances are he is alone or in the company of a very few persons as he listens to your message. Be friendly and matter-of-fact. Keep your sentences simple and relatively short, and use words and terminologies that will be familiar to your listener. In preparing your talk, you may find that reading your remarks aloud as you write them will help you achieve the conversational tone you are striving for. There is no need to orate. In fact, you are likely to lose listeners if you do.

Remember, too, that your listener cannot see you and therefore is not in a position to rely on the facial expressions and hand gestures you would normally use to emphasize points in a face-to-face conversation. You have to blend all this expressive quality into your words and voice inflections, stressing words and phrases to emphasize your ideas and to lend variety to the pitch of your voice. Finally, don't try to cover too much ground. As you would in an interview, confine yourself to imparting a few basic points. Some useful guidelines for organizing and delivering a radio talk are these:

1. Begin with a pleasant greeting to the audience.

2. Fashion an opening statement or paragraph that will capture the listener's attention and arouse his interest in what you have to say.
3. Summarize the points you intend to cover.
4. Elaborate on those points as interestingly as you can.
5. Clinch your points with a final, but brief, summary.
6. Tell your audience how to get additional information or offer suggestions for whatever action you want taken. Keep this closing information simple and repeat it.
7. Make at least three copies of your radio talk, one for yourself, one for the engineer to use as a guide while you are delivering the talk, and one for the station's files.

PLAN SIMPLE TELEVISION DEMONSTRATIONS

An intelligently conducted television demonstration can be extremely effective in illustrating a *method* (mouth-to-mouth resuscitation), an *effect* (what happens when borers attack field corn), or a *process* (how to build a bird feeder). Simplicity of idea, thorough planning, wise selection of visual aids, and logical presentation are essential to the success of any such program. It also is best if the demonstration can be confined to a relatively small area, such as a tabletop. Action is desirable, but movements should be deliberate rather than quick or impulsive. Limiting the space and slowing the action will allow cameramen the time and opportunity to adjust smoothly for the varied shots called by the director.

If your demonstration is to feature working models or apparatus of any kind—make sure they work. It is pretty embarrassing when the idea you are trying to present falls apart because the demonstration equipment does not function as you had planned. This is just another way of reiterating the importance of simplicity. The complicated and complex normally are not suitable for television presentation, unless the concept can be simplified enough so that it will be understood and remembered. In any television demonstration, time should be provided at the close to repeat the basic points covered. As you discuss your demonstration with station personnel, find out from them what is wanted in the way of a script, what specific form to follow in writing it, and how many copies to prepare.

KEEP PANEL DISCUSSIONS UNDER CONTROL

One of the most persistent problems in presenting radio-television discussion programs involves identification of the participants. It is both confusing and frustrating for the listener-viewer when he does not know who is saying what. The problem is a particularly difficult one for radio, because the listener cannot see the participants. But it is present in television, too, especially where recognizable nameplates have not been provided, or where identifications are not superimposed over the picture often enough. Ordinarily this is a problem for the program producer to solve. Knowing that it exists, however, can serve as a reminder for you to refer to other panel members by name during the course of any program upon which you might appear.

Discussion programs generally are most successful if the number of participants is kept relatively small—say at five or fewer. Limiting the number makes it possible for listeners and viewers to become more thoroughly acquainted with the participants than would otherwise be the case. It also improves the opportunity for a broad exploration of the topic and, at the same time, reduces the tendency to stray afield. The most interesting discussions are lively as well as informative, but liveliness does not imply that emotion should be permitted to outdistance reason. That possibility usually can be minimized where an opportunity is provided before the program begins for the participants to get acquainted and to agree on general ground rules for the discussion.

SUMMARY

To summarize, broadcasting is an exciting and highly personal mass communication medium. It can be of enormous help to you in any publicity effort—if you use it wisely and with intelligence. That means you will need to devote creative thought to (1) what you hope to accomplish by using the broadcast media, (2) what audience you want to reach, and (3) what program device or devices are best suited to your purposes. Discuss your publicity plans and problems with appropriate station personnel. They will be more than happy to help.

SUGGESTED READING

ABBOTT, WALDO, AND RIDER, RICHARD L. *Handbook of Broadcasting*. New York: McGraw, 1957.

BROWN, DONALD E., AND JONES, JOHN PAUL. *Radio and Television News*. New York: Rinehart, 1954.

CBS NEWS STAFF. *Television News Reporting*. New York: McGraw, 1958.

CHESTER, GIRAUD, AND GARRISON, GARNET R. *Radio and Television: An Introduction*. New York: Appleton, 1956.

HILLIARD, ROBERT L. *Writing for Television and Radio*. New York: Hastings, 1962.

WILLIS, EDGAR E. *Foundations in Broadcasting*. New York: Oxford U.P., 1951.

★ *Good pictures represent a powerful means of telling a story in a way that words alone cannot.*

★ 6 ★ Tell Your Story With Pictures

PICTURES ARE INCREASING in number and improving in quality in almost all forms of mass communication. Journalists have found that good pictures attract attention, arouse interest, and represent a powerfully effective means of telling a story in a way that words alone cannot.

Television is the medium that perhaps has done more than any other to make twentieth-century America picture conscious. Now that the viewing public can be transported almost instantaneously to the scene of a news event and can watch it unfold, people no longer are satisfied solely with word descriptions of what is going on around them. They want to see what the people and places in the news look like. They expect pictorial reports in virtually all mass media and on all manner of topics.

Recognizing this growing demand for pictorial communication, the professionals who work for newspapers, television stations, and magazines are anxious to obtain and use as many pictures as possible. This means there are outlets for your publicity pictures; you have the opportunity to convey a favorable impression of your organization, your project, or your company. But conveying that favorable impression depends, at least to some extent, on how much creative effort you invest in getting a good picture—one that is worth publishing.

TAKING THE PICTURE

Whether you take the picture yourself or have a photographer from the newspaper or television station carry out the assignment for you, you will want that picture to say what you intended. A professional photographer can help you arrange subject matter and adjust lighting. It is his responsibility to expose the picture correctly and produce a satisfactory print. But his work will be eased considerably if you have a clear idea of the picture's purpose and can tell him what it is.

If you must take the picture yourself, it will be up to you to select and arrange subject matter, plan the background and create lighting effects so the picture will carry out its purpose. Any camera you use should have a lens capable of producing an 8 x 10-inch enlargement that is sharp and clear from corner to corner. This generally rules out box cameras with their simple lenses, but almost anything else will work if you use it properly.

When you cannot do the photography yourself, arrange to have the newspaper or television station send a staff photographer. This minimizes cost to you, but you will have to sell the people you contact on the news value of the event and the worth of the picture before they can justify assigning photographers. Wherever possible, you should start working with the media at least a week ahead of the time you want the picture taken so the assignment can be fitted into photographers' schedules.

If the picture is for a newsletter, brochure, magazine, or some publication that does not have a staff photographer, you may be able to hire the newspaper or television station photographer to take the picture on his own time. Still another possibility might be the local portrait or wedding photographer. Even an amateur who has access to a darkroom and produces photographs of good quality can do the work for you. In these cases, you should expect to pay his expenses and up to $5 for the first print of each picture. Additional prints of individual pictures should cost less than the first one.

In general, it is safe to publish news pictures without obtaining releases from persons pictured. If you want to be safe, however, it is wise to obtain a written release from every person whose picture appears in advertising, promotional, or news-editorial pieces. Here is an all-purpose release form recommended by the Photographers' Association of America.

City_____, Date_____

For value received, I hereby consent that the pictures taken of me by _____, proofs of which are hereto attached, or any reproduction of the same, may be used or sold by _____ for the purpose of illustration, advertising, or publication in any manner. I hereby certify and covenant that I am over twenty-one years of age. (A parent or legal guardian must sign for a minor.)

_____
Signature of model or subject

_____
Witness

STRIVE FOR TECHNICAL QUALITY

Before a picture can be reproduced with any degree of success in a publication or on television, certain mechanical and technical requirements must be met. Perhaps the most important of these involves picture clarity. The images must be sharp and distinct. If the picture is blurred or fuzzy, one or more of several errors is responsible:

1. *The camera was moved when the shutter was snapped.* Practice releasing your camera shutter gently and slowly, just as the crack marksman squeezes away a rifle shot. The slightest poke or jab at the shutter will jar the camera sufficiently to blur the entire picture, even at relatively fast shutter speeds.

2. *The subject moved at the moment of exposure.* Try to catch your subject during a relaxed moment when sudden or violent movements are unlikely. One way is to have the subject concentrate on a point away from the camera but plausible to the story you want to tell, so that you can take several successive exposures without disturbing the basic composition of the picture.

3. *The camera was not focused properly.* The photographer who persists in prolonging the focusing operation unnecessarily is a trial to everyone, but it is important to focus the camera carefully. On a camera with a ground glass focusing screen, one way is to rack the focusing knob forward and backward through the point of greatest image sharpness, reducing the amount of turn each time until you are right on target. The camera with a rangefinder system seldom presents a focusing problem. Just remember to perform the operation!

One of the reasons technical excellence is so essential is that some quality inevitably is lost whenever a picture is reproduced in newspapers or magazines or on television. For the continuous tone photograph that you carry around in your billfold or purse to be reproduced in any medium, the tones in it would have to be broken into a pattern of dots or lines (see illustrations on page 93). In the process both tone and clarity are reduced somewhat.

The photograph that reproduces best is one that has a full contrast range from jet black to clear white, with most of the picture area composed of the various shades of gray between these two extremes. There also should be visible detail in the picture's shadow areas as well as texture in the white areas. If you think about it, you will realize that the shadows cast by objects seldom are completely black and that even pure white shirts or blouses have visible folds and fabric patterns. The technically excellent picture will portray these nuances of tone faithfully.

As you judge a picture for reproduction purposes, look for *tonal separation* between the objects that are important to the photograph's story. If there is only slight contrast, the objects will tend to blend together and become nearly indistinguishable from one another in the reproduction process. It is also likely that the picture that looks muddy or washed out will be unacceptable for publication, as will prints that are full of dust specks and scratches.

PREPARING PICTURES FOR PUBLICATION

Now here are some mechanical considerations you will want to observe as you take, select, or prepare pictures for publication:

A photograph is composed of continuous tone gradations ranging from black to white, with the majority of the picture made up of the various shades of gray. Black printing ink on white paper can produce only two tones, black and white. Unless it goes through the half-tone engraving process, a continuous tone photograph will reproduce like the stark example on the right.

To get the gray tones necessary for reproduction, the picture must be broken into hundreds of tiny pieces. The method used for the examples on this page breaks the picture into dots of varying sizes.

Once that has been done, dark tones in the photograph are represented by large dots of ink with very little white paper showing between the dots. As the tone in the photograph becomes lighter, the dots in the engraving become smaller and the white space between the ink dots is more prominent.

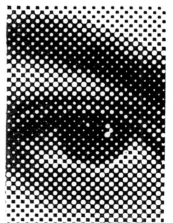

Thus, areas of the photograph which were black will not be completely black in the reproduction. Likewise, the white areas of the photograph will contain tiny dots of black ink in the reproduction. The result of all this is a reduction in the tone range of the picture. If your pictures are to survive the engraving process and retain as much quality as possible, the photographs must contain the full range of tone from black to white.

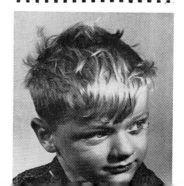

1. The white borders around the edge of the print should not be cut off. The editor may want to use this space to indicate the exact area of the picture he wants to reproduce.

2. Don't write on the back of a picture. Almost any mark on the reverse side of a print will leave an impression on the surface and show up in the reproduction process, even though the surface impression may not be visible to the eye.

3. All legends, identifications, or instructions which are to accompany a picture should be typed on a separate piece of paper. Use rubber cement to fasten the upper edge of the paper to the back of the print so the message is visible below the picture. Adhesives other than rubber cement tend to wrinkle the photograph.

4. Avoid banding the picture because surface cracks will show up in reproduction. If you are sending a photograph by mail, sandwich it between two pieces of stiff cardboard and label the envelope "Photograph. Do Not Bend."

5. Most larger newspapers and magazines prefer 8 x 10-inch prints. Many smaller daily and weekly newspapers, however, are not equipped to change the size of a picture in the engraving process. For this reason, you ought to check with the publication to see if you should submit the pictures in the exact sizes they will be when published and what sizes are wanted. Another possibility is to measure the paper's column width and then submit prints that are one, two, and three columns wide, thereby offering the editor a choice.

6. If the picture is to be used on television, an 8 x 10-inch horizontal format is best because it conforms quite closely to the rectangular shape of the television picture tube.

7. For either printed media or television, matte dried rather than glossy prints will do nicely. The shiny surface of the glossy print causes reflection problems in the television studio, and any unevenness in the gloss will cause engraving problems for newspapers.

8. Television stations can and do use 35 mm. color slides, but magazines and newspapers normally will not accept

A good picture tells its story in an original or unique fashion without distorting the message. Avoid the overworked lineup arrangement and look for a creative way to convey the message.

People are interested in other people. When an editor is faced with a choice between a picture containing a person and one which does not, he almost always will pick the one with the person. The human element suggests action and adds a sense of reality. Even though the picture of the machine may convey the information you want, how many people will it attract and how many would take the time to study it for the information it contains? Adding a workman to the machine will almost always capture more readers and hold their interest for a longer period of time.

them because they are not equipped to reproduce them.

9. The standard motion picture film for television is 16 mm., but because of the expense involved and the rather high level of competence required, it is best to use film only when the station is willing to do the shooting, processing, and editing.

PICTURES MUST TELL A STORY

Although these technical and mechanical considerations are of great importance, observing them will not necessarily guarantee a picture that will interest an audience or convey a message. In the last analysis, it is subject matter—what it is and how it is presented—that determines the communicative worth of a picture. Happily, there are no eternal rules governing how any particular subject should be photographed. If there were, all pictures of a given type would come close to being exactly alike. As a matter of fact, that happens all too frequently—even in the absence of such rules. How often, for example, have you seen group shots or award presentations where picture after picture looked the same? Or how many times have you seen the little knot of basketball players with arms stretched upward toward the ball or hoop? When each successive picture begins to look like the previous one, no one can blame the audience for ignoring the photograph or giving it only a passing glance. Those same pictures, however, taken with a little planning, a few props where that is possible, and some imagination can be new, interesting, and informative experiences for the audience.

You don't need to be a veteran photographer to blend these ingredients into the picture-taking process, although the more practice you get the better you should become. Just observing two fundamental principles can improve almost anyone's photography in only a matter of hours: (1) Put action into your pictures, and (2) keep them simple.

USE IMAGINATION TO SHOW ACTION

Perhaps the easiest and most useful way of getting action into your pictures is to include people, or animals, or both. If you are photographing a machine, for example, show its operator as well, and have him turning a dial, pushing a button, or engaging in whatever activity he normally would under the circumstances. Even having him wipe the sweat from his brow might be logical. The important considerations really are two: (1) That the action be plausible to the situation, and (2) that the action be of the kind the camera can portray.

In not many circumstances is it plausible or desirable to have persons looking into the camera. That is the sort of action you don't want. If the person is supposed to be driving a tractor, operating a lathe, or removing a cake from the oven, he ought to be paying attention to what he is doing and not gazing into the camera lens. Otherwise, all the realism is lost. The person becomes someone having his picture taken rather than a man performing a task.

The second consideration—action the camera can portray—is equally important. Reading, for example, is a mental rather than a physical process. The camera can show a person in the act of reading, but the picture will be more interesting if that person is shown turning a page or frowning in puzzlement over some difficult passage in the book. It is the suggestion of physical action that makes the difference.

It is not always necessary to have the entire person or animal in the picture. In fact, when you are photographing rather small objects, just showing the upper torso of a person, or a face, or even a hand will be enough. For example, if you wanted to photograph a fisherman tying a fly or a homemaker sewing on a button, these rather intricate operations would become almost meaningless in a picture that included the entire person. Instead, try a closeup of the key objects, and include just the face and hands, locating them as strategically as possible. The human element will introduce action, arouse interest, and provide a means of establishing the relative size of the central subject matter— the fly or the button. The world's largest ear of corn will look just like any other ear of corn unless some comparison is made in the picture.

Finally, the reality you are trying to portray in a picture

by using living creatures to introduce action can be lost if they are not in a realistic situation. That is, under most circumstances you should not expect a farmer to be feeding hogs in his best suit. Unless he is cautioned against it, however, he might show up wearing a dress suit because he is going to have his picture taken.

CUT CLUTTER FOR IMPACT

The second basic guide to setting up effective pictures—simplicity—is achieved in part by getting the subjects as close together as possible, positioning the camera as close to the subjects as possible, and selecting a camera angle which will eliminate everything that does not contribute to the meaning of the picture.

When an individual looks at a group of people or objects, they are seen as part of a larger panorama. There can be considerable distance between the objects, but they will appear to be unified because the human eye can cover the surrounding space with great speed and remarkable efficiency. In a photograph, however, this space effect is eliminated. The scene becomes a restricted one and, instead of a reasonably unified group, you are likely to have a series of disunified individuals. The spaces between people or objects may seem insignificant to the eye, but they stand out in a photograph like the gap left by a missing tooth.

This principle applies to all pictures, not just to those involving groups. If you were photographing a home economist and her prize-winning cake, for example, she normally would hold the cake at about waist level—a pose that looks perfectly natural to the eye. In a photograph, however, her face would be at the top of the picture and the cake at the bottom, leaving too much unused space between the two. The picture would lack unity. In fact, instead of a single picture you have two: one of the head and one of the hands and cake. To achieve unity, you might have the woman hold the cake up to her face—so close that she undoubtedly would protest. This might not look natural to the eye, but it would be effective in the finished picture. Another way of solving the problem would be to raise or lower the

When the subjects in a picture are looking at the camera, all the reality you were trying to capture is gone. It merely becomes a picture of people having their picture taken. One of the most difficult parts of your job will be to keep the people interested in what they are doing and not in what the photographer is doing.

Pictures tend to exaggerate the distances between objects. To produce a unified picture, the objects and people must be close together—to the point where they may seem crowded to the eye. Also, select a camera angle which will minimize the space between the images.

Any time you are trying to show the size of an object in a picture, it is necessary to compare the object to something of known size.

If you wish to make something appear very large in a picture, select a very small object for comparison. For example, the watermelons seem larger when a small boy is used to establish scale than when an adult is used for the comparison.

If you were trying to show the reader that a transistor is a very tiny object, the meaning of the picture would be clearer if you used a large masculine hand rather than a small feminine hand.

It is also possible to control the illusion of size by the position of the objects in a picture. To make an object seem larger, place it closer to the camera than the object of known size used for comparison. This is a photographic trick every fisherman learns early in his career.

101

camera enough so that very little space existed between the face and the cake, even though there was considerable actual distance between the two objects.

One of the most difficult impulses to overcome in photography is the one that motivates you to make sure that "everything is in the picture." When grandpa decides to take a picture of little Ralph opening presents on Christmas morning, his first move is likely to be a step backwards to make sure that he gets all of little Ralph and his package in the picture. Then he takes another step back to include the Christmas tree, then another step to get Uncle Charlie and Aunt Mabel in the picture. The result may be an interesting picture for the family album, but it would quickly find its way into an editor's wastebasket. What he is more likely to want is a picture characterizing the emotions of a child on Christmas morning. So instead of backing up, move in closer—then move closer still. In our example, all you would need is the expression on the boy's face and a recognizable fragment of the Christmas present. It is the expression that conveys the human interest and the gift that conveys the meaning. Everything else merely serves as a distraction from the main point.

It is easy to move back, but it takes real courage to move in close and sacrifice all those things which it might be nice to show in the picture. If you think the editor might want a picture of the family, move them in close to the boy so they form a unified group. Then take a close picture of the group.

Even in a case where it is possible to get a simple picture from some distance away, the picture is likely to be more interesting if taken from a closer viewpoint. This emphasizes detail—detail that people fail to notice in their busy everyday lives. If the picture is of a loaf of bread, a shot taken from 6 feet away will show the bread, but one taken from 3 feet away will show the loaf and the texture of the bread itself.

BACKGROUND—AID OR DISTRACTION?

The background against which a picture is taken is probably the greatest source of confusion in pictures. The

Simplicity is one of the key factors in all good pictures. When you are setting up a picture, avoid clutter in either the background or the foreground.

Another way to simplify a picture is to move the camera in close to the subjects. Even an already interesting picture can usually be made more so by taking the picture from the close rather than the far viewpoint. This brings out textures, facial expressions, and other detail the human eye often overlooks.

human eye is extremely selective. That is, your eyes see only a very small area at a time. Look at an object, even something as small as a pencil. You see the pencil after your eyes have moved from end to end and side to side. The eyes examine small parts of the object and the mind puts the image together. This is especially significant for the person setting up a picture because the eye sees only what it is interested in and ignores or screens out the unwanted or the distracting. A camera lens, however, is not nearly as selective as the human eye. If something exists in what is being viewed by the camera lens, the film records it, whether it is related to the subject of the picture or not.

To make things worse, the camera has only one eye and consequently cannot perceive depth. If there is a telephone pole 40 feet behind a person when his picture is taken, that pole in the finished photograph will look as though it is growing out of the person's head. The consequence is that an unwanted object steals interest from what the photographer was trying to say in the picture. Almost anything in the background can dominate and confuse a picture if it has no business being there. Distractions can be as common as a light switch on the wall or a "No Parking" sign and still ruin an otherwise good photograph.

Safe backgrounds for most picture situations are a bare wall, clear sky, or open ground. If you use a wall, move your subjects 4 or 5 feet away so they will not cast confusing shadows on the wall. If you decide to use the sky, select a spot where the horizon is relatively free of trees or buildings and take the picture from a low viewpoint. If you wish to use the ground, pick up any litter that might be scattered around and take the picture from a high angle.

There often are situations in which the background can help tell the story. To carry out that function, however, the background must be well organized and everything in it must relate to the picture. Avoid any background which seems uniform at first glance but actually is made up of little patches of light and dark. This includes trees, shrubbery, radiators, venetian blinds, figured draperies, and the like. Backgrounds of that sort make pictures seem cluttered.

One of the best ways to eliminate a cluttered background is to have the photographer shoot the picture from a high camera angle. He may have to stand on a chair or hold the camera over his head, but the subjects will not blend into the trees, brush or other background distractions.

A low camera angle frequently can be used to eliminate background clutter. The low viewpoint will place subjects against the sky rather than against trees or other unrelated objects.

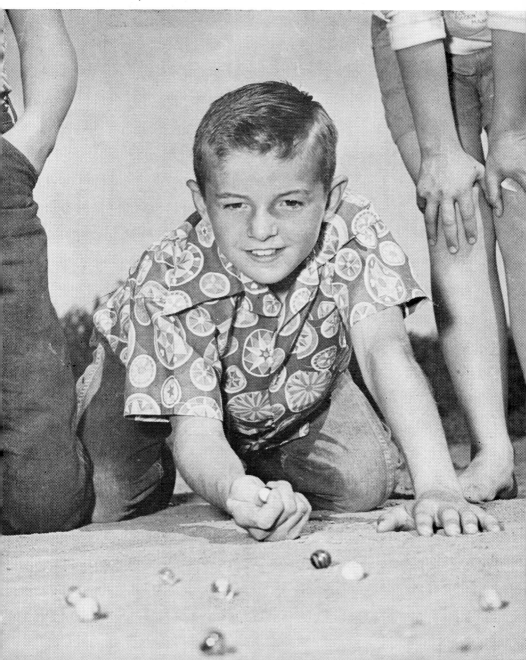

At times the background of a picture can be used to help tell the story. In such cases, the background objects must be carefully arranged. Anything which does not contribute to the meaning of the picture should be eliminated or avoided by shifting the camera position.

In general, if you are taking a picture of a dark object, place it in front of a relatively light background. If you tried to photograph a black Angus cow in front of a dark red barn, for instance, you would have trouble in a black and white picture trying to decide where the animal ended and the barn began. The reverse situation is also true. If you arranged to photograph a blonde woman in a white coat against a light background, your picture might turn out to be a face and two hands floating around in space.

PLAN LIGHTING TO FIT SCENE

In addition to keeping your pictures simple and loading them with action, learning as much as you can about lighting and composition and applying that knowledge will do much to make your pictures more meaningful and psychologically interesting to those who see them.

As you consider the lighting question, you must decide what mood you want the picture to portray. Do you want the subject matter to have a strong and forceful appearance, or would it be more appropriate to convey the impression of softness and gentleness? If you decide upon the former, set up the picture in bright sunlight or light the subjects with incandescent light bulbs. In both situations, the light will be intense and direct, resulting in bright highlights and strong shadows. This is a type of lighting that is appropriate for machines, buildings, men at work, and the like. It would not be the lighting to use for a picture of a young girl or a child with a new puppy where you wanted to create the effect of gentleness and affection. To do that, select a spot in the shade, take the picture on an overcast day, or use fluorescent lighting. All of these lighting conditions produce relatively less contrast between highlights and shadows.

Another aspect of lighting that may be subject to control is the angle at which the rays strike the subject. If there are people in the picture, have them face directly away from the light unless it is not particularly bright or intense. In that case, it is all right to have them face the light source. Either way, you will avoid harsh and ugly shadows

Lighting is almost as important as subject matter in a good photograph. Strong lighting conditions, such as those found in direct sunlight, lend a feeling of strength and forcefulness to the persons and objects in the picture. These feelings are primarily the result of the sparkling highlights and dark shadows produced by bright sunlight.

When the contrast between highlight and shadow is reduced, the subjects take on a soft, warm, and gentle feeling. Pictures taken on overcast days or in the shade will have these soft qualities.

110

It is usually best to have people face either directly into or directly away from the sun. This avoids the harsh shadows which frequently form an unattractive pattern on faces.

With inanimate objects, on the other hand, it is usually better to have the light skim across the surface. This will result in patterns of highlight and shadow which create the illusion of volume in the flat images. This type of lighting also brings out the surface texture of the object.

A camera cannot perceive or record depth in a picture. When the images of objects touch or coincide with each other, the illusion of depth is lost. Even though there may have been a great distance between the objects in the scene, the images may merge in the photograph. This creates the illusion that someone has a tree or a lamp post growing out of his head or, as this picture illustrates, a fence running through his ears.

and lines on their faces. If, on the other hand, you are photographing an object such as a cake, a building, or a machine, the picture will be more interesting if the light strikes that object from a side angle. This creates the highlights and shadows which will separate the various planes of the object in space, giving it volume and providing the illusion of depth in the picture. This type of lighting also brings out surface texture, illustrating for the viewer whether the subject being photographed is rough, smooth, shiny, or dull.

PLAN COMPOSITION FOR MOOD, STORY

Although composition is a term about which volumes have been written, we will use it here to mean *the arrangement of images within the picture.* As you compose a photograph, you should be less interested in the arrangement as seen without the camera than you are in the arrangement as seen through the viewfinder. When you are doing the camera work yourself, study the scene carefully through the camera's viewing system. As you do so, move the subjects to be photographed, the camera, the lighting, or all three until you are satisfied with the arrangement. If someone else is taking the picture for you, cut a small rectangular hole in a cardboard sheet, close one eye, and study the arrangement this way from the camera position. Again, shift things around until you like what you see.

One quality that people like to see in pictures is repetition of lines, shapes, or objects, so long as there is some variation in the pattern. If, for example, you were taking a picture of the winner of the county fair pie baking contest, you might show her in the foreground holding the prize pie while in the background would be a table holding all the other pies in the contest. You could tell the story by photographing just the woman and her pie, of course, but the picture would have greater appeal with the pie repetition feature added.

Another way to make your publicity pictures more attractive to editors and viewers is to arrange the subjects in a spot where there will be a natural framing situation.

The repetition of an image within a picture will almost always add interest. The repetition can be in the background, in the foreground, or in both.

The simplest example would be to pose a person in a doorway and use the doorjamb as your framing device. The framing idea you decide upon does not need to be as obvious as a doorway, and it is not always necessary to have the subject matter completely framed on all sides. Sometimes, just the corner of a building at the edge of the picture is sufficient. One of the most common framing devices used by photographers is a tree. Usually, the trunk is located at the edge of the picture on one side and the lower limbs and leaves complete the frame at the top.

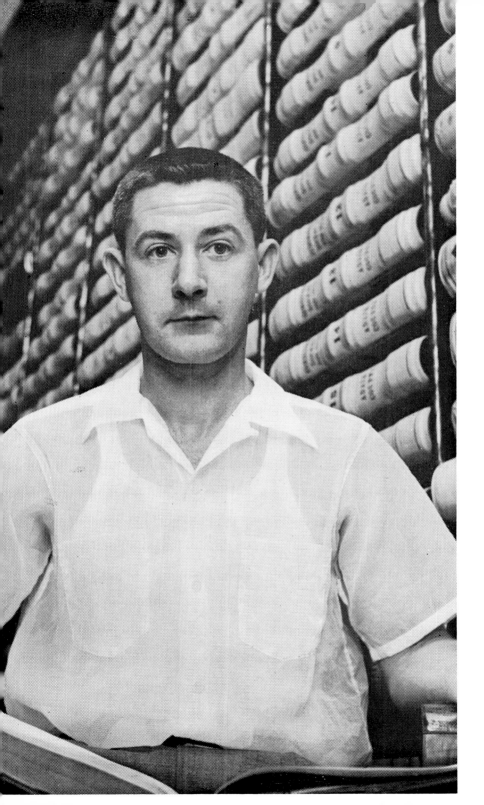

A picture which has a vertical shape and contains vertical lines or a vertical arrangement of
subjects conveys a feeling of dignity and respect.

Providing a picture with some sort of natural frame is another way of getting reader interest. A tree, a door, or almost any object can serve as a frame, but the best frames are those which actually help tell the story. Frequently you can combine objects to get both repetition and a frame in the picture.

There are some other aspects of composition you might find useful in setting up a picture. One of these is the shape of the picture itself. In general, the picture's shape ought to fit the subject. That is, if you are picturing a tall object, such as a silo or grain elevator, the photograph probably will be more effective if it is taller than it is wide. Similarly, if you are photographing a horizontal scene such as a bean field or an arrangement of food on a dinner table, a horizontal picture will best fit the subject matter. It is also widely believed that a rectangular picture, either horizontal or vertical, is more interesting to the viewer than a perfectly square picture.

Where you are free to arrange your subject matter, a horizontal grouping in a horizontal format will convey a restful or quiet mood. A vertical arrangement in a vertical picture, on the other hand, is thought to convey an impression of dignity or strength. A diagonal arrangement through either a horizontal or vertical picture will suggest action to the viewer. For example, if you wanted a picture of a conveyor loading corn into a crib, the picture would suggest more action if it were based on a diagonal line. You could position the camera so that the wagon and the bottom of the conveyor were in the lower left corner with the conveying device running diagonally to the upper right corner where the corn was falling into the crib.

SUMMARY

You are responsible for the pictures you want to place for publicity purposes whether you actually operate the

Pictures composed of horizontal lines or a horizontal arrangement of images will tend to produce a quiet or restful feeling.

camera or not. Keep them as simple as possible and load them with plausible action so they will seem real to both editors and viewers. Where possible, use lighting, repetition, and natural frames to emphasize subject matter.

SUGGESTED READING

ANON. *Enlarging in Black and White and Color.* Kodak Publ. No. 6-16, Eastman Kodak Co., Rochester, N.Y., 1960.

ANON. *Flash Pictures.* Kodak Publ. No. C-2, Eastman Kodak Co., Rochester, N.Y., 1959.

BETHERS, RAY. *Photo-Vision.* New York: St. Martins, n.d.

FOX, RODNEY, AND KERNS, ROBERT. *Creative News Photography.* Ames, Iowa: Iowa State, 1961.

RHODE, ROBERT B., AND MCCALL, FLOYD H. *Introduction to Photography.* New York: Macmillan, 1965.

SIDEY, HUGH, AND FOX, RODNEY. *1,000 Ideas for Better News Pictures.* Ames, Iowa: Iowa State, 1956.

You also are encouraged to read carefully the instruction booklet accompanying your camera and the instruction sheet accompanying the film you buy. Both provide reliable information which can be combined with the picture-making guides discussed in this chapter to improve both the technical quality and the content of your photographs.

Diagonal lines or a diagonal arrangement of objects will enhance the feeling of action and movement in a picture.

★ *Understanding the organization and processes of various news media will make your reporting more efficient.*

★ 7 ★ Learn How the Media Work

THE JOB OF MASS COMMUNICATION MEDIA is to gather and report information of interest to their particular audiences as quickly, completely, and accurately as possible, and they are organized to perform this task most efficiently. If you are seeking space for publicity, you can operate effectively only if you understand media organization and can identify key personnel.

WEEKLIES COVER THE LOCAL SCENE

Publicity workers in towns with weekly newspapers have the easiest task of identification. Weeklies are characteristically published in small towns, or homogeneous suburbs of larger cities, and their staff members are among the best-known persons in the community. Since local news is the lifeblood of the weekly's existence, local publicity is a desirable and welcome commodity.

There are about 9,000 weekly newspapers in the United States, with 363 of them semiweeklies (twice-a-week publications) and 39 published as triweeklies. The smallest of these weeklies are called "family newspapers" because they usually are operated by a man and his wife, sometimes with the part-time help of older children. These family newspapers, existing typically in communities so small they can support only the most marginal of publications, appear to be a dying institution. The key man in such operations is the publisher, who also serves as editor, business manager, and frequently printer.

Substantial weeklies, even the largest, are staffed in their "front offices" (for editorial and business functions) by from three to seven persons. The publisher may provide overall direction and write editorials, although he sometimes doubles as his own news editor or business manager. If the publisher does not double in a major position, his newspaper will have a news editor and a business manager, a women's editor (who also may have charge of country correspondence), a reporter-photographer, and a secretary-bookkeeper. A number of persons are employed to perform the printing tasks under the direction of a foreman—these are the "back-shop" workers. Variations may exist, but this is the basic organizational pattern. Most publicity seekers work with the publisher or news editor, both of whom are familiar figures in a weekly's community.

The country correspondent, usually a housewife who takes the job for extra cash, can be helpful to the publicity man. Most weeklies, and a good many dailies, employ correspondents to report happenings in the small towns and countryside within the paper's circulation area. These correspondents are part-time employees who ordinarily are paid by the amount of their material the paper publishes. They are happy to have news tips and frequently supply the first contact between a newspaper and the person seeking space for publicity.

THE BROADER SCOPE OF THE DAILY

The major difference between a weekly and the smallest of daily newspapers is the fact that the daily must report the most significant happenings of the day no matter where the events may occur. The weekly is concerned only with the news of its immediate trade area, but the daily must report not only the hassle on east 12th Street but also major occurrences in Paris and London, not only on Henry J. Johnson, town mayor, and Mrs. Leona Slotnick, the fifth-grade teacher at the local grammar school, but also on the prime minister of Great Britain and the president of Harvard University. Thus, the some 1,750 daily newspapers in the United States are organized to gather news on a broad geographical basis.

The editorial division of the daily newspaper is organized into local, area, and national-international departments or "desks." Most dailies have an editor in charge of each desk, usually referred to as the city editor (local), the state editor (area or regional), and the wire or telegraph editor (national-international).

The city editor is the person with whom you would be most apt to deal in scheduling publicity if your organization is located within the city limits. He is in charge of the newspaper's reporting staff and assigns staffers to "beats"— news generating centers such as city hall, the courts, police and fire stations, and transportation and housing offices— or to specific stories as they arise.

The state editor—sometimes called the regional or area editor—is responsible for the staff of correspondents. A newspaper's "area" is determined by the geographical limits of its circulation, which, in turn, tend to be determined by those of the trade area of the city of publication. If your organization is located within the trade area but outside the city limits, your best contact with the nearest daily newspaper may be with one of the paper's correspondents, although direct contact with the area editor is highly desirable. In any case, you should be well acquainted with both the editor and the correspondent.

Most daily newspapers acquire the greatest portion of their national and international news from the two major American news services, The Associated Press and United Press International. These news services—called "wire services" in the profession—transmit most of their news via teletype. Nearly 100,000 persons contribute material daily to The Associated Press, a membership organization to which about 8,000 newspapers and radio and television stations belong. UPI, which has a staff of about 10,000 part-time and full-time newsmen and women, has about 7,000 subscribers to its services. The wire services have bureaus in most of the major cities of the world and employ correspondents in other critical news centers. Teletype news is handled on the local level by the telegraph or wire editor.

If your publicity release is of such a nature as to be newsworthy beyond the distribution areas of local and regional news outlets, the news associations may be depended upon to disseminate it further. The local newspaper often sees to it that such news is brought to the attention of the wire services, particularly member newspapers of the AP. Associated Press newspapers are required by the terms of their membership to pass on to that organization all news of significance beyond the publication's circulation area. It is wise, however, for a publicity chairman or director to become acquainted with the local wire-service correspondents or bureau staff members.

Even the smallest daily newspapers have editors in charge of specialized news, such as sports and women's information. Many small dailies, and all the large ones, in agricultural areas have farm editors. Larger newspapers may have other editors responsible for gathering, writing, and editing news of the home, science, labor organizations, business, education, and cultural activities. If your newspaper does have an editor specializing in the kind of news you have to offer, you should deal specifically with him. If, for example, you represent a cooperative feed organization whose annual stockholders meeting is being planned, the farm editor will be happy to meet you and consider for publication the information you have to offer. Similarly, information concerning the home, women's fashions, food, social activities, and children are of concern to the woman's page or home editor of the newspaper.

RADIO AND TV—MOST WIDESPREAD NEWS MEDIA

Nearly 5,100 radio and 680 television stations in the United States are important to the alert publicity chairman seeking the widest possible distribution of his information. For news programming, the electronic media are organized in roughly the same way as newspapers. They have reporters—and cameramen—as well as correspondents and the services of the AP and UPI, both of which produce a "radio report" written for voice delivery. The person most important to the publicity seeker is the station's news director, who supervises preparation of the medium's frequent newscasts. If you have an idea for an entire program, rather than single news items, or a series of programs on your subject, it should be discussed with the program director rather than the news director.

The newspapers' geographical orientation is also present in the electronic media's handling of the news, with reporters, correspondents, and the wire services carrying out identical geographical responsibilities for both. Network programming adds another dimension for radio and television, however. The major networks are the National Broadcasting Company, the American Broadcasting Company, and the Columbia Broadcasting System. For entertainment and information, they offer a service which would be the equivalent to a newspaper printing only national and international news and feature material. The closest approach to such a daily newspaper is the economics-oriented publication, the *Wall Street Journal*. Only information of widespread interest or importance is offered by the networks, which rely, of course, on the local stations to air their programs. The latter supplement network offerings with local and regional fare.

COPY GOES UNDER THE EDITOR'S PENCIL

After your publicity release has been delivered to the newspaper's city or area editor, or to a special-interest editor, it is edited—sometimes rewritten—for accuracy, clarity, and to conform with the newspaper's style of presentation. A determination is then made as to its relative importance as news and a headline (varying in size and style of type depending upon the relative newsworthiness of the story) is assigned and written. After these tasks have been accomplished, the printer takes over. For the electronic media headline writing is omitted; and after editing and rewriting, the information is simply assembled along with other stories into a news program and read over the air.

KEEP ALL NEWS MEDIA HAPPY

Since a publicity campaign is most efficient when it finds acceptance on the part of all the media, it is important for you to understand that newspaper and electronic-media newsmen are competitive and do not like to be placed at combat disadvantage. Timeliness, as pointed out in Chapter 3, is an important news value; and should you place a story with a radio station several days before the local weekly newspaper is to be published, you will destroy the value of that information to the latter. The prudent publicity man avoids alienating any of his potential outlets.

Generally, publicity is most effective when distributed widely, so plan to submit releases to all the outlets within your area. Whenever possible, it is desirable to tailor stories for specific outlets—localized for newspapers and written for the voice for radio and television. Tailored releases require additional effort, but the results are almost always greater media acceptance. Tailored releases are appreciated by all newsmen, who know they indicate professional sensitivity toward media competition on the part of the publicity man.

If you are constantly aware of all the media in your area, you will make certain that picture possibilities for your stories are thoroughly explored. Acceptance of your release is improved considerably if accompanied by good photographs or photograph ideas designed to aid in storytelling and to attract attention. Radio newsmen cannot use pictures, but equal treatment for all newspapers and television stations on your list insofar as pictures are concerned is necessary.

The thoughtful publicity man does not give favored treatment to some outlets at the expense of others. The only way to convince the more reluctant editors is to treat them as fairly as the most cooperative—they may come around.

MAKE A PUBLICITY CAMPAIGN BLUEPRINT

The first step in planning a publicity campaign is to break the event down into story possibilities. For the sake of illustration, let us say the event is a banquet to honor outstanding salesmen for your firm. Here is a checklist of possible stories:

1. Announcement of the banquet (nature of the event, the time, and place).
2. Committee appointments for the banquet.
3. Names of speakers, master of ceremonies, and of those who will present the awards.
4. Statements on importance of awards by a company spokesman.
5. List of award recipients. Sometimes this list is released before the awards are presented, but if dramatic suspense is desired and the names kept secret, it should be released to the press for postbanquet publication.

Strike a reasonable balance between too few and too many advance stories. Some events require several stories to tell, but the technique can be overdone. If you find yourself preparing several releases on a story best told in one, you probably have overreached the probabilities of acceptance.

Often a publicity man will sigh with relief once the publicized event has passed into history. His publicity has succeeded in capturing the share of public attention he desired, and he relaxes in anticipation of his next big event. He is relaxing too soon and is ignoring a basic public relations necessity—the follow-up story (sometimes stories). Newsmen feel an obligation to fully inform their audiences, many members of which may have read or heard a number of your releases prior to the event. These readers or listeners now want to know what happened during the program: What did that noted speaker say and how many persons heard him say it? Even those who attended may now want to read about the happenings they observed and the words they heard.

The follow-up story is another opportunity for your organization to get its name and activities to a mass audience. And the follow-up may well be regarded as the opening release of the next event, particularly when the event is held annually.

Consult your list of media outlets early in the planning

stages. An event such as your banquet probably would have included (1) all newspapers, (2) radio and television stations in your immediate geographical area, (3) newspapers and radio stations outside your area but having extensive circulation or listenership within it, (4) specialized publications (such as church or industrial newspapers or periodicals), or those dealing with your subject matter or product—if you represent an agricultural firm or organization, certain farm publications may be naturals for your releases, and (5) all school publications within your area.

KICK OFF WITH A NEWS CONFERENCE

Publicity on some important special events may best begin with a news conference, a relatively new phenomenon in communication made popular by its frequency at top government levels. Members of the press are invited to the conference at which they are given information concerning the event and allowed an opportunity to ask questions.

The news conference may be overdone as a publicity device. Newsmen have many demands on their time; they will not attend a news conference if the information could have been presented through standard release techniques.

An example of an event of sufficient importance to merit a news conference—or conferences—might be an industrial firm's decision to construct a plant large enough to require employment of several hundreds or thousands of persons in a particular community. Obviously, the economic and social implications for that community are considerable and extraordinarily newsworthy. Another example of an event for which a news conference might be scheduled would be the movement of the national offices of an organization into or out of an area.

The publicity man's job for the news conference requires scheduling; issuing invitations; and briefing the experts, who will present the information, on their tasks and the probable nature of newsmen's questions. He also should prepare materials designed to supplement the information presented during the conference—usually the organization's history, purposes, and statistical facts and figures. His responsibility is all-inclusive—even to seeing that the newsmen's vehicles are conveniently and legally parked.

If at all possible, time the news conference in such a way as to give all media sources the best possible competitive break.

HONESTY—THE ONLY POLICY

Despite the efficiency of your planning and your sensitivity to timing and other requirements of the media, you will fail in your relationship with newsmen if you forget the most important of the publicity man's rules—honesty.

Inevitably, embarrassing situations and events occur in any organization. Your instinct, as a human being, will be to keep these embarrassments secret. You cannot succeed, unless your organization is so highly exclusive it has only two members. It is a journalistic truism that any story known to as many as three persons is not a secret. Should you be so foolish as to try to hide a newsworthy event from the press, inevitable subsequent disclosure may well destroy the confidence and goodwill you have carefully built for your organization not only with the press but with your publics. Once lost, that confidence and goodwill may never be regained. And that is a disastrously high price to pay.

Honesty is the only practical policy. A candid publicity man—and his organization—survives embarrassment. A less than candid one becomes the victim of rumor—usually distortions much more damaging than the facts—and may not be around to make his next attempt to hide the truth.

A SAMPLE GUIDE TO PUBLIC RELATIONS

The following material was prepared by the National Electrical Manufacturers Association. It is intended to answer fundamental questions about the public relations function, to present the essentials for understanding its role as a basic management function, and to describe opportunities for utilizing public relations viewpoints and techniques

to assist the overall organization in accomplishing its objectives. Selected portions are included here as a good
example of *The Publicity Process* in action.

NEMA GUIDE TO PUBLIC RELATIONS*

THIS GUIDE PROVIDES management with considered viewpoints
on the following questions:

What, essentially, is public relations?

Who establishes public relations policy?

What can the public relations function contribute to business operations? To sales? To profits?

Is public relations an integral part of the corporate structure?

What budgetary yardsticks can be used in planning and
executing a public relations program?

What public relations opportunities exist for all NEMA
member companies?

How should a public relations program be implemented,
and by whom?

Can NEMA's public relations department help smaller
companies in effective communications programs?

PUBLIC RELATIONS DEFINED

There are many different concepts of public relations. For
many years, public relations was synonymous with publicity.
Today, public relations embraces much broader concepts—
counseling with management on public attitudes affecting the
company's operations, government relations, building company
stature, human relations, employee communications, shareowner relations, and the measurement of customer and general
public attitudes toward product lines, company policies, sales,
distribution and other aspects of a business.

Distilled to its essence, the following definition appears to
be particularly applicable to the electrical manufacturing industry:

> Public relations is the continuing process by which management
> endeavors to obtain, maintain, and enhance the good will and
> understanding of customers, shareowners, employees, corporate
> neighbors, government, and the public at large—inwardly,
> through self-analysis and correction; outwardly, through all
> means of expression.

Publics

Publics are both internal and external. Here are examples
of each.

* Reprinted by permission of the National Electric Manufacturers
Association, 155 East 44th Street, New York, N.Y. 10017.

One of the largest and most important of all *internal publics* is a company's own employees. These may be separated into various classifications: production and clerical employees; union and nonunion employees; top management, middle management, and first-line supervisors; scientific and engineering personnel, and so on.

External publics include customers, shareowners, security analysts, community leaders, professional societies, educators, public information media (press, TV, radio) and, of course, the man on the street.

All individuals comprising internal and external audiences constitute present and potential shareowners.

Publics and Attitudes

Public relations includes many different publics: individuals, groups, organizations, and governmental bodies—in fact, all audiences which a company or association wants to reach with an important message.

Because each is composed of individuals, personal attitudes toward a company have an important bearing on its programs, policies, sales, and financial results.

For example:

Greater efficiency in a plant may depend more on improving the attitudes of employees than on the introduction of new equipment.

Personnel problems may be related more to the kind of employee attracted by the company's reputation, than to its personnel policies.

Financing may be more affected by stock market trends, rumors, and passing comment than by a company's actual financial structure.

Customer acceptance of a product may be more closely linked with the company's reputation, employee relations, or other factors than the quality of the product itself.

Under these circumstances it becomes necessary for the practical-minded public relations practitioner to make a special effort to seek out and evaluate attitudes of those with whom he must deal and act accordingly in counseling management on a course of action to take under all circumstances. Also, he must take such attitudes into consideration in planning and implementing his program to help management reach its desired goals.

It Begins at the Top

In the broadest sense, public relations begins in the office of the chairman of the board or president. He, more than any other man in the corporate realm, is most properly concerned with what others think about the company he heads. It is to the top officer that the public relations director must turn for guidance on the company's basic policies and objectives.

The chief executive knows that it will do little good to send a salesman out on the road with a sample case full of lightning arrestors, wire and cable, motors, or any other products and expect him to return with a full order book unless his company has established the kind of reputation which will motivate his customers to buy with confidence. An effective public relations activity can contribute to both a company's reputation and confidence in its products.

Public relations programming based on sound corporate policies and activities presells a firm's products, smooths the way for salesmen, puts the stamp of reliability on its equipment, and makes financing easier. Also, it attracts dependable and competent employees, enables customers to evaluate the company fairly and accurately in comparison with other companies, builds community confidence, and establishes a company's position in its industry as a leader in those fields in which it excels.

Must Be Part of Management Team

Whatever its scope, public relations—if it is to contribute to a company's success—must not be on the periphery of business pursuing corporate popularity for the sake of popularity. It must be wanted by top management and have top management's cooperation and support. To obtain that support, public relations must be fully integrated with top management and dedicated to the performance of useful activities that will help assure the continuation, growth, and profitability of the company.

Public relations practitioners have a responsibility to educate top management by defining public relations programs as fully as possible in terms of company profits and in providing management with an understandable means of measurement by which these programs can be evaluated. While management has the responsibility to clarify the company's business philosophy, effective planning can only be done by the chief executive if he is made fully aware of the benefits of a public relations program in terms that he knows best, that is, the profitable operation of the company.

Public relations should help build and maintain a climate of acceptance for the company's products and services. A program that lacks this objective will eventually fall apart because it does not deserve the support of management.

VALUE OF PUBLIC RELATIONS

The value of public relations to a company or organization has been debated at length in many corporate circles. Smaller companies, particularly, have a tendency to look upon the public relations function as a fringe activity and to equate it with activities which either are unwanted or far too costly for serious consideration.

As a result, some reject public relations entirely or concur reluctantly that it may play some role in business. Behind most negative evaluations lie misconceptions of public relations, a lack of understanding of what it can do, and a disregard of its limitations.

Smaller companies often are discouraged when they try to develop a public relations program which matches that of a much larger competitor. What they overlook is that the size of a company has much to do with the character of program undertaken but that all companies—large and small—can benefit from a properly conceived, expertly implemented public relations activity.

There are many sound reasons for differences between public relations programs conducted by big and small companies. Here are a few specifics: A regionally-oriented firm or even a small, national-line company will not have to face the multiplicity of public relations responsibilities or problems which beset a big multiproduct corporation. Because of its limited objectives, therefore, a small company's public relations program need not be as all-inclusive as that conducted by a large company.

For example:

Although continuing, effective government relations at all levels are essential to maintaining a favorable business climate, few, if any, small companies maintain representatives in Washington for that purpose. Their governmental problems and contacts tend to be local in character though, of course, every business manager should know his congressional representatives in Washington. And businessmen do look to their industry associations—National Association of Manufacturers, Chamber of Commerce of the United States, and NEMA—for news of developments in Washington.

In other areas, problems of only passing interest to small companies become major headaches to large corporations, which are highly visible on the national scene and tend to become targets for criticism relating to the whole industry.

A small, single-town firm can take its community relations in stride, doing what it can within its comparatively limited resources to establish itself as a good corporate neighbor. But a large firm must multiply these efforts manyfold to reach every locality in which it has a plant and then reconcile its plant-city efforts with overall policy at headquarters. To do so requires a variety of different programs and corporate and local staffs to implement them.

Product publicity, another arm of public relations, is also a more extensive activity with large companies, because they usually have a larger variety of products to publicize and markets to reach. With more to do, larger companies need more people and more extensive publicity programs.

The same situation applies to many other activities—industrial relations, shareowner relations, marketing, customer relations, and public affairs, to name a few. In larger companies, decisions on such matters are often played out on the national scene in the full glare of the press and the inquiring public. Smaller companies, as a rule, are better able to confine their actions to local or regional levels than are their big competitors. While each firm—big or small—must do its public relations job effectively, such programs need be only as large as the services they are called upon to perform.

Another comforting thought for small companies is that a big public relations program is not necessarily any more effective than a small, sharply targeted program. No program can do more than meet its objectives: limited objectives—small program; big objectives—big program. It is as simple as that.

Direct Objective

Simple, too, and just as direct, is the single aim of all public relations programs regardless of their components. It is the top rung of today's business ladder—profitability.

To prosper, companies need capital, labor, supplies, and services. Also, they need a favorable climate of law, policy, and public opinion. Companies cannot create these elements themselves. Therefore, the business must maintain constructive relationships with the people who provide what it needs—customers for income; employees for labor; shareowners for capital; suppliers for materials and services; and government, the public and community leaders for a favorable climate in which to operate. To provide and maintain such constructive relationships is the job of public relations.

In today's constant battle to improve profitability, it is essential for public relations departments to provide factual and convincing financial background data on a company's operations which will help persuade vendors and employees to keep costs in line so that the company can remain competitive and operate at a profit for the mutual benefit of all.

PUBLIC RELATIONS GAINING ACCEPTANCE

Despite divergent views on the role of public relations in an industrial organization, the function is gaining steadily increased prominence and acceptance. This is indicated by the National Industrial Conference Board's latest survey of Business Opinion and Experience. Of the 205 companies participating in the survey, many indicate an intensification of their public relations programs, and others report having added a public relations department where none existed before.

The board quotes one of the respondents as follows:

> We sincerely believe that the respect and regard for our company and its products has increased substantially in the past two years through our concentrated effort to accomplish that end. We had a narrow choice of up or out. We chose to go up. Public relations has done its part in the recovery of the company, and to pave the way ahead for advancement at a steady pace.

TOOLS OF THE TRADE

The techniques employed to help a company achieve desired results should be looked upon, simply, as tools of the trade—not ends in themselves. Thus, publicity, for example, becomes just one of many techniques in the vast field of communications. And a collection of clippings becomes only so many pieces of waste paper unless they establish the fact that readers have been motivated to buy the company's products, look upon the company in a more favorable light, agree with its policies, or perform in some other way consistent with the intent of the announcement or statements made in the original news release.

Management, having approved the approaches recommended to reach predetermined public relations goals and set up the necessary budget, need not become bogged down in techniques. Just as the executive never dreams of inspecting the mason's tools before he has a sidewalk built, he should not have to concern himself with the details of preparing a news release or the more complex "how to" phases of conducting government and community relations programs. What he can expect and should get are results. It is the public relations director's job to deliver what his top management wants effectively, economically, and legally in a way which reflects credit on the company.

Organized for Action

To reach audiences considered most important to them, whether they be composed of the man on the street or the man in the White House, companies organize on different levels, and go about their efforts in different ways.

Elements of a public relations program vary from company to company in relation to the goals which corporate executives want to accomplish.

In most large and in many medium-sized companies, directors of public relations or communications are on the vice-presidential level. Some of these officers deal only in communications. Others also may have under their direction such functions as marketing services, public affairs, industrial relations, government relations, shareowner relations, and legal matters. In fact, a number of those who handle public relations are also general counsels for their companies or are listed as vice-presidents of industrial relations or, simply to connote their broad responsibilities, vice-presidents of relations services.

Smaller companies may delegate public relations work to advertising managers or employ agencies to perform whatever public relations activities they feel are essential. Presidents of many small as well as medium-sized companies are, in fact, public relations directors.

PUBLIC RELATIONS RESPONSIBILITIES

Whatever the title may be, if the person is responsible for his company's public relations, his duties will cover most of these cardinal points:

1. Measuring attitudes of all publics of importance to the company.
2. Counselling management on the impact of decisions, actions and statements to be taken, applying his judgment on their effect on all audiences—internal and external.
3. Developing sound positions on public policies.
4. Communicating views and ideas to those who make decisions for a company.
5. Conducting or being a part of any government relations activity and counselling management on actions to be taken in connection with present and projected legislation or attitudes affecting the company's operations.
6. Formulating and recommending policies and programs designed to promote and maintain favorable attitudes toward the company on the part of the various publics with which it is concerned.
7. Administering and supervising press relations, including the development and distribution of all news releases.
8. Coordinating with general department and/or division heads the systematic formulation, approval, and scheduling of relevant publicity.
9. Maintaining files of publicity affecting the company and/or its operations. Analyzing current newspaper copy for evidence of adverse or favorable publicity, reviewing it with appropriate officials, and making recommendations, if necessary.
10. Guiding and assisting department, division, and district managers in the development and coordination of programs involving the company's participation in special events.
11. Coordinating and guiding the public relations program of the company insofar as it involves personal appearances and speeches by officers and executive personnel before various groups, clubs, conferences, and organizations.
12. Preparing the regular budget estimates for the Public Relations Department and approving disbursement of all funds allotted for its operation.
13. Planning and supervising local and national advertising programs, when advertising is a part of a public relations director's responsibility.
14. Coordinating company-sponsored memberships in clubs and organizations and recommending the extent of the company's participation in such activities.

15. Administering and supervising policy and practice concerning contributions.
16. Approving requisitions for materials and supplies necessary to the functions of the department.
17. Performing special assignments and duties designated by the president.
18. Supervising the employee communications program, including publication of company newspaper.
19. Coordinating and arranging for publication of materials to shareowners.
20. Planning, assigning, laying out, and supervising work of the public relations staff.

Objectivity Essential

A public relations man needs objectivity, a clear understanding of company goals, the ability to analyze quickly what is to be communicated, and experience in internal and external media. He must earn the confidence of his superiors and acceptance of his role in the corporate structure. He earns confidence and acceptance by his ability to communicate effectively with widely varied publics. A public relations man must be willing to work hard—and love it—many hours of the day and night until his company's goals have been reached.

Smaller Companies, Broader Duties

While it may seem paradoxical in some ways, the smaller the company for which a public relations man works, the broader his duties may become, and concentration on targets may diminish in direct ratio to time and help available.

Larger companies with a large volume of public relations work can assign specialists to perform different jobs. Small companies with one or two people available and more limited needs expect their public relations men to perform a variety of duties—some of them in fields of promotion as well as in communications and other public relations functions.

Thus, some public relations directors also will be charged with developing informational or sales letters, booklets, promotional brochures, and other types of literature. They may consult with sales executives to develop informational tools to help sell products as well as to communicate company news and policies. Out of these conferences may come sales flip charts, films, and other customer relations aids.

Included, too, may be advertising at all levels, shareowner messages, along with product "reader" articles for customer-oriented trade journals, speeches for top executives, programs for plant tours, participation in community programs, awards for veteran employees, employee communications, liaison with

plant or company unions, coordination of marketing information, preparation of materials for management and sales conferences, and membership on committees of associations to
which the company belongs.

PUBLIC RELATIONS "GOES TO MARKET"

With public relations so closely allied with business operations of a company, its relations to marketing have become an
increasingly vital part of the program. Here are six different
approaches to marketing and ways in which public relations
can—and has—helped management turn opportunities and
problems into profits:

Increased Brand Preference

Approach Number 1: Public relations can help to increase
brand preference for a company's product by helping to build
an understanding of the "company behind the product."

In most companies, the public relations component has the
assignment of building public understanding and support for
the company as a whole as contrasted with the direct sales and
promotion of individual product lines. Some companies, however, have always assumed, and rightly so, that building the
reputation of the company also promotes the sales of its
products.

For example, one NEMA member's Major Appliance Division recently surveyed a substantial number of housewives to
determine their brand preferences and their reasons for recent
appliance purchases. Although other elements such as price,
product features, previous experience with company products,
word-of-mouth recommendations, and product service were
frequently mentioned, the housewives indicated that the company's overall reputation was the most powerful factor in their
choice of products.

To Sell Products

Approach Number 2: Turn public relations audiences into
customers.

Public relations people are being unrealistic if they leave
all the selling to the sales force and concentrate all their
energies on noncommercial relationships. After all, public
relations audiences know companies are in business to sell
goods. When customers are in the market to buy, companies
certainly should make sure that their products receive fair consideration.

Consider shareowners, for example. They have already
shown enough confidence in the company to invest their money

in it. Here, then, is a large and favorably inclined market that ought to be cultivated.

Employees represent another important, and sometimes overlooked, market that ought to be cultivated also. With the proper promotion, employees are proud to buy and show off their company's products, and can rather easily be persuaded to go out and stir up sales leads among their friends. Other public relations audiences can also be turned into customers as well as salesmen for a company's products.

Establish Image in a Market

Approach Number 3: Public relations can help a company establish an identity and leadership image in new or expanding markets.

Perhaps a company is entering a market where it is not well known. Perhaps it is a new field, growing fast, where leadership has not been clearly established by anyone. Perhaps it has established its leadership but now needs to keep that reputation for leadership distinctive in the face of aggressive competition. In all these cases, it is not enough merely to push product features, price, and delivery. The more important need in these cases is to establish a company's identity as a competent and responsible organization—a leader in the field.

This can be done through creative selling gestures, which might include company-sponsored forums in which nationally known individuals participate and discuss a field in which the company is expanding, such as space, national defense, or transportation. Other ideas might be: a dramatic motion picture which links a company with a new development, interviews with company officials and their research directors, photographs of executives of companies producing key components for electrical systems with defense or other officials responsible for such systems.

Also, consider press conferences at which authorities discuss such things as national security, energy resources, or world trade with a top company official, or simply signed articles by prominent people identified with a market the company is entering or with which more identification is desired for publication in a company magazine or pamphlet going to selected lists of customers or influential people in the financial community.

To Develop or Expand Markets

Approach Number 4: Public relations can help develop or expand the total market for company products—particularly products where the public will have to foot the bill.

A classic example is a campaign initiated by a company producing motors, controls, and other electrical equipment for sewage treatment plants. This was a profitable but slow market in the 1930's and the 1940's. When a community installs a sewage treatment plant to dump clean water rather than raw sewage into rivers, the main beneficiaries are the cities downstream—which do not share in the cost. At the time, very few cities were investing in sewage treatment plants and many rivers were becoming running sewers, unfit for recreational use, killing off wildlife, and destroying property values. Here, simultaneously, was a public problem and a market opportunity for the manufacturers of sewage treatment equipment.

So in the late 1940's, the company took the initiative; it produced a motion picture illustrating the problem and the solution, and developed a manual telling how to rouse and organize public demand for action to clean up the rivers. The film and the manual, together with low-cost promotional material, were packaged in a kit for purchase—at cost—by any organization that wanted to join the crusade for clean waters. There were no plugs for the company in this material; rather it was selling an idea. The activity became a centerpiece for public action programs.

The market for sewage treatment equipment expanded and extra business was generated for the company—and its competitors.

To Gain Corporate and Social Acceptance

Approach Number 5: When public relations is building an understanding of the company's social performance—as it must, these days—it can simultaneously promote the company's products.

There is always a latent suspicion of business—particularly "big business"—that can be exploited by hostile critics. In order to minimize the harmful effects of this criticism, public relations must continually interpret the company's performance in social terms, pointing out the company's contributions to the life of the community and nation.

Social interpretations of companies can center primarily around the goods and services it produces—how they benefit individual people and communities, as well as the national interest.

To Overcome Adverse Opinion

Approach Number 6: Public relations can sometimes help to overcome serious obstacles to sales and market growth, obstacles that are rooted in public misunderstanding.

One example is atomic energy. The public was introduced

to atomic energy by the astonishing announcement that a single atomic bomb killed 300,000 people in Hiroshima. This image lingers around the words "atomic energy."

Billions of dollars have been invested in developing atomic power plants to the point where they are safe and efficient. But the growth of this market, and progress of atomic energy for peaceful purposes, has constantly been threatened by people who spread the fear that atomic power plants are dangerous.

However, industry has found that fear of atomic power plants varies inversely with knowledge. Public relations can provide the knowledge to combat this fear; in fact, it is doing so now in several different ways: through visits to reactors for explanations on atomic energy, by developing and distributing educational material, and by informational advertisements.

Fear of atomic power plants represents an outstanding example of an obstacle to sales and market growth that can be reduced by public relations effort. But there have been many others over the years—some dramatic, others prosaic: fear of airplane travel and adverse early reactions to sleeping under electric blankets, for instance.

As in the atomic power plant example, public relations, working with sales and marketing people, helped to change the public's view in these cases, too, through well-documented, customer-oriented programs.

Although some objectives may be reached by comparatively short, intensive campaigns, all activities must be a part of a long-range public relations program. For public relations, to be successful, must be a continuing process—not a one, two, or three-shot effort. It functions best for a company when managements realize their responsibility to communicate regularly with all groups important to them.

SHAREOWNER RELATIONS

With more companies going "public," the matter of what to do about shareowner relations becomes highly pertinent to the operations of many corporations. And, it becomes a problem, too, for public relations which, in most cases, gets the job.

The showcase of many shareowner programs is the company's annual meeting. Generally, it represents the only opportunity for personal communications between company officers and investors. To facilitate this interchange of ideas, a number of companies are holding their annual meetings in different parts of the country—going to meet the stockowners, rather than confining meetings to headquarters' cities.

Other typical functions of shareowner relations which fall within the province of public relations are annual reports, quarterly statements, periodic announcements of new products, financial statements, and occasionally, comments from the chief executive officer which refute rumors or confirm changes in corporate structures and policies.

Because of the limited time available and the problems involved in controlling large audiences in the presence of one or more publicity-seeking hecklers, at least one major company has supplemented its annual meetings with personal interviews with stockowners. Such interviews are not for the purpose of selling the company's products or services, but to answer questions about its operations. Subjects include the company's financial condition, research projects, problems, and major activities under way.

Recommendations for success in a shareowner program, as one company's public relations director sees it, cover these points: Decide on a well-defined activity and tell the shareowners what it will include and how it will benefit them; involve as many of the top executives and other employees as possible in a saturation information job among investors, and make it a full-time assignment for the public relations staff in cooperation with the company's administrative officer.

PRESS RELATIONS

The cardinal rule that applies in dealing with the press, and all other informational media, for that matter, is BE HONEST.

Don't mislead and don't get upset when you are asked embarrassing questions. Reporters are not being impertinent. What may seem strictly your business may also be the reporter's business. His job is to get news. What he asks may be what his city editor has told him to ask. And city editors, more often than not, are the sole judges of what newspaper readers want.

Get acquainted with the men to whom you send your news. They may not give you any better treatment, but at least they will know who you are and give you a chance to tell your side of the story in case of unfavorable news or criticism.

Be objective and don't speak off the record unless the reporter knows you are doing so and accepts your comments as background information. Some will accept off the record comments; some won't. It depends on the policy of their papers. Chances are they will be candid with you if you are truthful with them. But better yet—know the men with whom you are dealing.

If you have something to say, say it; but don't give the impression that you have a big story dangling and that you would like your media friends to sit up and beg for it.

Here are some tips on what to do when a news media man calls and wants answers on company operations.

Newsman Calls—Relax

When a reporter calls, relax. Be cordial and natural. Most questions can be answered promptly, provided you have all the facts. If you can't answer, or don't want to answer try to help the reporter understand why.

There always are reasons for not wanting to comment at a particular time on some touchy subject. Perhaps policies have not been formulated, people who have the answer are not available, or to answer now would be premature for certain reasons you should be able to give.

Whatever the case for delay, it is good public relations to try to get the information desired as rapidly as possible and to pass it on to your news contact without delay. Editions can't wait and reporters on the job will write something anyway— so give them what you would like to have published. If you are fair with them, they will be fair with you. Stories which are written past deadlines are history, and today's sandwiches are wrapped in yesterday's newspapers. Nobody wants stale news.

DOS AND DON'TS OF PRESS RELATIONS

And, here is one major company's list of *dos* and *donts* for press relations. Keep it handy. It will save a lot of confusion and provide an essential guide on what to do under trying circumstances.

Do

Get to know your local newsmen.

Learn what they consider news—what you might be able to supply from time to time.

Answer their questions honestly, frankly, fully, courteously, and as briefly as possible. If they want more, they will ask for it.

Call them back when you say you will.

Call them whenever you think you have something of interest.

Say "I don't know," when you honestly don't. But find out! And then get back in touch with a reporter or editor.

Make every effort to get answers quickly if you don't know those answers, then relay them immediately.

Keep a reporter's confidences as you expect him to keep yours. If he asks you for information on a news matter and the man from his opposition paper does not ask, supply the information only to the man who asks for it. However, if in the meantime the opposition paper calls and asks for the same information, give it to both and explain to the first caller what you are doing and why.

Welcome reporters and press photographers to your plant, office, or shop.

Don't

Give guesswork, off-the-cuff, hence possibly wrong, answers. They have to be right.

Promise to call back with the answers, and neglect to do so.

Ever give a blunt "no comment!" It isn't an answer.

Ever ask the advertising man to get a story into the paper.

Ask to see the story as written, before it is printed.

Go "off the record" unless the reporter consents and understands that you are doing so.

Forget to tell the reporter when you go back "on the record" in your answers or remarks.

Demand or expect corrections or retractions of insignificant, unimportant errors. Reserve such efforts for the very occasional important errors.

PUBLICITY—NEWS

Publicity is the oldest arm of public relations and can be one of the most rewarding—particularly on a small budget. Companies thrive on being known, and notice of them and their activities helps customers to identify themselves more closely with the products they make and the services they offer. A salesman is more likely to come away with an order when prospects are presold on the name and reputation of the company for which he works. A sound publicity job can create a favorable impression in advance of the sales approach.

Company public relations directors generally consider publicity in two categories—news and product information.

Many company activities make news—the opening of a new plant, the promotion or retirement of employees, quarterly and annual reports, and others.

The public relations director who wants to publicize his company's name—as who doesn't—will never have a better opportunity than through the medium of a straight news story. Because his contribution is news, acceptance of it is exceptionally high among editors and business commentators on radio and television.

Despite the obvious opportunities to publicize a company through news channels, the job is often overlooked. Perhaps it's a matter of not seeing the trees for the forest—or of thinking that many activities are so routine inside the plant that there is no interest outside. Maybe there just isn't anyone available to prepare the story. Or, more to the point, the news value of an activity goes unrecognized.

Regardless of reasons, most companies can do more to get

their corporate names and those of their employees before their customers and the general public through the satisfying expedient of publicity, expertly handled and carefully placed in media which will do the most good for all concerned.

Opportunities Unlimited

Opportunities for publicity are almost unlimited. A partial list of several, together with some helpful suggestions on how they can be turned to a company's advantage, follow:

1. Few companies have prepared *histories* of their operations. How did they start? How have they changed? What products are now produced? How have they grown? And why? What are the personal backgrounds of chief executives that are unusual in the business community? This and similar information is grist for any writer in preparing articles for local papers on the occasions of special editions and important company anniversaries or at any time when a new product, system, or process is announced to the press. Seek out trade journal reorters and go over your material with them. They are as hungry for good stories as you are to get your company's name mentioned, and your material might present them with intriguing story possibilities.

2. *Promotions and retirements* always make good copy. How long have the employees been with the company? What are their past records? If promoted, what will be their new duties? If retired, what are their future plans? When dinners are held to announce promotions or retirements invite the press to attend and bring along a photographer. Have copies of company statements available if issued and arrange interviews where appropriate. In the matter of promotions, portraits of the employees often accompany press announcements.

The distribution of this type of company news depends on the importance of the move—up the ladder or into retirement—and on the present position of the employee. The promotion or retirement of a corporate officer, obviously, is more important than a change in the status of a punch press operator. Although news of both should be offered to local newspapers, the corporate officer will rate consideration by wire services; editors of trade publications serving the company's primary customers, newspapers in the company's plant cities, and radio and television business commentators.

3. *Encourage talks* by your chief executives or engineers before civic clubs, church groups, and at school assemblies about the electrical manufacturing industry, with special reference to your company's progress and plans for the future.

4. *National Electrical Week*, an industry-wide observance held annually during the week of Thomas A. Edison's birthday (February 11), provides an ideal opportunity for companies to

establish themselves as good corporate citizens and their employees as assets to the community. The observance puts a welcome switch on community participation problems. Companies which seek ways to work more closely with their plant cities throughout the year discover that for one week, at least, their communities are asking them to play prominent roles in a national program.

National Electrical Week is one of the most effective local level "platforms" ever devised to assist an electrical manufacturer to identify himself, his employees, his products, and his company with a great industry and his community. More than 900 local NEW community programs are held each year. They are sponsored, more often than not, by local utilities and run the gamut from community-wide dinners and luncheons to week-long home shows, electrical safety campaigns and promotions of electric products of all types—appliances, electric heating, shop tools, for example. Many NEMA members join with utilities and other sales allies to help support these events.

In addition, they sponsor plant tours for high school students, community leaders and families of employees; arrange for executives to address civic clubs, schools and youth groups; exhibit products in prominent downtown store windows; publicize the Week and their company's contributions to the industry and the nation through newspaper advertising, radio spots, and on television; conduct employee meetings to explain the company's position in the community, in the state, and in the nation; announce new programs, products, and developments; present awards for safety and long service; conduct essay contests on the value of electricity; promote educational campaigns on adequate wiring, including surveys by students of home wiring layouts; and conduct other activities—all designed to better inform townspeople of the importance of electricity and electric equipment in their daily lives.

5. *Nema Awards.* Every company has a number of executives who devote many hours of time voluntarily to Community Fund drives, Boy Scouts, Girl Scouts, YMCA, and other organizations. Let NEMA know who they are and whom we are to contact in the local chapter of such groups, and we will determine whether that organization considers him sufficiently active to qualify for a Community Service Award. These awards are made available by NEMA to electrical manufacturers who have performed outstanding, voluntary civic services to their communities. Presentations are made at local ceremonies, arranged by NEMA in cooperation with sponsoring organizations, and resultant publicity proves of value to the volunteers, the groups for which they have worked, and—of course—to the company by which they are employed.

6. *Do you do business abroad?* If so, the chances are

that you have foreign representatives call at your office. Ask them if they would be willing to talk to your local reporters on conditions in their home countries or on the world situation. Then check their views with a few pointed questions to be sure they won't go off the deep end on company policy. If the situation looks promising, call in the local reporters and arrange for a press luncheon or a discussion around the coffee table.

7. There are many other publicity opportunities in local papers. Here are a few of them:

Change of hours of work, bonuses, pay changes, benefit programs, promotions and transfers, company picnics and parties, safety records, unusual production records, news of profit-sharing plans, company schools or training activities, building operations, activities of company sports groups, signing of labor contracts, expansion programs, unusual orders, inventions, improvements, unusually large shipments of supplies or products, sales meetings of some significance, development of new marketing approaches, business statistics, attendance of executives at association meetings, reports of conferences in which executives have participated and in which the community is interested. Executive comments on industry trends, business outlook, business climate, economic issues, government policies, community needs and, other factors that affect business operations.

Patience a Virtue

Most new publicity writers will await anxiously the next editions of magazines to which they have sent their editorial "brain children," and suffer pangs of heartache and suspense if the article does not appear. To them we say, "Have patience."

Trade magazines, particularly, will run articles two or three months after they have been received. Newspapers are much tougher. If the article isn't run the day it is received, or the day after, the chances are that it won't appear at all. Professional public relations men take a more or less charitable view of this situation, although they, too, can't help feeling upset. But, they know that most newspapers receive hundreds of news releases per day and that they must take their chances in competition with many of their associates. Being out of luck one day doesn't necessarily mean that all is lost. There will be other days, and other opportunities. Like a good salesman (which he is), a public relations man keeps plugging and hoping—winning some and losing some.

New company writers will, in time, develop the same philosophic approach to this age-old public relations problem. They will learn that, unless they own the newspaper, they can't expect preferential treatment for publicity. Even when companies buy space they are not always guaranteed the best location for their advertising.

PRODUCT PUBLICITY

Of all the activities in the public relations galaxy product publicity appeals most to small companies. This is the job which consists largely of producing news releases about a firm's products and placing them in publications which customers read.

The function can be conducted successfully and economically for a company by a small agency or can be operated on a "do-it-yourself" basis. Many companies which have followed the "do-it-yourself" approach as an experiment have stayed with it and report gratifying results.

With a little imagination and experience, company product publicity writers can become proficient in expanding their knowledge of preparing news releases to cover other phases of a company's operations for home-town papers and, thus, build stature for their firms and executives with local residents. A small, but sound, community relations program can flow from this initial approach.

News about plant activities and those who participate in them can also help improve personnel relations. Practice in the art of writing will place the product publicity man in a gradually ascending position where he creates sufficient confidence in his ability to take on added chores of communications—the issuance of corporate statements, for example.

The program can be easily expanded to include customer newsletters containing much of the information prepared for product releases plus statements from company executives to impart the company's strongest messages to those who buy its products. Brochures along the same line can be produced—all stemming from the identical source material used in news copy.

The main element in success in the first stage of a "do-it-yourself" publicity program, however, is to start small. Begin with the customer "news" approach and assign a capable person to do the job.

The objectives of the program are the essentials of any going business: To let customers know who you are, and what you make, that your products have quality and reliability, and that the company's policies are consistent with the highest standards in the industry.

Getting Necessary Source Material

A story is only as good as the source material used in its preparation and the better this material is the more interesting and acceptable the story will be.

It is good business to have your publicity writer review with engineering and sales departments new products and older products about which no news has been prepared. They can help, too, in compiling a list of systems, processes, or services which may be "old hat" to company employees but which may be news to trade magazines and, therefore, good material for product releases.

This comprehensive list of proposed subjects should be reviewed with top management and approaches suggested for news articles. Out of such conferences may come: additional news stories, where to place the greatest emphasis, what is best to say, what to delete, recommendations for special placement in certain magazines, or perhaps a suggestion that one publication be brought in to do an exclusive feature on a product or service peculiar to the company.

Short product releases can often be expanded into longer articles, and writers should be alert to this possibility. In the main, however, product publicity stories relate to the design of a product, its production, and application. News stories can also be produced to illustrate some unusual application of a product or system, size of installation, or dramatic use. Stories of this kind may be provided by design engineers or spotted in the field by salesmen for reference to the public relations department.

Product releases are often accompanied by 8 × 10-inch or 4 × 5-inch glossy photographs. The photographs should be clear and sharp. This requires a professional photographer and not an enthusiastic amateur with a box camera. A poor photograph will kill a good story. Costs of photographers will vary but average from $10–$20 per picture, with service for a day running from $150–$300. Complicated, full-color photographs can cost $200 or more each; it all depends on what you are shooting at and for.

SPECIAL NEWS PROBLEMS—SUGGESTIONS FOR HANDLING

Becoming expert in press relations is a necessary adjunct to being able to handle problem news stories. Many of them "break" in the course of a public relations man's life, but few are more critical than accidents, strikes, and shutdowns.

Despite all safety programs and precautions, accidents do happen—and they are news. Disasters are public property. In such instances, public relations policy dictates these two rules: Get all the facts as quickly as possible. Don't try to cover up an accident.

With the information at hand, mobilize your communications forces for action. If the accident is a serious one, reporters, photographers, and TV reporters may be knocking on your door or even wandering around the plant as soon as the news is flashed to the police and fire departments.

Some pretty sour stories have resulted and company relations have been damaged to a large degree because of three serious omissions of concern for those who communicate news to the public: News media men refused permission to enter the plant to see exactly what happened and how, company officials not available for comment, and the public relations man or plant communications specialist unable or unwilling to give adequate information. The uninitiated might expect that these so-called voluntary or involuntary safeguards to prevent news leaks might send a reporter back to his office to report that he could not get enough facts to write a story.

Not so, however. Policemen, firemen, and the coroner will speak freely about most accident cases. They are public servants and quite uninhibited about providing whatever information they have or can surmise. So some sort of story will be written whether company heads want it or not. By the time the damage can be corrected, the cause is often lost; and what might have ended with the issuance of a rather simple statement of a workman's failure to heed safety rules or the unauthorized removal of a safety guard from a big punch press is now blown out of all proportion.

Of course, there will be follow-up stories in reporting disasters. But, they can be held to a minimum by first giving all available facts at the time of accidents and then following up yourself later that night or the next morning with a more complete assessment of injuries, plant damage, and estimated date of resumption of plant activities if these were stopped for any reason.

Industrial Relations—Communications Responsibility

Strikes and plant shutdowns are something else again. Usually, they don't happen overnight—and there is time to lay a sound groundwork for action in advance of the time when either might happen. This is when your personal relationships with reporters and other news media men can pay dividends.

In these instances, a company's top level officers and its industrial relations manager work closely with the public relations department unless, of course, there is a combination of duties and one or two men have the communications responsibility for the firm. In other words, the company may be so small that the president functions in all capacities, or the industrial relations man serves also as the public relations director.

However the corporate structure is designed, the work load is approximately the same. When labor negotiations begin—or even earlier—some companies prepare and send letters to the homes of their employees explaining the company's position in relation to union demands. Phase two consists of presenting the company's position in all news media. This usually is countered by union statements so the public is aware of the issues in each case. Too often, the union gets front-page attention first, and management is on the defensive. Why not move first for a change?

If a strike does occur, Purple Hearts are in order for many public relations people who find themselves sleeping and eating in the plant while busily engaged in answering news media questions and turning out statements to present management's side effectively, objectively, and clearly. There are two sides to every labor controversy, and it is the job of a public relations man to make sure that his company's position is presented and accepted in the best light. The survival of his company may be at stake. Also, the community and sometimes the nation should know the importance of his company to its employees, the locality, and to the economy as a whole. This kind of situation often makes it essential to tell everything possible about the company, its growth, present stature, comparative wage rates, competitive position in the industry, employee policy, and any and all other information which will focus attention on the best of everything which the company represents in the life of the community, its industry, and maybe, the defense capabilities of the country.

But even the most serious of strikes will end. This is the time for public and industrial relations people to bind up old wounds, bring management and employees together in statements of mutual trust, and distribute pictures of both sides figuratively sheathing their swords until the next round.

Plant Shutdowns—Tough But Necessary

Business is up against competition from all sides. And sometimes it becomes an economic necessity for a company to close one or more plants, merge with another company, move from one location to another, or just go out of business.

When this happens a community often is stunned, particularly if the plant is a big one and layoffs of employees reach proportions which stagger its economic well-being. Loss of contracts or loss of business in one or more lines can trigger a complicated series of developments.

Here again management, industrial relations, and public relations must work together. Program planning is important. Timing is important. Communities and employees must be prepared through thoroughly documented statements and news releases explaining exactly why this economic disaster is about to befall them.

The effort will not be easy, and the results are never fully satisfactory. However, if the economic facts are presented well, the community and a company's employees will, at least, understand the reasons for drastic action being taken.

THE AGENCY APPROACH TO PUBLIC RELATIONS

Agencies are a public relations department's "right hand" in performing jobs which cannot be done with a small staff. In many cases, too, they do the complete job for smaller companies which prefer to operate on any agency rather than a company staff level.

If an agency is to be employed, discuss the matter with your associates and others outside the company. Get their views of an organization which can do the job you want done.

Selecting an agency is just as important as selecting the right people for any company job. The wrong agency can cashier a public relations program before it can get off the ground. But even with the right agency, it takes plenty of effort and know-how to get the proper return from your investment.

Here are some tips on selecting an agency from a major NEMA member company which works with a number of agencies in various product lines:

1. Be willing to invest a reasonable amount of time—and money—in screening agencies.
2. Focus in on three to six agencies that seem well qualified for the particular job you have to farm out.
3. Give the agency, verbally or in writing, a good summary of your program—what it is you want to communicate, why, and whom you must reach. Allow the agency to come back with questions so it has ample information on which to base its presentation and proposed program.
4. Visit all agencies under consideration, if possible, to see their offices and meet key people; but beware of superficial appearances. A big agency with fancy offices and lots of people who have nothing to do but meet with you all day with no interruptions may be a bad sign. Smaller shops, with more modest quarters and people in shirt sleeves, may get you more real attention, effort, and *results*.
5. Look for the people who will roll up their sleeves and start pounding the typewriter.
6. Ask for written presentations to *you*. Cost is, of course, a part of this, as is the question of who will be working on your account and how much of his time will be assigned to you. Then you make a nomination and have your in-house client (e.g., company president, division sales manager, etc.) hear only one formal presentation, with you and your client having the right of veto. You can revise the program and renegotiate the budget after the formal presentation, if need be. There is a danger in having too many presentations and having too many people listening to presentations. Buy a *program*—not a *presentation*.

Now You Have Your Agency—What Next?

Here are several points to consider in the "what next" category:

1. An orientation visit by the person who will actually be working on your account is very desirable.
2. Allow enough of your time—or the time of someone on your staff—to see that the agency receives plenty of direction and information and can get decisions or recommendations quickly when needed. Provide good basic direction at the outset.
3. Set up a regular system of reporting—perhaps written reports monthly and quarterly in-person reporting-review meetings. Also, there is a real need for plentiful day-to-day communications.
4. Don't be bashful about insisting on tangible evidence or results. Or—Where are the clippings?
5. Try to understand the agency and its problems. Be willing to talk over any problem, no matter how large or small, in an atmosphere of goodwill and candor.
6. Keep the agency—and your organization—flexible so as to take advantage of new opportunities, meet new problems, etc.
7. Offer your agency an opportunity to come up with new ideas, new programs, etc., even if this means more money.
8. See that the agency gets full credit within your organization—where it counts—if it is doing a good job.
9. Make a really soul-searching reevaluation of the program from time to time.

Small Agency Costs

Some agencies handle both advertising and public relations. Although under one company department head the two functions can be blended satisfactorily, they do not often mix well in an agency. Therefore, if you can, select an agency which is entirely public relations oriented.

Costs of agency time vary. Usually, however, time costs about $15 per hour. On an annual basis, a small agency may be hired for $6,000, which should give a company approximately one day of personal consultation time every two weeks plus whatever product work results from such contacts.

You will also be charged for printing and other out-of-pocket costs involved in producing booklets, news releases, and other literature developed plus mailing expenses if the agency performs this additional chore.

A full-scale product publicity program, only, including out-of-pocket expenses for services of a small agency may cost a company from $15,000 to $25,000 per year.

Agencies are seldom employed to do more than a communications job, although some are specialists in community relations. On the other hand, consulting firms do function for some companies in matters of government relations and public affairs, although the final program and its implementation rest with the companies themselves.

WHAT TO DO—HOW IT PAYS OFF

Looking back over the material presented, the question arises: What to do about organizing and implementing an effective, initial public relations program? Or what should be included in a present, modest program? Here are suggestions for such components:

1. Product publicity, supplemented with news releases about company operations (retirements, promotions, new programs, etc.) to papers in home towns, in the surrounding area, and in all plant cities.
2. Community relations, including active participation of company executives in civic affairs; assistance, whenever possible, in city improvement programs; also statements by chief executive or Board in support of worthwhile causes or in opposition to activities detrimental to a company's position in the community or its costs of doing business.
3. Participation in National Electrical Week by means of product displays in downtown locations; addresses on the industry, and the company's role in it, before civic clubs, schools, church groups, etc.; plant tours; interviews with company personnel on the present and the projected future of the company and what it means to its home city or plant cities.
4. Communications to employees through periodic newsletters or even bulletin boards and intercom systems to give them an unbiased picture of company status—today and as foreseen in the years ahead. Providing complete information as the company moves along will head off rumors which could be detrimental to the company and win employee support for the profit-making objectives of the business.
5. Government liaison to keep on the alert for changes affecting business brought about by local, state, or federal government actions. Be helpful, giving your frank views, seeing appropriate government officials from city councilmen to congressmen as required. Your interest and helpfulness will usually be appreciated.
6. Shareholder or owner relations in the form of an annual meeting, supplemented by an annual report which gives a review of company operations in addition to the usual cut-and-dried balance sheet.

Start with these six proposed activities and you will have a basic public relations program which will help your company to:

1. Establish its reputation among customers for service and for the manufacture of high-quality, reliable products.
2. Give it stature in its own community as a good corporate neighbor and hence community support when it is needed.
3. Improve communications with its employees—a sound industrial relations move.
4. Assist, through cooperation with other companies, in helping to provide an acceptable business climate.
5. Provide useful data to shareowners on which they can make a fair and favorable evaluation of your company's shares and your managerial performance.
6. Bring in more orders and help to reduce the costs of running your business.

PUBLIC RELATIONS WORKS FOR EVERYBODY

Public relations is for everybody. Whether you think you need it or not, you are practicing the art of communications each time you talk to a customer; a news media man; an employee; or your associates at meetings of NEMA Divisions, Sections, Groups, and Committees.

Communications started when man first learned to make his thoughts understood by his fellow cave dwellers, and it will be with us down through the ages so SPEAK UP professionally, forthrightly, and with competence. *Make public relations help you, your company, and your industry.*

SUGGESTED READING

BOND, F. FRASER. *An Introduction to Journalism,* 2nd ed. New York: Macmillan, 1961, chaps. 9–12, pp. 127–200.

CHARNLEY, MITCHELL V. *Reporting,* 2nd ed. New York: Holt, 1966, chaps. 4–8 pp. 50–106.

EMERY, EDWIN, AULT, PHILLIP H., AND AGEE, WARREN K. *Introduction to Mass Communication,* 2nd ed. New York: Dodd, 1965, Part IV pp. 173–363.

RIVERS, WILLIAM L. *The Mass Media.* New York: Harper, 1964, chap. 2, pp. 15–58.

★ *There is a ready-made audience among magazine readers for your publicity story if you do your job properly.*

★ 8 ★ Write for a Magazine

ONE OF THE MOST USEFUL of the media for many publicists, and often one of the most overlooked, is the magazine market. Whatever your interest, there is a magazine to match it and a ready-made audience waiting to hear what you have to say, if you do your job properly.

The first magazines in America appeared three days apart in 1741—Andrew Bradford's *American Magazine* and Benjamin Franklin's *General Magazine.* The country had some 75 magazines at the beginning of the nineteenth century and about 700 at the close of the Civil War. During the next 20 years magazines proliferated until there were about 3,300 in 1885 and about 5,500 in 1900. By the mid-1960's we were counting about 9,000. In addition corporations and institutions issue 6,000–9,000 house magazines for employees, stockholders, customers, and other persons.

A MAGAZINE FOR EVERY INTEREST

The first things about the magazine field that are likely to strike an observer who does anything more than glance at the copies on a drugstore shelf are the volume, the range, and the utter lack of uniformity among American magazines. There is *Reader's Digest* with its 14,500,000 circulation, and there is the *Florida Entomologist,* circulation 390. There are glossy, color-splashed books (magazine editors' terms for their products) and there are drab, smeary jobs. There are magazines for bakers and for stamp collectors, for motorcyclists and for astrophysicists, for lonely hearts and for probation officers.

But the number of magazines does not give an adequate measure of their impact on our society. Nor is the influence of a particular magazine always to be measured by the size of its reading audience. There are several things to suggest this.

For instance, it costs an advertiser more than $8 to buy 1,000 readers for a page of advertising in *Vogue*. But it costs only about $2 to put a page of *TV Guide* before 1,000 readers. Buyers of advertising in the two magazines obviously believe there is something different about the two sets of readers. Here is another measure. The magazine that is most read by newspaper editorial writers, an influential group, is *Harper's*. And *Harper's* has a circulation of only 275,000. Another magazine that is read by a significant number of editorial writers, *Commonweal*, has only a minuscule 21,700 circulation. Opinion leaders have written for and have read such magazines since magazines began. And today, as always, we can trace the development of many important public discussions from ideas that first appeared in relatively small journals of opinion or quality magazines, through the more popular magazines, into the newspapers and general public debate.

A MAGAZINE AUDIENCE IS UNIQUE

The publicist who wants to see his story within the covers of a magazine must know his market and know it very well. His problem is more difficult than that of trying to please a newspaper editor. The newspaper audience is more or less alike, no matter what the newspaper. It varies from area to area, of course—the rural reader of a community weekly does not have the needs and interests of the reader of a metropolitan daily in New York, for instance. Nonetheless, the newspaper is directed toward a general audience. It seeks to serve all of the adult population of its area and some of the children as well. This means that the newspaper writer, once having determined the wishes and needs of people in general, is sure—almost—that he knows the interests of his readers.

The magazine writer's case is different. Our discussion of the wide variety of magazines will already have suggested this. The self-selected readers of *Popular Mechanics* are quite different from those who have paid their money to read *Foreign Affairs,* or *Grit.* If we are to please the audience of a particular magazine, we must know what the special interests of its audience are. Professional writers expend a great deal of time and energy in trying to discover just who it is they are writing for.

TOOLS OF THE TRADE

There are several methods of helping the writer or publicist with this task. The writer may learn what he can about an editor; he may study one or several of many reference works which describe magazines and their needs; he may study the magazine itself. Personal contact with a magazine's editor is, perhaps, the quickest and surest road to understanding what that editor will buy. But it is by no means a prerequisite for placement of magazine articles. Many a writer has never seen the editor who signs his checks.

There are a great many tools which are designed specifically to help the person who wants to deal intelligently with magazines. Some are directed specifically toward the writer or would-be writer. Some are built to ease the task of the man who must decide where to spend his company's advertising budget. Some are designed to help the scholar or researcher. All are useful to the writer.

Written specifically for the writer who is trying to find out, "What does this editor want?" are a number of market guides. Three are aimed directly at the free-lance writer: *The Writer's Market* (Cincinnati: Writer's Digest, yearly), *Writer's Yearbook* (Cincinnati: Writer's Digest, yearly), *The Writer's Handbook,* (A. S. Burack, editor, Boston: The Writer).

Three magazines of importance to a U.S. or Canadian

writer—*The Writer, Writer's Digest,* and *Author and Journalist*—offer articles designed to instruct or inspire. Each month they carry news of changes in magazine personnel, locations, and needs, as well as the all-important market lists.

Another group of references, while designed for the advertiser or others rather than for the writer, hold significant clues to the kind of materials that a publication desires. Among these are: *Consumer Magazines and Farm Publications* (Standard Rate and Data Service, Inc., Skokie, Illinois), *Business Publications* (Standard Rate and Data Service, Inc., Skokie, Illinois), *Ayer Directory of Newspapers and Periodicals* (Philadelphia: N. W. Ayer and Son, yearly), *House Magazine Directory* (New York: The Gebbie Press).

Some of the publications mentioned here are available at any good library or bookstore. Most can be found in a large library, although you may have to go to a newspaper office or an advertising agency to find the SRDS publications.

Publications in another category, while most difficult of all for the ordinary person to come by, can be the most useful of the lot. These are the market analyses produced by some large publications and designed to attract potential advertisers. Such analyses, produced at considerable expense to the magazines concerned, offer a wealth of information about the readers of the publications.

SUCCESSFUL WRITERS READ

As useful as these references may be, however, they are not enough. The ultimate clue to what a magazine wants—lacking an editor to tell us—is the magazine itself. No writer in his right mind, unless circumstances are very peculiar, will attempt to write for a magazine he has not read. If, among the many frustrations that give an editor ulcers, one can be said to lead the rest, it is probably this: To receive in his morning's mail a well-researched, handsomely written story that might fit another magazine but is patently unsuitable for his own.

Most successful writers—especially those who make their living by sales to the specialized publications, the business and trade magazines—will tell you that they spend an appreciable part of their working days reading the markets to which they would like to sell.

The professional writer does not read a short story merely to enjoy the plot nor does he read an article—except when he is gathering data for a story of his own—solely to obtain information. He reads to see how the other fellow did his writing job. He analyzes technique. He does not read to find out whether the hero wins through in the end. He reads to find out how the author made the reader worry about the hero.

Nor does the professional read only the articles or the stories. He reads everything. He reads the magazine's departments to see who they are written for. He reads the ads and tries to visualize the age and sex and income and church affiliation, and so on of the ad writer's target audience. He looks at the letters to the editor to discover who is reading the magazine.

ALL MAGAZINES "SLANT"

When he has completed his study of a magazine, the publicist or writer has a firm grasp of what, in the trade, is called "slant." Some people feel that a slanted story is one which warps or distorts the information it is conveying, and that to say a magazine is slanted is to say that it is, in one degree or another, untruthful or biased. It should be obvious that magazines, since they are produced by human beings, are subject to human frailties; and there are publications which are incomplete in their reporting, one-sided, or even untruthful. But when we talk about slant, we are talking about something quite different.

We are talking about the special interest that a magazine and its readers may have in a particular subject or subjects. And we are talking about the special approach to that subject that readers have come to expect. A woman buys *Better Homes and Gardens*, for instance, because she expects to find within its covers stories that deal with home

and family. If she chooses *Good Housekeeping*, she anticipates that some of the content will be the same, some different. But she is not disappointed to find that the approach to
the topics covered is quite different. She would be disappointed if this were not the case. It might be said that
every good magazine has a theme song. And that the writer
who wants to publish in that magazine will write a tune
which harmonizes with that theme song.

WHAT MAKES A MAGAZINE FEATURE?

The typical reader is well aware that there is something
about magazine stories that makes them different from other
reading matter. But he has trouble putting his finger on
the difference. The would-be writer and the publicist may
have the same difficulty. The modern American magazine
story can be distinguished from other prose forms if we
recognize that it has certain unique characteristics.

The magazine story deals with facts. The feature story
reader expects the writer to supply him with information.
He expects to learn something new; if he does not, he goes
away disappointed. True, he frequently wants his facts to
be sugarcoated, but even this is not always the case.

The magazine story deals with people. Or at least it
deals with facts as they relate to people. Facts in the abstract may be of interest to researchers in pure science.
They hold little interest for the magazine reader. He wants
to be able to see "how this applies to me—or to the people
around me." Good writers recognize this. Even Einstein,[1]
introducing his special theory of relativity to a general
audience, used familiar pictures:

> In your schooldays most of you who read this book made
> acquaintance with the noble building of Euclid's geometry, and
> you remember—perhaps with more respect than love—the
> magnificent structure, on the lofty staircase of which you were
> chased about for uncounted hours by conscientious teachers.

The magazine story deals with an idea. A feature story

---

[1] Albert Einstein, *Relativity: The Special and General Theory*
(New York, Henry Holt & Co., 1920).

is not a mere catalog of facts. It is a recital of facts which have been selected and arranged in accordance with the particular genius, the particular viewpoint of a particular author. In other words—to steal from any good book on English composition—it states a theme.

The magazine story deals in satisfaction. A feature story must make a definite promise to gratify reader wants and needs in some way or another or it wins no reader. And it must satisfy those wants and needs or it sends its customers away grumbling. A story may satisfy its readers by offering information they need, by appealing to interests that are inherent in them (sex, hunger, or power-seeking) or trained into them (patriotism or religion), by offering escape from grim reality, or by reinforcing convictions the reader already holds.

LIKE NEWSPAPER REPORTING, BUT . . .

The job of gathering information for a feature story is not much different from that of gathering it for any other purpose. This has been dealt with in Chapter 2. It is worth noting here, however, that there is one fact-gathering technique that has no great place in the daily journalist's life but which can be important to the magazine writer. This is the technique of the long-distance interview. There are many writers who have missed stories or have written incomplete stories because it has not occurred to them that they might ask questions not only in person but by letter or telephone. A postage stamp can sometimes save time and shoe leather—or the price of train or airline tickets plus hotel bills. So can a telephone call. The person who uses these splendid reporter's aids should, of course, instruct himself well in the minimum courtesies that are expected of a user.

It may also be worth supplementing here what has already been said about using written sources in story research. The library is the typical starting point for many kinds of story research. A more than academic familiarity with its organization and its contents are a must for the professional writer. He should know how a card index is organized; he should know the names and locations of the major bibliographies—those which classify the books that he might be interested in and those which can keep him posted on new articles appearing in recent newspapers and magazines. He should know also how to find what he wants in the vast flood of government publications. He should know the librarian.

At a minimum he should know these basic references and what they can do for him:

Winchell. *Guide to Reference Books*
Essay and General Literature Index
Agricultural Index
Reader's Guide to Periodical Literature
Social Sciences and Humanities Index
Education Index
The World Almanac
"Who's Who in America"
Ulrich's Periodical Directory
Business Periodicals Index
New York Times Index

One more caution is in order before we turn away from the problems of dealing with information sources. Human beings are fallible. This means, quite simply, that the searcher after facts must not be naive or gullible. He must be ever skeptical, checking and double-checking one source against another until he is satisfied that he is as sure of his data as a reasonable reader—or editor—can demand.

Sometimes the writer is an expert in his own right in the area with which he deals. He then may run the danger of being blinded to facts by the theories and the points of view that he holds. If he is not an expert, he runs the risk of failing entirely to understand his facts. For the first danger there is no cure except humility—willingness of the expert to admit to himself and to others that there may be other ways than his own of looking at the world. For the second, the cure may be research, research, research—borrowing the brains of the experts. The good reporter, in an unfamiliar field, will hunt down men who know the field well and will lean on them heavily. He will ask them for suggestions to guide his exploration; he will ask their opinions as to the meaning of what he discovers; he will carry his finished story to them and ask, "Does this make sense?"

SELLING THE STORY TO AN EDITOR

Because writers and editors may never see each other, communication between them becomes particularly important. There are certain amenities which, if observed, make the communication quicker and easier. These govern the correspondence between writer and editor and the form of the manuscript which the author submits.

Basically, the only thing that an editor is interested in from an author is the author's story. If it is good and suits his needs and the editor recognizes this to be the case, he will buy it. Otherwise, he will reject. This means that a writer's letters to an editor, explaining what his story is about or why he wrote it or what it means, are likely to be not only superfluous but self-defeating. The editor does not care why an author wrote a story. He only cares what his readers will make of it. And if an author must explain what his story is about or what it means, there is something missing in the story itself. Occasionally there are circumstances that call for an explanation by the author of something that would not interest readers. Under such conditions, a cover letter is called for. Otherwise, the manuscript and its package will explain themselves if they follow accepted procedure.

The package that an editor receives should contain, at a minimum, the following:
1. The cover sheet. (See illustration.) This is, on the one hand, a sales device with which the author helps prove his competence to deal with his topic and, on the other, a prospectus which shows the editor at a glance what he is buying.
2. The manuscript. (For examples, see illustration.)
3. Self-addressed, return envelope.
4. Adequate return postage, clipped to return envelope.

All of this goes into a manila envelope large enough to carry the manuscript flat—9 x 12 inches, at least. Weigh the

To be paid for at   for <u>The Iowan</u>
your usual rates or
returned to: mailed Dec. 5, 1966

Diane Dior
2118 Sunset
Ames, Iowa

She's Not Getting Any Older

by Diane Dior

                    Note:

    This article is about an Iowa woman who has a unique way of staying young --
she makes bridal dresses. The article contains approximately 500 words.

    Georgia Mullex, Ames, has more than just a grandmotherly hobby. She's been
making dresses for 20 years and through that activity stays vital and "alive."

    The article should appeal to adults concerned with their elderly parents'
welfare and to the elderly themselves-- Georgia is one of them.

    The following pictures are inclosed:
        1. Fitting time.
        2. Delicate handwork is part of the process.

                    The Cover Sheet

Diane Dior
2118 Sunset
Ames, Iowa

500 words

SHE'S NOT GETTING ANY OLDER

By Diane Dior

She's 70 going on 20.

Georgia Mullex, an Ames, Iowa, senior citizen, has a unique
way of staying young. She doesn't golf; she isn't chairman of the
woman's group.

She designs and creates bridal dresses...for young brides.

"Each time I hear the romantic wedding details I get excited
all over again," says Georgia, a woman so tiny that she has to stand
on tiptoe to "fit" some of the brides. And she's outfitted about five
bridal parties a year for 20 years -- more than 100 in all. It's no
wonder Georgia still enjoys life so.

"I enjoy the girls and I stay useful," says this woman with
snow-white hair and snapping eyes.

(more)

Page 1 of a manuscript

package to verify postage needed. Do not guess. Nothing can spoil a sale in some offices faster than a purple "Postage Due" legend stretching across the envelope.

QUERY CAN SAVE TIME, SELL STORY

When you have a story that you think an editor will like, should you write him about it? The answer to this question varies. If he has never heard of you or your company before, the answer is "No." He will not know until he sees the story whether he can trust you as a reporter and a writer. However, professional writers seldom go to the work of researching a story completely until they have a go-ahead from an editor. A well-written query can save an author's time by helping him avoid useless work. Or it can help him make his reporting more efficient by eliciting suggestions from an editor as to the way he would like to see a story handled. A good query letter will (1) indicate an article's theme, (2) demonstrate the slant and tone of the story, and (3) prove the writer's ability as a reporter and as a writer. A badly written query is a sure road to refusal.

One of the magazine practices that puzzles nonjournalists is the profession's refusal to accept multiple submissions. If you have a story that is perishable, why not offer it to several magazines at the same time and accept the offer of the first—or the highest—bidder? The only answer to this is that, with minor exceptions, it just is not done. This is a case where the man who wants to place a story simply has to play the editor's game or find himself ruled off the field.

PLANNING BRINGS UNITY TO WRITING

Achieving unity in a piece of prose is really quite simple. The writer merely has to decide what it is that he is trying to say, and say it, and say nothing else. The difficulty for the beginning writer in doing this usually comes as he is attempting to decide just what it is that he is trying to say.

"What is my theme? My thesis? My controlling purpose? My central idea? The main point that I am trying to put across?" Whatever you wish to call it, you need a very clear notion of "what it is that this story is going to add up to." For the beginner a rather simple way to get at this is to ask this question: "If I had to boil this whole story down into one or two sentences, what would those sentences be?" Write those sentences down, tack them over your typewriter, and refer to them as you write.

Having clearly determined your theme or central statement, you find the rest of the story of how to achieve unity is quickly told: Simply make sure that you include no paragraph or sentence or word in your story that does not contribute to that central statement. In other words, the second step in achieving unity is selective discarding. So far, so good. We have assembled a set of facts; we have looked at those facts and decided what they add up to—what they say in essence—and thrown away those facts that do not fit the total picture.

But there is more to be done. We now must serve up these facts in a way that makes sense—makes sense so far as the facts themselves are concerned and makes sense to the reader. We cannot reach blindly into our grab bag of information and pull sentences out at random. The result would be gibberish. This brings us to the problem of coherence.

COHERENCE RESULTS FROM ARRANGEMENT

We achieve coherence by proper arrangement. In arranging story elements, we must do two things: (1) Choose an arrangement that makes sense, and (2) make the reader see what that arrangement is. In deciding the order in which we will present our story statements to the reader, we have a number of patterns from which to choose. Some of these patterns or arrangements of material are discussed in the following paragraphs.

Order of time, or chronological pattern, is useful for many topics. It is easy for the reader to follow; he is thoroughly familiar with the way it operates; he is not likely to get lost if we start at the beginning and go straight through to the end.

Order of space is another easy-to-follow pattern. Suppose we want to describe an automobile assembly line. We might simply walk down the line, describing what we see at each station as we come to it.

Order of ascending importance is a useful technique if we decide that certain points we want to make are more important than others. We may simply start out with the least important and work up to the most important. Speakers tend, on the whole, to follow this pattern. Once they have caught the attention of their audience, they usually offer their lesser arguments or statements first and work their way up to the most important statement at the end of the speech. It is worth noting that the opposite order also is possible, the order of descending importance, but that only one accepted prose pattern uses it—the "inverted pyramid" news story which we have discussed in Chapter 2.

You may find it more effective to arrange facts from the *familiar to the unfamiliar*. The writer who wishes to give his reader new information must start with what the reader already knows. He must start where the reader is before trying to lead him into the unknown.

A simple yet almost always acceptable pattern is summarized as *easy to difficult*. Any teacher or student knows that when trying to teach something, he starts with the easier concepts and works gradually into the more difficult ones.

Following a similar psychological reasoning, we may begin with *pleasant* and move to *unpleasant* material. If we are going to tell an audience some unpleasant truths, we usually save them till later in the speech. The speaker who is going to try to put across a point that his audience will not readily accept starts out by making statements that he knows they agree with and builds gradually toward his unpleasant propositions.

Inductive arrangement may be used when we wish to prove a general statement and find it convenient to do so by citing a series of examples which add up to the point we wish to make at the end.

Deductive arrangement, on the other hand, involves making our general statement first, then supporting it with a series of examples. Of the two, the deductive pattern is ordinarily more useful to the feature writer, because when he announces his general statement in the beginning of his story, he indicates clearly where the story is going.

Similarity is illustrated by the old saying, "Like goes with like." Story materials that are comparable or similar may be clumped together. This frequently is the way in which the professional writer determines his story divisions. He scans his notes until he sees similarities of certain facts, then drops these notes together.

Order of contrast is used when it would be most effective to put opposites together. If describing the right and wrong ways of doing something, you may choose to set the "right" beside the "wrong." This not only provides an arrangement that makes sense to the reader but the contrast also may provide emphasis.

CONSIDER YOUR READER

Having chosen a story arrangement that makes sense, the writer has still another task if his story is going to be coherent. He must make that story arrangement apparent to the reader. Not only must the writer know where the story is going but the reader must know, too. This is accomplished with paragraphs and smaller units of introduction, of summary, and of transition. An old cliché of teachers states: "First you tell 'em what you're gonna tell 'em; then you tell 'em; then you tell 'em what you told 'em." The feature writer does something similar.

The story beginning, if it does not summarize what is coming, at least gives very strong indications of what the story is all about. Near the story's end, the writer commonly looks back over the route that has been traveled and summarizes what has been seen. In a long story there also may be in the body of the story structural paragraphs which simultaneously review what has been covered so far and look ahead to what is coming up. Transitional sentences or paragraphs between major divisions of the story must not only lock the divisions together, they must also remind the reader of the way in which each portion of the story ties to the story theme.

START WITH AN OUTLINE

The writer's most useful tool in getting an arrangement of his story materials that makes sense is the outline. Once you have gathered your material, sketch out an outline. This will make your arrangement visible to you, and it will help you discover whether you have left out information that is necessary to your story or if you are trying to include extraneous material—material that diverts the reader from the points that you are trying to put across. Few professional writers work without some kind of outline. And the less practiced a writer is, the more important it is that he use one to help him see, as he writes, where he is going and where he has been.

EMPHASIS—EASIER SAID THAN DONE

It sounds easy, yet one of the trickiest practical problems that the feature writer must solve is that of stressing the story points he wants to stress and playing down those he does not. Several methods are available.

To emphasize material, give it more space. If our stories do not always say exactly what we intend them to say, we may find the cause here. As we gather information for a story, we find that some facts are easier to get than others. We may eventually find that we have too many notes on one phase of the story and skimpy notes for another. If we merely write what we have at hand—and our inclination always is to use everything—our story obviously will be out of balance. We may need to throw away extra material that fits one part of the story and wear out shoe leather to gather additional facts for another part.

If something is important, simply say so. Announce in a story that "the crucial years in the development of the Nazi party were 1928 and 1929." The reader may quarrel with the statement but he cannot escape your meaning.

Contrast is one of the easiest methods of giving emphasis to material. If you have been writing long, loose sentences, a sudden shift to short, curt phrases will alert the reader to the fact that something is different—something is happening in your story that he had better look at. Just as black against white emphasizes each, the juxtaposition of contrasting language, ideas, or images will underscore them.

To emphasize an idea, put it first—or put it last. The middle part of a story is easily forgotten. But a reader will remember a well-executed climax.

HOW TO CATCH A READER

Unlike the inverted pyramid news story, a feature story has a beginning, a middle, and an end. The beginning should arouse the reader's attention and interest. It should give him a clear idea of what the story is going to be like. And it should push him smoothly into the body of the story.

"To make rabbit stew, first you must catch your rabbit." To make any kind of headway with a feature story, you must first catch your reader. The methods of stimulating reader interest are many. (See discussion of human interest in Chapter 2.) Many magazines like anecdotal openings—openings in which the author uses a "yarn" to introduce his topic. Also, striking statements that jar a reader's preconceptions about the way the world operates are popular. We may tell the reader forthrightly what a story is going to be about. Or we may choose to save such direct statements for the climax. In any event, the opening must indicate in unmistakable terms the kind of story that is coming up. The beginning must be honest and appropriate to the story.

In the body we get down to business. This is where we serve up the information or ideas that are the story's reason for being. Typically, the body is made up of a series of general statements (subtheme statements) alternating with proof of these statements. The proof can take many forms—statistics, statements from authorities, physical description, logical argument, illustrative anecdotes, and so on.

Pay particular attention to anecdotes. Most editors love them dearly, as you can prove to yourself by leafing through a few published stories. As you dig out the information that is going to make your article, keep your eyes and ears open for the little stories of people in action—stories that will help make *your* story's point.

ORGANIZE YOUR CONCLUSION

When we have finished our main story, we have one more task. We need to wrap it up gracefully. The ending offers both an opportunity and a challenge. It is our last chance to drive home the point that we have been trying to make. Story endings generally fall into one of the two classes, the *summary* or the *snapper*. The summary is exactly what it says—a last, quick look at what the story has said. The snapper tries to send the reader away with a chuckle, or a gasp, or a "wow."

So much for the "rules" (all of which are broken by good writers every day). Now let us look at the way a working writer uses them. The article which follows is very short, but it demonstrates many of the principles that you will use in writing at any length.[1]

VENTURER IN DENTURES
by William V. Adams

As the wheel purred, the apprehensive expression on the patient's face softened to one of interest. Across the room John Greenwood, surgeon-dentist to President George Washington, was drilling a hole in the base of an artificial tooth. The drill resembled a spinning wheel and, indeed, that was what it had been until Greenwood appropriated it from his mother-in-law and converted it to his purposes.

Anecdotal opening. People in action. And the theme has been sounded. We know—unless the author is fooling us—that the story is going to concern a dentist and dental equipment.

---

[1] William V. Adams, "Venturer in Dentures" *Steelways*, XXII:2 (Mar.–Apr., 1966) p. 24.

The patient's fascination was understandable. The standard drill of the day was the bow drill which operated with the alternating circular motion of a Boy Scout's bow for starting fires. It was a tedious operation requiring both hands. On Greenwood's machine a treadle turned the large wheel which spun a smaller wheel by a pulley drive. A steel bit was affixed to the spindle of the small wheel. The new foot drill had three advantages over the bow drill. It was much faster because the pulley drive multiplied the rotation of the large wheel several hundred times, the treadle left both hands free to hold the workpiece steady and the bit could be driven in one direction continuously.

We have begun to get solid, technical information. But the writer is keeping the unfamiliar tied neatly to the familiar—to "the patient," to "Boy Scout's bow," to Greenwood.

Greenwood often used hippopotamus ivory to make artificial teeth. Carved to match the decayed teeth they would replace, the ivory was drilled to the correct depth and a gold pivot was screwed firmly into the tooth. After wrapping the protruding end of the pivot with cotton to ensure a snug fit, Greenwood inserted it into a previously drilled hole in a root of the old tooth. To drill the root he used an instrument with a pear-shaped point.

Note how the general statement of the first sentence in this paragraph is illustrated and amplified—"proved"—by the rest of the paragraph.

Greenwood's drill, like most dental armamentarium of the time, was homemade, for dentistry was a mechanical sideline rather than a science. But Greenwood did much to change the state of dentistry and is often hailed as the "Father of American Dentistry."

Transition to a new idea-statement.

It has been recorded that Greenwood learned dentistry from his father, Isaac, and from a neighbor, Paul Revere, both part-time dentists. More recent research proves that John left home before his father took up dentistry to serve first as a cabinet-maker's apprentice. Greenwood's own account of his introduction to the profession in New York City has a macabre charm: "Out of fun one day by the desire of Dr. Gamage I attempted to draw a tooth for him. I had never seen one drawn before in all my life. It came out well and encouraged me to attempt others."

Greenwood biographical data, amplifying the "Father of American Dentistry" statement. Note the anecdotal material. Readers like to see people in action and hear them speak.

Study, work and Yankee ingenuity soon carried him to the top of his profession. His theories on the causes of tooth decay were far ahead of his time. Even his foot drill was eighty years in winning general acceptance. He was probably the first in this country to swage gold plate as a base for artificial teeth and may have been the first American to use porcelain teeth brought to him from France by Aaron Burr. George Washington whose notoriously bad teeth should have made him an excellent judge of dentists wrote Greenwood, "I shall always prefer your service to that of any other in your profession."

More proof. We are still tying new and unfamiliar facts to familiar names and ideas.

The next major advances were not until the 1870's. At that time the first dental foot engine was introduced, and an agile foot could pump out drill speeds of over 3,000 revolutions a minute. The electric drill was also introduced in that decade, but even as late as 1938 the highest speed of electric drills ranged only around 4,000 revolutions.

We step ahead. Chronological arrangement makes the sequence of ideas easy to follow.

Today the low torque, air turbine-driven drill is wafted at speeds as high as 400,000 rpm. Shanks for these drill bits require steel of top quality and finish, and the cutting edges or burrs are usually of tungsten carbide. These are the refinements which bring a heartening measure of compassion to the dentist's exacting work. But still, one hundred and seventy-five years after John Greenwood, the dentist's sensitive sole still starts the drill.

We have brought the story up to date. The reader leaves the story with a strong feeling that although most of the things he has learned are historical, they have important meaning for him here and now. And note the twist of the final sentence. The author has taken us full circle—back to where we started, watching Greenwood and his spinning wheel. Everything has been wrapped up in a neat package of orderly ideas. We have learned things we did not know before (including a few things about steel!), and the author has made the learning process a pleasurable experience.

A publicist can expand the range of his effectiveness by learning the rudiments of writing for magazines. To do so, he must learn to analyze markets and audiences in order to meet their needs. He must learn how to dig efficiently and deep for story materials. He must learn how to analyze his materials to determine their meanings. And he must learn to organize them so that they are clear and interesting to the reader.

SUGGESTED READING

BAIRD, RUSSELL N., AND TURNBULL, A. T. *Industrial and Business Journalism.* Philadelphia: Chilton, 1961.

BIRD, GEORGE. *Article Writing and Marketing*, rev. ed. New York: Rinehart and Cox, 1956.

CAMPBELL, WALTER S. *Writing: Advice and Devices.* Garden City, N.Y.: Doubleday, 1950.

FOSTER, JOHN, JR. *Science Writer's Guide.* New York: Columbia, 1962.

GEHMAN, RICHARD. *How To Write and Sell Magazine Articles.* New York: Harper, 1959.

GILMAN, WILLIAM. *The Language of Science.* New York: Harcourt, 1961.

HOWARD, CLIVE (ed.). *A Guide to Successful Magazine Writing.* New York: Scribner, 1954.

LEDERER, WILLIAM J. *Spare-Time Article Writing for Money.* New York: Norton, 1954.

MORRIS, TERRY, AND OTHERS. *Prose by Professionals.* Garden City, N.Y.: Doubleday, 1961.

PETERSON, THEODORE. *Magazines in the Twentieth Century*, 2nd ed. Urbana, Ill.: Univ. of Ill., 1964.

SCHOENFELD, CLARENCE. *Effective Feature Writing.* New York: Harper, 1960.

WOLSELEY, ROLAND E. *Understanding Magazines.* Ames, Iowa: Iowa State Univ., 1966.

★ *Advertising is the most straightforward of all publicity techniques. A wealth of information can be conveyed by a properly prepared ad.*

★ 9 ★ Advertising—
What It Is and
How To Use It

"TURN IT OFF; I can't stand that commercial!" Or: "That's the most misleading ad I've ever seen!"

You have heard people react just as negatively, just as emphatically, to specific advertising messages. Perhaps you have even done it yourself. But the coin has its other side, too. People everywhere depend heavily upon advertising for information they find useful, or helpful, or both. The housewife, for example, studies food-store advertising as she prepares her weekend shopping list. The farmer checks the advertising in agricultural publications for new ideas or products that will help him increase production or improve his management methods. The camera fan keeps abreast of late developments in the photography field by reading the advertising in his favorite photography magazines.

PROS AND CONS OF ADVERTISING

Because they are sensitive to the public's demand for and dependence upon advertising, many respected members of the American business community maintain that advertising is the primary fuel that energizes our private enterprise machine. They contend that it stimulates demand, causing people to spend money which, in turn, buys goods and services and creates jobs. This "chicken and egg" relationship then spurs business so that people have still more money to spend, to buy more goods, to create more jobs. Without advertising, say these protagonists, our whole private enterprise system would collapse.

On the other hand, many presently popular authors—among them Vance Packard—contend that advertising approaches sheer economic waste. They point to its use in creating "planned obsolescence"—the highly advertised new model that makes your car "old" regardless of mileage. They also maintain that the millions spent in urging consumers to shift from one brand to another do nothing but add to the cost of the product.

The arguments don't stop there. Some will insist—and cite convincing examples as proof—that "you can't believe a word you see (or hear) in advertising." Others will declare that a large number of public agencies police the business and that advertisers themselves are constantly on guard to root out and eliminate the untrustworthy.

Finally, there are those who point out that all the media—newspapers, magazines, radio television—are carried into American homes on the back of advertising. Without advertising, they say, the vital task of keeping a democratic society informed and functioning could not be performed as effectively and efficiently as is being done today.

Whatever your personal opinions about advertising, it is at least clear that it is an interesting and controversial subject. In this chapter we will examine in some detail differing points of view about advertising practices. What you learn should be of value to you as a consumer and as a citizen. We also will discuss some of the bread-and-butter aspects of advertising so that you may use this tool more effectively in connection with your business, your profession, or your personal affairs.

DISTINGUISHING CHARACTERISTICS

First, let us get some terms straight. What is advertising? To the publicist, advertising may seem quite similar to other communication techniques. It contains many of the qualities associated with news, publicity, and propaganda and is used widely by public relations specialists. But advertising has at least three other distinguishing characteristics:

1. It is almost always purchased.
2. The buyer of advertising is assured that his message will will be published or broadcast.
3. Advertising is displayed in such a way that it can be identified as having been paid for.

In some ways, advertising is the most straightforward of all publicity techniques. Whereas the source of the planted news story, the public relations gimmick, or the propaganda device may be hidden, the advertisement is marked as a persuasive message motivated and paid for by an individual or agency with a selfish interest. The language of an advertisement may be deceptive but seldom is its purpose a mystery.

ADVERTISING CATEGORIES

Advertising can be categorized in several different ways, the most common types being:

National advertising. This is what you see or hear on many radio and TV shows, see in magazines, on billboards, and—to some extent—in newspapers. It promotes goods and services which have wide distribution—petroleum products, for example. It says: "Buy my brand."

Local advertising. This is sometimes called retail advertising because it is used by the local retail establishment (such as your local food store). It says: "Buy at my store."

Classified advertising. This is the advertising on the so-called want-ad pages.

Other. Various other kinds of advertising may be classified as institutional, trade, idea, or industrial. But in this text our purposes will be served if you become familiar with National, Retail (or local), and Classified advertising.

ATTITUDES TOWARD ADVERTISING

Now let's go back and examine some of the arguments which make advertising such a controversial subject. Conrad Hill of the University of Nebraska in *The Aberrant Image of Advertising* has summarized the criticisms and defenses as well as anyone.[1] The following are some of the issues raised by Hill.

Economic

Critics say that advertising is an economic waste, that it inflates the cost of goods. Supporters claim that it promotes mass demand which makes possible the economies that can be realized by mass production; thus advertising lowers the cost of goods. Hill's analysis: "Neither side makes sense . . . it all depends upon a host of variables, including the product, the market, the economic times, the competition, and so forth."

In the hard goods industries, where production is complex and costly, advertising may bring lower prices. It is likely that automobiles, refrigerators, and other such products would be more expensive if advertising had not stimulated millions of persons to buy them, thereby allowing manufacturers to introduce the efficiences of mass production. On the other hand, manufacturing soaps and cosmetics involves far simpler production problems than are faced by most hard goods producers. These industries have less to gain from mass production techniques. It follows that advertising may not lower the cost of such products. Analysis of the advertising expenditures by various industries supports this premise.

According to *Advertising Age*, automotive firms spent from 1.3 to 2.4 per cent of sales for advertising in 1961.[2] Among appliance companies, the range was 1.4 to 1.8 per cent. On the other hand, the major soap companies spent from 8.2 to 21.2 per cent of sales for advertising. Cosmetics

---

[1] Conrad Hill, *The Aberrant Image of Advertising*, Univ. of Nebr. Publ. No. 202, 1960.

[2] Conrad Hill, "The World of Advertising, *Advertising Age*, Jan., 15, 1963, p. 29.

producers allocated from 15 to 57 per cent of sales to advertising. It is unlikely that advertising lowers product costs for a company which spends half of its receipts on promotion.

Psychological

The charge is made that contemporary advertising relies heavily on appeals exploiting deep-seated weaknesses which the consumer has but of which he is not aware. The critics cite approaches which dwell on hidden sexual drives, the desire to achieve mastery over others, the hope for immortality, and so on. Vance Packard has been the most outspoken, if not the most scientific, critic on this score. He claims that advertisers use the knowledge of human behavior to manipulate the buying patterns of consumers.

Advertising is filled with psychological appeal. It has been for centuries. Whether advertising should use psychological techniques more normally reserved for those involved in healing mental ills is an interesting philosophical question. Certainly politicians, educators, lawyers, and commercial and governmental publicists—professionals in all fields who have a selfish interest in persuading human beings—use the psychological approach. These appeals in advertising have long been recognized as effective, but it would appear that Packard and his advocates have exaggerated the extent to which such appeals can motivate behavior. The unpredictable responses of consumers to advertising messages indicate that advertisers do not possess talents which allow them to mold consumer opinion or force buying behavior.

At this point in time, it is doubtful that the American consumer is being hypnotized by overpowering psychological devices commanded by advertisers. One day the techniques of psychology may become so effective that concerns such as those of Packard will merit more serious consideration.

Cultural and Ethical

Critics charge that advertising emphasizes the material at the expense of the cultural. Defenders claim that advertising spreads culture by subsidizing the communication media which provide Americans with information, entertainment, and culture at levels to satisfy all tastes.

Hill looks upon advertising as a bystander in its relationship to culture. It "mirrors the fashions, the moods and mores of the nation . . . but is not culture itself." Perhaps the most important point of this debate is that through the years both advertising and culture have flourished in the same societies.

It is unwise and unfair to generalize regarding the ethics of all members of any profession or occupational group. But one need not search long to discover unscrupulous businessmen-advertisers. Although a very small percentage of advertising is false by legal standards, too much is misleading and exaggerated. For instance, an advertiser may "hide" important copy if he thinks it will hurt sales. Everyone is familiar with the tiny lines of type often used in advertisements betraying limitations or qualifications of an apparently attractive offer made in large type elsewhere. Such practices deserve no defense. Although the courts allow "normal trade puffery" in advertising, there can be no justification for deliberate attempts to mislead the consumer. Even though it is impossible to determine accurately the amount of advertising that is purposefully misleading, the most casual observer will probably conclude that there is far too much.

Legal

It is claimed that advertising men knowingly violate laws that have been established to protect the consumer and insure responsible performance by advertisers. When cited by a regulatory agency, there is a tendency for business to fight the citation rather than desist from the practice that prompted it. In nearly all instances, these agencies notify an advertiser when they think he is violating a regulation and ask that the practice cease. Only if the advertiser fails to comply is he likely to be prosecuted. The antagonistic behavior of advertisers to the rulings of the regulatory commissions probably stems from the traditional fear Amer-

ican business has of governmental control. A large number
of the firms contesting the decisions of these commissions
are major U.S. businesses—the giants in such industries
as tobacco, cosmetics, food, and drugs. Hill sums up the
situation this way: "If businessmen would become recon-
ciled to the existence of Big Government along with Big
Business and Big Labor, their petulance and morbid fears
would vanish."

Logic and Language

The language and logic used in much advertising has
offended the sensitivities of the American public and in-
sulted its intelligence since the early days of the patent
medicine advertisers. As the consumer has become better
educated and more sophisticated, however, there has been
a decrease in sloppily written, illogical advertising. A great
deal of contemporary advertising is entertaining, well written, and informative. This trend will probably continue.

Much of the quarrel with advertising revolves around
the practices of those firms which produce low-cost, mass-
demand items that vary little from their competitors' wares.
In promoting such goods, the advertising man sometimes
feels he must overstate minor differences between his and
competitive products. Generally speaking, this is not true
of companies producing high cost, durable goods. The copy-
writer who must create an ad differentiating between two
brands of cigarettes has a more difficult job than his cohort
who writes copy for an automotive account.

A large share of the complaints about advertising are
directed at national advertising; local or retail advertising
escapes relatively unscathed. Soap ads promising a successful love life, cigarette ads that imply there is a relationship
between the brand smoked and the masculinity of the
smoker, and soft drink ads suggesting that elders who con-
sume the product will feel like teen-agers understandably
trigger hostility in rational persons. Seldom are complaints
aimed at the advertising of a women's apparel store, a
grocery store, or almost any other retail outlet. The fact that
40 per cent of the money spent on advertising goes for retail

advertising escapes the notice of most critics when they train their big guns on the practices of a relative handful of national advertisers.

These are only the briefest kinds of references to some of the arguments and differing viewpoints concerning advertising. They are intended to help you rest your own opinions on a broader base of information. They may be of value to you as a consumer of advertising.

Watchdogs of the Industry

On any subject where there is such divergence of opinion, some will declare, "There ought to be a law against that." The truth is that already a number of laws are concerned with the regulation of advertising, and there also is considerable self-policing within the industry itself.

Federal, state, and local governments regulate advertising. Some degree of self-regulation is accomplished by associations within the industry. Consumer-supported groups also exert pressures on the advertising industry and on individual advertisers.

The number one watchdog of advertising is the Federal Trade Commission. It is empowered to take action against firms engaged in interstate commerce which practice false or deceptive advertising. The FTC also enforces laws regarding the labeling of textiles and flammable products. The Food and Drug Administration is mainly concerned with the labeling and packaging claims (considered advertising) of food, drug, and cosmetic products.

The Federal Communications Commission is the licensing agency for all television and radio stations. Although its primary interest is not in advertising, the commission may be reluctant to renew the license of a station which has been in trouble with other agencies because of the advertising it has carried. The Post Office Department is involved in constant surveillance of advertising because of federal laws regarding fraud by mail, the advertising of lotteries, and the mailing of obscene materials.

Other federal agencies have varying degrees of control over advertising. These include the Alcohol and To-

bacco Tax Division of the Internal Revenue Service, the
Securities and Exchange Commission, the Civil Aeronautics
Board, the Federal Deposit Insurance Corporation, and the
Federal Home Loan Bank Board.

State and city governments have passed a multitude of
laws or ordinances related to advertising. Some 45 states
have enacted false advertising laws. Many states have laws
prohibiting or curtailing advertising by certain professions
and occupations. Other state laws are directed at the advertising of insurance companies, loan firms, and the pur-
veyors of food and liquor. Political and outdoor advertising
is closely controlled by many states. And almost all states
have statutes prohibiting obscene advertising, the advertising of lotteries, and the use of the American flag in
advertising.

Attempts at self-regulation are made by a variety of
organizations within the advertising industry. Among these
are advertising agency, magazine, newspaper, radio, and
television associations. Each of these provides codes of
ethics and standards of behavior for its members. The
degree of influence of these groups varies. Probably the
most effective is the National Association of Broadcasters.
Its television and radio codes specify standards of good
taste, types of products that can be advertised, and the
amount of time that can be devoted to advertising on television and radio. The broadcast media probably police themselves better than other media because broadcasting is so
closely controlled by the federal government. If they do not
behave, the FCC is likely to step in.

Individual media units—the newspaper, magazine, or
television station—also exercise some control over advertising. Most large, responsible media employ advertising
censors who screen copy before it is approved for publication or broadcast.

Perhaps the most efficient and comprehensive nongovernmental policeman of advertising is a voluntary organization, the Better Business Bureau. Better Business
Bureaus are located throughout the country and are loosely
affiliated with the National Better Business Bureau. These
agencies are composed of companies and retail business

firms interested in promoting fair advertising and selling practices. Although they possess no legal authority, the bureaus are vigilant monitors of advertising. They act on their own and upon complaints by consumers. When an improper practice is discovered, the advertiser is notified and requested to change his ways. If this fails, advertising media are notified and asked not to accept advertising from the business in question. Also, other Better Business Bureaus are alerted. If these moves fail, evidence is supplied to local, state, or federal authorities so they can bring legal action against the offending advertiser.

One private agency, Consumers Union, has been quite successful in combating false and misleading advertising. It is a nonprofit organization that tests products and publishes its finding in Consumers Report, a monthly magazine whose circulation is edging toward one million. The product test reports often put the lie to advertising claims made by manufacturers.

With this as a general background, we will devote the remainder of this chapter to the various media and some of the techniques of the advertising business.

AN OVERVIEW OF THE MEDIA

By way of quick overview, a national advertiser has at his disposal some 1,750 daily newspapers, 9,000 weekly newspapers, 9,000 magazines, 4,000 AM radio stations, 550 TV stations, 320,000 outdoor advertising signs—plus the cards in buses and subway trains, motion picture advertising, calendars, trading stamps, novelties, and direct mail —to name only the major media. A large American business firm may use several or nearly all of these outlets. How selection is made among them is a highly sophisticated process that will not be dealt with in this text. But the relative advantages and disadvantages of the various media should be noted.

NEWSPAPERS—HERE TODAY, GONE TOMORROW

Approximately 1,750 daily newspapers are published in the United States with a total circulation of about 60 million. Weekly newspapers number about 9,000 and have a total circulation of some 25 million. Newspapers have survived the emergence of magazines, radio, and television to remain the primary promotional vehicle for retail advertisers. About 30 per cent of the total advertising dollar goes to newspapers.

Newspaper advertising has these major advantages: *It penetrates.* Typically the newspaper which has no competition reaches 75 to 90 per cent of the homes in the town where it is published. *It is flexible.* A national advertiser can select newspapers in the specific areas where he has distribution. *It has breadth of audience.* Virtually everyone—regardless of income, or occupation—reads his hometown or area newspaper. *It is timely.* The advertiser can inject immediacy into his advertising through newspaper ads.

But newspaper advertising is short-lived; it is here today and gone tomorrow. Newspaper reproduction (although vastly improved) is still inferior to magazines because of cheap paper and high-speed presses. And to achieve national coverage through newspapers an advertiser must deal with many papers. Newspapers, even the very largest, are essentially community papers serving at most a major metropolitan area, a state, or a region.

MAGAZINE ADS LACK TIMELINESS

Of the approximately 9,000 magazines in this country, only a small percentage are a major factor in advertising. They include some 300 so-called consumer and farm magazines such as *Life, Look, Reader's Digest, Farm Journal,* and *Successful Farming* plus about 2,500 business and trade publications. Business publications are classed as horizontal or vertical. The horizontal publication is aimed at individuals, such as engineers or personnel officers doing the same kind of jobs in various industries. Vertical publications are aimed at all individuals employed in the same business , such as everyone in the petroleum industry, whether a vice-president or an apprentice.

One-issue circulation of the 300 consumer and farm

publications is well over 200 million. The 2,500 business publications have about 45 million subscribers. About 8 per cent of all advertising is done in magazines and almost all of this is purchased by national advertisers. When television attracted many of the blue chip national advertisers, the magazine industry looked to some of the smaller firms including companies with regional rather than national distribution. To attract these advertisers, many magazines now offer zoned or regional editions. *Reader's Digest* has nine regional editions. *Life* allows advertisers to choose any three of 26 marketing areas.

In recent years a number of controlled or free-circulation magazines have been highly successful. These are distributed free to audiences tailored to satisfy certain classes of advertisers. Most of these magazines are business or farm publications.

The advantages of magazines include:
1. An above average audience in terms of income, education, social position, and buying power.
2. A longer life than newspapers.
3. A much better quality of ad reproduction.
4. Audience selectivity. An advertiser can, through selecting the right magazine, aim his message at men, women, professional people, certain income groups, or whatever audience he chooses.

The disadvantages of magazines are:
1. Limited market penetration—magazines deliver national and regional audiences but they do not offer extensive penetration of any one territory.
2. Lack of timeliness since advertisers must plan anywhere from two weeks to as much as months in advance.
3. There is some waste circulation since only those advertisers whose products are available in all markets realize maximum efficiency from magazine advertising.

TELEVISION—COSTLY BUT EFFECTIVE

Television is the newest and most flamboyant of advertising media, and it is considered the most effective by many advertisers. The 670 television stations in existence in 1965 were beaming programs into more than 90 per cent of the American homes. The typical family has its set turned on about five hours per day.

Of the $2.2 billion spent annually on television (about 15 per cent of the total spent for all advertising), about 85 per cent is contributed by national or regional advertisers, some 15 per cent by local advertisers. Television time is classed as network, spot, and local. *Network* refers to full, alternate, or multisponsorship of network-originated programs. *Spot* is the purchase of programs or announcements on several stations without regard to network affiliation. *Local* is the purchase of programs or announcements on one or more stations in a single market by businesses in that market.

The advantages of television are:

1. *Audience size.* Prime time network television offers the advertiser the largest audiences of any medium.
2. *Exclusive features.* Television is unique among media in that it combines sight, sound, and motion.
3. *Personalization.* Personal selling is considered more effective than any other type.
4. *Breadth of audience.* Television provides an audience similar to that of newspapers. It reaches more young people than newspapers, but there is evidence that it is less popular among the highly educated.
5. *Market penetration.* Television penetrates as many or more homes in each market as do newspapers, but its exposure is considerably different. The reader can digest all of the content of all of the newspapers available in a market. He can view the offerings of only one television station at a time and thereby is denied exposure to whatever is being aired by other stations.
6. *Audience selectivity.* Although television probably reaches as broad a segment of the population as any of the mass media, it can offer selective audiences. By tailoring content and by carefully selecting time periods, the television advertiser can reach predominantly male, female, or young audiences.
7. *Integration of advertising with nonadvertising.* The advertiser can relate the content of the program to his

product. Popular entertainers can be used as commercial presenters. Their involvement usually heightens interest in the commercial.

8. *Exclusive appeal to small children.* Television is the only medium which communicates with children before they themselves can verbalize.

Some of the disadvantages of television are:

1. *Initial cost.* Although there is evidence that television is an economical medium on the basis of cost per viewer reached, the initial cost is high. It is beyond the budget of most advertisers, both local and national.

2. *Short life of advertising message.* The broadcast advertisement lives only 10 seconds, 30 seconds, or one minute.

3. *Inability to deliver complex messages.* The brevity of broadcast ads makes it difficult for the advertiser to present detailed product information.

4. *Difficulty of measuring audience.* Rating services and other types of surveys are used to measure broadcast audiences. These rely on sampling methods which provide only estimates of audience size, whereas the exact circulations of print media can be verified.

RADIO IS GROWING

Radio, which was counted out by many experts when television began to flex its muscles, not only has survived but has grown. Today there are some 4,000 AM radio stations and more than 1,000 FM stations. About 6 per cent of the advertising dollar is spent annually on radio advertising with more than half coming from local advertisers. Network expenditures are about $50 million as compared to the $200 million spent for this type of advertising in the late 1940's. However, the increased use of radio by local firms has more than made up the loss.

As an advertising medium, radio possesses several of the advantages and disadvantages of television. These include personalization of approach, use of program talent to deliver advertising messages, selectivity of audience, short life of message, inability to present complex information, and difficulty of determining size of audience.

Radio does not offer advertisers sight and motion. Therefore, the radio commercial usually carries less impact than its television counterpart. Although the signals of many radio stations reach further than those of competing television stations, radio audiences are generally smaller. The initial cost of radio advertising is low. Most local advertisers can afford it and radio reaches more customers out of the home than does any other medium except outdoor advertising. Listenership is high among commuters on their way to and from work. During the summer, radio accompanies people to the beach, on picnics, and on vacations. Of the 185 million operative radios, more than 40 million are in cars and 10 million are located in public places. More than any other medium, radio has an impact without receiving full attention. A housewife, for example, can listen to the radio while she irons or does the dishes.

OUTDOOR ADVERTISING ON DECLINE

Outdoor advertising is the only major medium in which expenditures have been declining in the past few years. This drop is at least partly due to a widespread movement to restrict the placement of billboards on American highways. The federal government now offers bonus highway funds to states which regulate outdoor advertising on the interstate highway system.

Some 700 outdoor advertising companies or plants are responsible for about 320,000 signs located in some 15,000 cities. The cost of an outdoor location is based on the number of potential viewers who pass the location daily. Plant owners offer the advertiser package deals of several signs which assure him of exposure to a specific percentage of the population in a local market. A No. 100 showing supposedly exposes a population equal to that of the entire market to the advertiser's signs in a 30-day period.

Although outdoor expenditures represent less than 2 per cent of the total advertising outlay, some types of businesses and noncommercial organizations make heavy use of some form of outdoor advertising. At the local level hotels, motels, and restaurants find it a valuable medium. Nationally, automotive manufacturers, gasoline and oil companies, and soft drink companies use it extensively. Outdoor is also an important vehicle for political advertising.

DIRECT MAIL REACHES SELECTED GROUP

About 15 per cent of the advertising dollar is spent annually on direct mail. More than one-quarter million businesses use this form of advertising, and it is an important medium for noncommercial agencies such as churches and political parties. Some types of firms spend more money on it than on any other medium. Book publishers spend almost half of their budgets on direct mail. Other heavy users include automotive dealers, drug companies, clothing stores, and investment brokers.

Direct mail offers several advantages: (1) The advertiser can select his audience carefully, (2) he can personalize his message to an unusual degree, (3) he can use a wide variety of formats, and (4) he can measure his response with considerable effectiveness.

The disadvantages of direct mail include (1) its cost (mainly because of the postage bill), (2) the problem of securing and maintaining mailing lists, and (3) the attitude of the public toward direct mail.

ADVERTISING COSTS VARY WIDELY

How much does advertising cost? As with most other items offered for sale, the price depends upon the kind and quantity purchased. But there is another factor, too—the size of audience reached. Before examining some typical charges for the various media and the methods by which advertising is sold, let us quickly review this subject from the standpoint of the individual businessman or merchant. What does advertising cost him in relation to his other business costs?

Some 14 billion dollars per year is spent on advertising

in the United States. In relation to our gross national product, this amounts to about 2 per cent. And this figure—2 per cent of gross sales—is a rule-of-thumb figure frequently used by businessmen in establishing an advertising budget. There are wide variations, of course. Some business firms on every main street will spend a tiny fraction of 1 per cent of gross sales; others may spend 5, 6, or 8 per cent. But many fall in the bracket between 1 and 4 per cent of gross sales.

Some businesses will spend more than others. Entertainment and luxury items will be on the high side of any comparison. Food, despite its large ads, will—percentagewise—be on the low side. But persons who maintain that the average businessman spends 15 or 20 per cent of his gross sales to buy customers through advertising are grossly misinformed. Certainly, at times, the merchant will spend more than at others—in getting his store established or in introducing a new line of merchandise. But typically his advertising expenditures will be fairly stable in relation to his gross business. The merchant will use his advertising program to help level out his business cycles. If his advertising program is well planned he will tend to overadvertise in periods when business is normally slow and underadvertise in times of ready sales.

The merchant must decide where to spend his advertising dollar. He quite naturally wants to know where it will do him the most good. Each situation is different, depending upon media available, costs, the merchant's particular needs, and many other factors. Following are some of the yardsticks he will use as he begins to make decisions in this area.

NEWSPAPERS USE THE COLUMN-INCH

Local advertising is usually sold at the column-inch rate. A column-inch is an area one column wide and one inch deep. A paper 8 columns wide with 20-inch columns will therefore—in a full page ad—offer for sale 160 column-inches of advertising. On small community newspapers this may cost a good deal less than $1 a column-inch and the page might cost less than $100. On a metropolitan newspaper this same page would cost several thousand dollars. This reflects the differing circulation. (National advertising appearing in newspapers is billed at so much an agate line. There are 14 agate lines in one column-inch; but this is jargon of importance only to those who are actively in the business.)

The yardstick used to measure comparative costs of newspaper advertising—larger circulation papers versus smaller ones, taking into account their varying advertising rates—is known as the milline rate. This is the cost of sending one agate line to one million readers. It can be figured by multiplying the line rate by one million and dividing by the circulation. Smaller newspapers customarily have higher milline rates than do metropolitan papers. But publishers of smaller newspapers maintain that their product is more thoroughly read.

MAGAZINES BILL AT PAGE RATE

Almost all magazine advertising is billed at the page rate or fraction thereof. A full-page black and white ad in a general consumer-type magazine with circulation of 7 million may run in excess of $35,000. Color will cost more. But a page in a business magazine with 25,000 circulation may cost less than $1,000. Again, it is a matter of circulation and the cost per thousand is the standard measure used to compare costs of magazines. This is calculated by multiplying the full page cost by 1,000 and dividing this figure by the magazine's circulation. The cost per thousand for some of the major consumer magazines may range from $2 to $5. In more selective magazines of smaller circulation the costs may go as high as $25 to $50. But the advertiser interested in that market may find the higher cost quite the best deal.

RADIO–TV RATES COMPLEX

The advertising rate structure of the broadcast media is far more complex than that of the print media. Rates are based on potential audience and on units of time and time of day. Broadcast audiences fluctuate greatly throughout the day. This fluctuation is more pronounced among television viewers than among radio listeners. Television is primarily a nighttime medium, radio a daytime medium. Network and station rates are scaled to take into account the general patterns of listenership—the greater the number of listeners the higher the rate. The most expensive time— the so-called prime time—on television comes in midevening, from 7 to 9. Peak listenership on radio, on the other hand, comes between 7 and 9 A.M. So here again the advertiser decides on the kind and number of listeners or viewers he wants to reach and the relative costs of reaching them. As has been mentioned, television tends to be a tool for national advertising whereas radio is more generally used for local advertising.

The cost of commercial time on a radio station located in a town of 7,500 may be as low as $3 to $5 per minute. In a city of 250,000 the cost may range from $50 to $70 per minute, depending upon the time of day. At the other extreme the cost of a half-hour show (including time, talent, and production) on one of the national television networks may run as high as $150,000. During this time the sponsor may have no more than three one-minute commercials which, under these circumstances, makes the actual commercial announcements cost at the rate of $50,000 per minute.

Cost per thousand is the measure used to determine the relative expense of television and radio advertising. This informs the advertiser of the cost of reaching a thousand homes with one commercial minute and is calculated the same as cost per thousand for magazines except that talent expenses, if any, are added to time costs.

PREPARING THE ADVERTISING MESSAGE

Almost all advertising is produced in either of two ways. If it is national advertising, it is probably planned, created, and placed in the media by an advertising agency. If it is retail or local advertising, it is probably planned and produced by either the local businessman or his own advertising department working with a representative from his local newspaper or radio or TV station.

The advertising agency, commonly associated with Madison Avenue in New York where indeed many of the large agencies are located, exists solely to help business enterprises plan, produce, and finally place in the various media the kind and type of advertising which they decide to use. Thus the national advertising appearing in local newspapers, in magazines, or on radio or TV has actually been placed there by an agency acting as a representative of the business firm. Agencies typically receive a 15 per cent commission on all of the time and space purchased for their clients.

Regardless of who prepares the advertisement—an agency, a small businessman, a volunteer publicity chairman—the same general approach should be followed. It should be the climax of a well-planned, thorough investigation of all pertinent factors—the product, the consumer, and the market. The advertiser must define clearly the objective of his program. Is it to sell a product? To improve the image of a company organization? To sell an idea? After the basic approach is determined, the advertiser is faced with the most demanding and important task of all—phrasing the message.

WHAT MAKES AN EFFECTIVE AD?

The importance of the advertising message has been pointed up in countless instances in which advertisers have experimented with different messages in the same media and have realized startlingly different results. In one instance, two ads of the same size offering the same product at the same price were carried in the same issue of a newspaper. One ad resulted in the sale of 1,000 units. The other ad sold only 70. There have been other instances where an ad costing $40 sold 3 units whereas an ad costing twice that much sold nearly 200 units. A change in a headline on a particular ad boosted sales from 4 units to 50.

Professionals frequently classify advertising copy into

reason why, humorous, testimonial, dialogue, narrative, or descriptive categories. The distinctions, some of them subtle, are beyond the scope of this text—although most of them are quite obvious to the average reader.

More important than this classification, however, is the selection of the words, phrases, and sentences that make up the advertising message—regardless of the approach being used. Dunn[3] says that an ad must have these five attributes if it is to be effective: It must be interesting, specific, simple, concise, and believable. Analyze your ad against these five points.

Actually, writing an effective ad takes the same skills as those required to write a good lead on a news story. The sentences are usually short. The verbs are active. The words are minimal in number—each has a good reason for being there. But ad writing need frighten no one away. The most effective ads are those built from words familiar to the average person.

Morton Levinstein, in a trade magazine article several years ago, cited eight guidelines to effective retail advertising. Although his remarks were directed toward merchants, they are helpful to anyone engaged in creating an advertisement.

1. The purpose of advertising is to sell—not to satisfy the personal ambitions of the advertising man, the artistic aspirations of the artist, or the vanity of the firm. . . . Advertising should try to sell and not call unnecessary attention to itself, its cleverness, or its flamboyant originality.

2. Every advertising man should assume that the customers do not want to read his advertisement. Therefore, he should make reading it as easy as possible. . . . If we write our ads with no illustrations beforehand, and make up our minds that people are not eagerly looking forward to our ads, the burden is on us to do a better selling job.

3. Think of the customer as essentially egotistic and self-

---

[3] S. Watson Dunn, *Advertising, Its Role in Modern Marketing*, (New York, Holt, Rinehart and Winston, 1961), Chap. 19.

centered. He is interested primarily in himself. Therefore, show what you can do for him.

4. Make ads simple and easy to read. What you don't say
    is often as important as what you do say. Unless a thing
    is really important, leave it out. It is better to have three
    important statements in an ad than six important ones
    mixed with fifteen that are not.

5. Ideas are important in advertising. Give your ads plenty
    of thought. Have definite reasons for doing what you do.
    Space is expensive. If you cannot give a good reason
    for running an ad, don't run it. When you have some-
    thing worth saying, that is the time to advertise.

6. Be yourself. Give your ads a personality. Let them ex-
    press the individuality of your store, so that the people
    who read your ads will feel that your store is composed
    of human beings and not bricks, showcases and store
    fixtures.

7. Don't be dogmatic. All rules can be broken, including
    these. The only hard and fast rule in advertising is that
    there is no hard and fast rule. Be flexible in your think-
    ing. Don't be afraid to be different.

8. Don't use advertising to cover up your past mistakes.
    Good advertising will not help move bad merchandise.
    Such advertising is expensive because it will not produce
    results, and it also gives people the wrong impression of
    your store. Sell the merchandise the people want to buy,
    at the time they want to buy it, and at the prices they
    want to pay for it.

KEEP AD LAYOUTS SIMPLE

The task of laying out an ad bewilders the nonprofessional unnecessarily. It need not, if he keeps in mind
the major function of the layout—to make the ad as easy to
read as possible. Accomplishing this calls for an emphasis
on simplicity. Leaf through any newspaper or national
magazine and you will find that the layout of most ads is
quite standard. They contain one main headline, a dominant illustration, a copy block, and a trademark or business
signature. Such sameness in layout does not mean that ad-

vertising agency employees lack talent or imagination. It means, instead, that they usually conclude the most effective layout is the simplest.

To prepare an ad for the print media (see illustrations on pages 204–6) follow this procedure:

1. Use a layout sheet large enough to accommodate ad and still leave room for printer's instructions in the margins.
2. Include name of advertiser, medium, date of insertion, and size of ad in the upper right hand corner (for newspapers, ad size should be listed in columns wide and and inches deep—2 cols. x 5 inches; for magazines, ad size should be listed in fractional page units—¼-page, ½-page).
3. Rule in borders to exact size of ad.
4. Paste proofs of illustrations in exact location desired in final ad. If proofs are not available, indicate position and size of illustration with blocked-out area.
5. Letter headlines in approximately the same size as desired in the final ad.
6. Indicate body copy with horizontal, parallel lines. Key copy blocks with numbers or letters corresponding to actual copy on copy sheet (see 8 below).
7. Indicate position of trademark, product name, or company name.
8. On an 8½ x 11-inch copy sheet type copy blocks and key them to correspond with location on layout sheet.

As you begin to talk with professionals at this stage of ad preparation, they will suggest approximate type faces and type sizes. There are type faces more suited to some ads than others. But that is the subject of a more detailed discussion than we can offer here. Type sizes are spoken of in points. An easy way to visualize a point is to remember that there are 72 points in an inch—72-point type is an inch high. Typically the body type, the straight matter in the news sections, is 8 or 9 point. Many headlines, both in ads and in news, are 14, 18, 24, 36, or 48 point in size.

The principles of good advertising are the same regardless of medium used. However, basic differences in the physical presentation of print and broadcast ads necessitate somewhat different approaches and techniques. Because

2 col. X 7 inches
Affiliated Men's Clubs
Register
Tuesday, April 2

Copy A

95m

12½

Pancake Days is a joint venture of all Boy Scout troops in Lyon County. All proceeds will be used for renovation of equipment at the Ka-Ho-La Scout Camp in preparation for next summer's activities. Tickets available from the scout who will visit your home this week or at the Auditorium's south entrance.

The copy sheet (above) and the layout sheet (opposite) have been prepared according to the standards discussed in the text. The layout is the same size as the completed ad will be. Type faces, type sizes, and line length (for example, copy block A has been marked for 9-point Spartan Medium to be set 12½ picas wide) have been indicated to assist the printer in building your ad the way you want it to appear. Make sure the printer has the type faces and sizes you specify. He will be glad to discuss makeup problems with you. Note that complete information has been given concerning source of illustrations. The completed ad resulting from this layout is shown on page 206.

2 col. x 7 inches
Affiliated Men's Clubs
Register
Tuesday April 2

ILLUSTRATION
Metro Mat Service
3944 Aug. 66 M.P. 19

ILLUSTRATION
Metro Mat Service
1905 Feb. 66 M.P. 65

3rd Annual Boy Scout

PANCAKE DAYS

Three Consecutive Saturdays
APRIL 6, 13 and 20

PANCAKES ALL YOU CAN EAT!

J and

SAUSAGE 50¢

Open 6 a.m. till 10:30 a.m.
Civic Auditorium Basement

AFFILIATED
MEN'S CLUBS

BREAKTHROUGH FOR YOUTH

3rd Annual Boy Scout

PANCAKE DAYS

Three Consecutive Saturdays

—— APRIL, 6, 13 and 20 ——

PANCAKES
and
SAUSAGE

ALL YOU CAN EAT!

50c

Open 6 a.m. till 10:30 a.m.

Civic Auditorium Basement

Pancake Days is a joint venture of all Boy Scout troops in Lyon County. All proceeds will be used for renovation of equipment at the Ka-Ho-La Scout Camp in preparation for next summer's activities. Tickets available from the scout who will visit your home this week or at the auditorium's south entrance.

AFFILIATED
MEN'S CLUBS

the broadcast message is presented in a more intimate manner than the print message, the commercial writer should incorporate a personal tone into the broadcast message whenever feasible. Also the broadcast message is short and fleeting, so there should be emphasis on simplicity and repetition in commercial copy.

Radio and television offer the advertiser a number of exclusive tools and techniques. These include the singing commercial, echo chambers, various forms of animation, puppets, and the like. The nonprofessional usually is not familiar with these techniques and must rely on assistance from experts if he is to make use of them. Some can be used without inflating production costs. Others are prohibitively expensive for the typical budget.

SUMMARY

This chapter has attempted to give you a general picture of the advertising industry and to provide you with information that may be of help if you are ever called upon to produce an advertisement. If you do find yourself in this situation, be sure to take advantage of the expert services that are available, usually at no cost to you. The advertising departments of the various media are staffed by well-trained, experienced professionals whose main job is to assist advertisers. Take your problems to these experts. Be frank with them. Supply them with accurate, complete information and ask their advice. Usually, it will be extremely valuable. In many cases, these people will undertake the entire chore of preparing an advertisement or a campaign. However, it is still important that you understand the principles of effective advertising so that you can evaluate their work.

SUGGESTED READING

BEDELL, CLYDE. *Your Advertising.* Park Ridge, Ill.: Clyde Bedell, Inc., 1953.
———. "The World of Advertising." *Advertising Age,* Jan. 15, 1963.

DUNN, S. WATSON. *Advertising: Its Role in Modern Marketing.*
New York: Holt, 1961.
KIRKPATRICK, C. A. *Advertising: Mass Communication in
Marketing.* Boston: Houghton, 1959.
LEVINSTEIN, MORTON. "Eight Ways To Strengthen Your Ad-
vertising," *Automotive Retailer,* June, 1946.
SANDAGE, CHARLES H., AND FRYBURGER, VERNON. *Advertising:
Theory and Practice.* Homewood, Ill.: Irwin, 1963.
WRIGHT, JOHN S., AND WARNER, DANIEL S. *Advertising.* New
York: McGRAW, 1962.

★ *Some representation of meanings, that can pass between people, is needed so that we can communicate with each other.*

★ 10 ★ Communication Is Process

SUPPOSE FOR A MOMENT that you are working for some company in a small city—a good company that is doing a fine job of serving its customers and the community. It is a growing organization and is about to move into larger quarters with modern new equipment. To show these new facilities to the community, the company president decides to have a big public open house. Because you have studied journalism a little, you are designated the communication expert on the staff. Your job is to get the word out to the people and persuade them to attend.

You really work on the stories. You find good solid news pegs to hang them on; you write them in clean clear language with crisp leads, short sentences, straightforward vocabulary, and tight copy. You write separate versions for newspapers and broadcasting stations, and you time release of the stories to give an equal break to the weekly papers as well as the other media. You send the material to all the mass media outlets in the county, and even to a few papers and stations in a city in a neighboring county that is only a few miles away.

You are proud of your work—until the day of the open house. Some 100 or so persons show up, instead of the 200 or more planned for. The boss is disappointed—and so are you. What went wrong? Did *anything* go wrong? Could

211

you have done better—or were you and the boss expecting too much?

You start checking around. You discover, first, that two of the five weeklies in the county didn't use the stories, and two of the others only used one of the three you wrote. Only one of the two dailies used them, the one right in your community. Your batting average was not much better with the radio and television stations. Not only that, but two of the radio stations used the stories only on their 7:00 A.M. newscasts—nowhere else.

You run into a friend, one you fully expected to see at the open house but didn't. You ask him about it. "What open house?" he asks. "Don't you read the newspaper?" you counter. "Sure," he says, "every day. But I didn't see anything about any open house." (You don't bother to tell him that the local daily ran all three of your stories, right on schedule.)

Another friend tells you that certainly he knew of the open house but thought it was just for employees and their families and friends. One person forgot the date, and another got interested in the TV ball game and didn't go. Still another tells you that this open house business is just a bunch of propaganda and he is not about to get taken in by such stuff. The final straw is when one acquaintance tells you he didn't understand all that talk in the story about new electronic data processing equipment, automatic billing, and the like, and could not see any point in being confused further.

WHAT WENT WRONG?

You are about ready to throw in the towel. But wait, let's go back and look at this again. Let's go all the way back to the beginning—to the point where the boss gave you this assignment. You were asked to communicate something to somebody. You wanted a definite response to your message—attention to it, understanding and acceptance of it, and action on it. So you told them—not one, but three times. The stories were good—the local editor said so. But some editors apparently didn't agree. And the readers and listeners of the public—they must be blind, unthinking, stupid, forgetful, or careless—or all those things.

Now this is not a case study of failure as it might well seem at first blush. After all, quite a number of people did attend the event and presumably learned some things about the company they did not know. However, there are several possible misjudgments about how an audience is likely to respond to a series of messages. There also is some possibility that both you and the boss were overly optimistic about what could be done to persuade people to attend such an event.

Consider the questions implied. Why should one editor see the open house stories as relevant and worthwhile while another editor did not? How could any person who reads a newspaper regularly not see at least one of the three stories about the event? How could people so misunderstand the stories as to see them as propaganda or as intended for persons other than themselves? Why would lack of understanding of the stories' content occur? And why were so many people apparently uninterested?

THEORY BEHIND COMMUNICATION

Mass communication processes are complex. There are some general operating rules as suggested in earlier chapters in this book—good rules that are useful and make sense in spite of what this case study may imply. But these rules require sensitive, flexible application, and this requires understanding. It requires understanding of people, and it requires understanding of ourselves. It requires a concept of the processes through which people go in communicating, and a point of view to use in analyzing the communication situations in which we find ourselves. So let us look at some theoretic ideas about communication and see what they may tell us about our open house problem.

At the heart of the business lies a simple proposition— simple to state, easy to understand, and enormously difficult to accept and use. The idea: *Words and events do not have meaning—people do.*

It is simple, isn't it? But how seldom we incorporate

it into our reflexive and emotional behavior! Listen to
people, and see how many ways they have of telling you that
the idea is not true, that meaning really *is* in words:

"You don't mean that's blue—you mean it's black."
"I meant just exactly what I said."
"That's not the correct word, the right one is . . ."
"But that isn't what you said."
"If you'd only say what you mean . . ."
"But I told you!"

Have you ever tried to explain our kind of democracy
to someone from Russia, or from some other "democratic"
country in the world? Or tried to show a foreigner why
"Peanuts" is funny? Or told somebody who never heard of
it what the Cooperative Extension Service is all about?
Have you ever tried to give somebody—or get from somebody—directions on how to get someplace they or you want
to go?

WORDS, WORDS, WORDS!

Lewis Carroll made the point with exceptional clarity
in his marvelously piquant *Through the Looking-Glass:*[1]

"I don't know what you mean by 'glory,' " Alice said.

Humpty Dumpty smiled contemptuously, "Of course
you don't—till I tell you. I meant 'there's a nice knock-
down argument for you!' "

"But 'glory' doesn't mean 'a nice knock-down argument,' " Alice objected.

"When *I* use the word," Humpty Dumpty said, in
rather a scornful tone, "it means just what I choose it to
mean—neither more or less."

"The question is," said Alice, "whether you *can* make
words mean so many different things."

"The question is," said Humpty Dumpty, "which is to
be master—that's all."

The meanings we have for words and events are inside
of us—they are ours. Another way of saying this is to

---

[1] Lewis Carroll (C. L. Dodgson), *Alice's Adventures in Wonder-
land, Through the Looking-Glass,* and *The Hunting of the Snark*
(Washington: National Home Library Foundation, 1932).

suggest that the meanings we have for events are our *expectations* about them—what they will and will not do, how they relate to other events, what difference they make to our daily lives.

MEANINGS COME FROM EXPERIENCES

Where do we get our meanings—our expectations? From experience. We learn meanings from our experiences with the events and words of our world, and from the people with whom we interact throughout our lives.

We can say that events—that is, objects, characteristics, relationships, ideas—that we have not experienced in any way have no meaning for us at all. As we experience them in one or another way, repeatedly, we acquire meaning for them in increasing richness and depth. These are not neutral meanings, either; we *feel* about these events as well as *know* about them. Chairs are not just chairs; they are comfortable or uncomfortable, pleasant or unpleasant to look at, strong or weak, graceful or crude, useful or useless. What they are to each of us depends on our experiences with them, with people in relation to them, and with what we have learned to expect of them as related to our needs in the many varying situations of our daily lives.

MEANING AND YOU

Basically, every human being seeks to acquire a stable set of meanings or expectations about himself and the world he lives in. He wants his life to be predictable; he must be able to go along without constantly stubbing his toe and bumping his nose. When he drives down the street, he wants to know that the lights on the cross streets are red and that people in those lanes will stop. When he smiles at and says "good morning" to a friend, he wants to know that he will get a smile and greeting in return. When his expectations about these things are violated in some way, he is usually not very happy about it. He dislikes such violations so much, in fact, that he frequently avoids situations that are unpredictable.

An extremely important part of this concerns what an individual knows or expects of himself. The most important object in a person's world is himself; perhaps, as psychologist Gardner Murphy says, because he has more experience with himself than anything else.[2] One cannot be unconscious of self—at least not for long. To get along, an individual has to know who and what he is, what he is capable of, and how others are going to respond to him. He has to have a stable set of expectations about himself, just as he needs them about other events in his environment. Without them his dealings with events and people become unpredictable and chaotic—for most of us a truly intolerable state of affairs.

MEANING AND THE OTHER FELLOW

To get along with people, to work and play with them, to communicate with them, a person has to be able to predict how they will respond and behave. Communication, especially, is an exercise in prediction—prediction of the meanings people have for events and for words. The source of an utterance invariably anticipates what meaning his audience will assign to the words he uses, just as the audience anticipates what he means. Successful prediction means effective communication.

People tend to organize themselves into groups, and groups into societies. Over the years, societies produce many meanings for the words and events and people involved in living. We might say that these meanings, these expectations, constitute the culture of the society. In spite of continuing differences, there comes to be some amount of common agreement about the events of our world, and a fairly standard way of reacting to and talking about them. A society, like that in the United States, for example, develops many common ideas about food, about music, about sexual relationships, about families, about cars, about most of the events we deal with day by day. These common, or

---

[2] Gardner Murphy, "Social Motivation," in G. Lindzey (ed.), *Handbook of Social Psychology* (Cambridge, Mass.: Addison-Wesley, 1954).

shared, meanings are the basis for our attempts to communicate with each other.

MEANING MUST BE SHARED, BUT HOW?

In order to communicate with each other, people have to have more than meanings inside their heads. Meanings cannot very well be dumped from one head into another or carried in a bucket across the space between persons, even though we sometimes act as if this were so. We need some way of representing meanings—something that *can* pass between people—if understanding and acceptance are ever to be achieved, if mutually beneficial action is ever to occur.

At the root of human communication is the idea that we can make something stand for something else, that we can have meanings for events that symbolize other events as well as meanings for the events being symbolized. At base this simply means that we see some events in the environment related to other events in certain sequential ways. Thunder and dark clouds, for example, come to mean that rain is likely, so that part of the meaning we have for thunder and dark clouds is part of the meaning we have

It is easy, though misleading, to think of communication as transferring a bucket of meaning from one head to another.

for rain. A siren comes to mean trouble, for someone some-where, although it hardly could be called trouble in and of itself. Part of our meaning for it is part of the meaning we have for fire, auto accidents, speeding tickets, crime, and death.

More important, though, is the stage at which we begin to let abstract symbols stand for objects and events and people. We may let a circle with radiating lines represent the sun, and we then come to mean by it some of the mean-ing we have for the sun. Obviously, the circle has no mean-ing by itself; there is no inherent meaning contained in it; nor does it arouse any meaning common to all people every-where. But we develop meaning for it by using it to desig-nate something else for which we already have meaning. And so it is with all symbols, including words.

THE MEANING OF WORDS

Basically, language is a system for classifying experi-ence in that most of its terms, its words or vocabulary, com-prise a set of labels for classes or categories of ideas and events. In English, for example, the emphasis is on nouns —words that label groups of events, objects, relationships, ideas—the things in our worlds about which we talk. These are things that act, or are acted upon—things that run, or jump, or fly, or are hit, or live, or die. We coin words to indi-cate these actions—to suggest that things occur or exist or happen or are happened to. These are verbs, and they con-nect nouns in various relationships.

We also create various logical words that help us struc-ture and pattern thought—words such as "of," "for," "and," "or." These do not say much about our worlds and the events in them, but rather control the relation of one thought to another. We have, additionally, words that are primarily emotional in nature—words like "beautiful," "dis-like," "unpleasant," and "good" that express how we *feel* about the events in the environment we have identified.

It is easy to assume that our way of building a language is the only way. But not all languages are constructed exactly like this, although all have a vocabulary and a grammar, that is, a set of terms and a set of rules for combining them. Navajo, for example, is not strongly centered on nouns as English is, but rather on verbs. Other languages show other variations.

There is no *necessary* connection between a symbol and what it is used to represent. The relationships between symbols and events in any society are largely a matter of convention, and the child is taught early in life what these conventions are. He is taught, for example, that "daddy" and not "boo-boo" is the agreed upon symbol for that big, grinning "thing" that stands over him once in awhile and tickles him under the chin. But, to quote American philosopher Alan Watts: "What is much less obvious is that convention also governs the delineation of the things to which the word is assigned. For the child has to be taught not only what words are to stand for what things but also the way in which his culture has tacitly agreed to divide things from each other, to mark out the boundaries within our daily experience."[3]

What this suggests is that there are a great many ways of carving up the world, and that how it is done is to a considerable extent arbitrary. Convention determines that an eel is to be considered a fish and not a snake and that men's trousers that go just below the knee are to be considered pants while those that go just above are to be considered shorts. Convention also determines what experiences shall be called objects and what shall be called events. For example, a closed or clenched hand is often labeled in English as a "fist." But what happens to the fist when the hand is opened? Is the fist an object, or is it, like the opening of the hand, an event? And if that seems like a peculiar question, ask yourself at what point in the closing and opening of a hand it becomes a fist and at what point it stops being one.

THE CONCEPT OF "PROCESS"

This brings us to an important idea—that the world in which we live is composed of a set of dynamic, moving,

---

[3] Alan W. Watts, *The Way of Zen,* (New York: Mentor Books, 1957).

changing *processes* rather than static, unchanging objects, and that our language conventions tend to hide this idea from us. Consider this concept of process for a moment. It says that nothing stands still—not rocks, not solid oak desks, nor castles, nor diamonds, nor people. Diamonds wear down, and desks and castles, like the Deacon's master-piece—the wonderful one-hoss shay—eventually wear out. No two renditions of a song are exactly alike—and John today is not John yesterday, nor John tomorrow.

The philosopher Heraclitus once said that you can not step in the same river twice. Even more to the point is the idea that you can not step in the same river once. For in the process of stepping in the river, both it and the stepper change—they are no longer the same. This suggests that events do not repeat themselves, only classes of events do. It also suggests something equally important—that which is observed is changed by the process of observation.

We do not know how to analyze processes very well. To analyze a process, we have to stop it, take it apart, isolate its units; and that can not be done without changing or de-stroying the process. Try some time to take the flour from a piece of bread without ending up with something other than bread.

Given the concept of process, there is a basic problem inherent in our approach to naming things and then invent-ing other words to help us think about, discuss, and relate these things. It is the implicit assumption that our world is composed of static objects unless and until we or something else moves them. We do not, as a result, find it easy to in-corporate movement and change into our basic view of things. For example, the word "wave" does not, by itself, arouse much of the idea of "water in a moving, changing, always different state." In order to handle this aspect of waves, we have to add some verb action—"the waves roll," or "the waves beat against the shore." It is true that, with something like a wave, we know it always moves. But we do not explicitly recognize this in our naming of it; and we name a lot of other things that do not move or change as quickly, and then frequently act as though they do not move or change at all.

LANGUAGE LETS US BE ABSTRACT

Language—words and the rules for putting them together—may well be the most important tool that man possesses. It extends his experience enormously—lets him acquire meanings for (know about) aspects of the world with which he never comes in contact and possibly never will. He can deal, in a limited way perhaps, with events that occurred long ago, or on the other side of the world, or that happened only in somebody's head. He can dig up elements of his own past experiences and move them around symbolically in his mind, seeking new interpretations of them, new relationships with other experiences—new meanings and expectations. Language lets us deal with people and events in ways other than purely physical and emotional reactions of the moment. It is the basis of our knowledge, our ability to accumulate experience and learn from the past and build into the future. In short, it is the most crucial difference we can find between man and the other forms of animal life.

Language has a great deal to do with the kinds of meanings or expectations a person develops; it both *aids* and *interferes* with experience. For one thing, it tells us what we see when we look at our world—or hear it or taste it or touch it or smell it. Another way of saying this is that language tells us how to respond or react to what we perceive. Certain articles of clothing, for example—both men's and women's—are dealt with quite differently depending on whether we call them swimwear or undergarments. (You may say that swimwear and undergarments really are different but consider carefully just what the differences are!) Some food items are what they are to us because of what we call them. Offer your friends some cooked, sliced, cold chicken breast sometime, but tell them it is rattlesnake meat. Or tell your guests that those delicious steaks served for dinner came from a horse instead of a cow! In so much

of our life, a rose by any other name is *not* still a rose—it is
something else.

DANGER OF "LANGUAGE LUMPING"

As a classifying device, language lumps things together
into classes—a highly useful characteristic in that it simpli-
fies enormously our dealing with the myriad objects and
events we encounter in our worlds. Think how complicated
life would be if we had to treat every event as unique, if we
had to give each its own individual label and respond to it
in a special and separate way. Happily, we put things together into useful classes so that we can overlook differences
that at any particular time do not make a difference.

Consider the class of objects we call "desks." There are
millions of them—rolltops, flattops, metal, wood, executive,
secretarial, schoolroom, red, brown, gray, large, small, and
so on. But we call them all desks, because for many purposes it is perfectly adequate and convenient to do so.
Lumping together all members of a certain occupation—
"police," for example—is also often adequate and convenient. No one is likely to argue that one policeman is
much different from another when dealing with a speeder
in a school zone.

But just as our language lets us ignore differences that
do not make a difference, it also prompts us to ignore differences that do. A young boy's experiences with one or two
policemen may lead him to conclude that "all cops are
creeps," preventing him from seeing that most policemen
are conscientious and genuinely concerned with his welfare.
For whatever reasons, certain makes and years of autos are
considered to be "good" or "bad." While it well may be that
some models give more or less trouble on the average than
others, this hardly seems a good basis for assuming that a
used auto of one model is all right to buy, while that of
another is not. Most prejudices involve just this sort of
overgeneralization.

HOW PERCEPTIVE ARE YOU?

The idea that reality is dynamic and ever changing and
that events do not repeat themselves except in classes ought

to suggest to us that when we look at the world there is no certainty that we see what is there. The idea that language influences our responses to the world's events, and perhaps also influences our idea of how things in the world are related, ought to suggest that perception may be incomplete and sometimes downright inaccurate.

Most people have had the experience of looking at the houses, trees, and lawns along a street or road on which they walk or drive every day and occasionally seeing something they had never noticed before—although it presumably has been there all the time. Most of us have played card games of various kinds at numerous times throughout our lives. How much of what apparently is there to see in the cards do we remember seeing?

For instance, how many "spots" or suit designators are there on the face cards of decks commonly made in the United States? How many are there on the other cards in the deck? Are these suit designators all the same size? How many one-eyed jacks are there, and which ones are they? Which jacks wear moustaches? What common object does each of the queens hold in her hand? If you look carefully at common U.S. playing cards, you will probably find that the way you answer these questions for one deck is pretty much the way you will answer them for any other deck. (But let us remember that until all decks have been inspected, the answers can hardly be said to be *true* for all of them.)

The point is this. We look at events in the world every day but never seem to see all that is there to see. Some, in fact, would argue that we cannot ever do so. What we do see is what we *expect* to see and to some extent what we *need* to see. But we should not try to deceive ourselves or anyone else that we know what is really there. And we ought to remember that we oftentimes do not see things that would be in our best interests to see.

HOW PERCEPTIVE CAN YOU BE?

The problem with the idea of *inaccurate* perception is that one is hard put to say what constitutes *accurate* perception, if it is true that (1) the world is composed of processes and (2) we apparently cannot see all there is to see. Perhaps a better word than inaccurate would be *inadequate*. To illustrate, consider this little story from the pages of the Lansing, Michigan, *State Journal.*

> HONOLULU—An island wo-
> man motorist approaching a
> railroad crossing saw a train on
> the tracks but decided to pro-
> ceed because the locomotive
> was at the far end of the train.
> She thought the train was leav-
> ing the crossing, Mrs. Solina
> Agudong explained to a police
> officer. But it wasn't. The loco-
> motive was pushing the cars—
> which, in turn, pushed in the
> side of her automobile.

How many times have you lost points on an examination or in a game, or damaged an appliance, because you failed to read instructions carefully?

In addition, there is evidence that our senses fool us at times—that what appears to be there only *appears* to be there. Note, for example, the many optical illusions that allow us to see a figure one way at one time and another way at another time. Recall the mirages of the desert or the wet look presumably dry highways appear to have under certain conditions.

You may have seen the following demonstration. Look at the triangles quickly and say what words you see. Did you say "bird in the hand" and "Paris in the spring" as most people do? Look again.

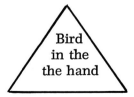 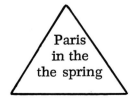

In general, we can say that the mind of man seems to abhor a vacuum. For each of us, things in the world have a way of fitting together, of rightness, of belonging. If the pieces are not all there—and sometimes even when they are—we fill the holes and order the parts in the way we think they *ought* to be, in the way they have to be to make sense—to us. We ignore process, and we ignore change. We ignore the concept that meanings are in people. We insist that we see what is really out there in the world and that we mean what we say about it. Lewis Carroll gently reminds us once again of the trap we often put ourselves in:[4]

"Then you should say what you mean," the March Hare went on.

"I do," Alice hastily replied; "at least—at least I mean what I say—that's the same thing, you know."

"Not the same thing a bit!" said the Hatter. "Why you might just as well say that 'I see what I eat' is the same thing as 'I eat what I see'!"

"You might just as well say," added the March Hare, "that 'I like what I get' is the same thing as 'I get what I like'!"

"You might just as well say," added the Dormouse, which seemed to be talking in its sleep, "that 'I breathe when I sleep' is the same thing as 'I sleep when I breathe'!"

PRACTICAL APPLICATION OF THEORY

At this point, you may well be asking just how all this applies to the problem of getting people to attend our company's open house. Some of the ideas may have seemed relevant; others quite possibly not. Let us recap briefly and then see whether we have some basis for suggesting why people might have failed to see the open house stories, might have distorted or misunderstood them, or otherwise did not act on them in the desired manner.

We have said that meaning is a property of people and that they acquire their meanings through experience. We have suggested that people want their lives to be predictable so that they can control their relationships to the world in satisfying ways. We have also implied that many of our meanings are learned from other people with whom we live and try to get along throughout our lives.

Language was seen as an arbitrary system of classifying experience, a set of symbols representing classes or categories of events, and a set of rules for combining these

---

[4] Lewis Carroll, *op. cit.*

symbols into meaningful discourse. People acquire meanings for these symbols in the same way they acquire meanings for everything else—by experience. In any society there is some agreement about what language symbols represent, hence some possibility for communication. But, since meanings are learned through personal experience, and no two persons can ever have exactly the same experience, some part of the meanings we have remains forever individualistic and private and can only be communicated imperfectly if at all.

We considered the idea that the world is a set of processes, and that our language does not fit this idea too well. Language both facilitates and interferes with experience, helping us to deal more efficiently with the events of the world while at the same time leading us to interpret the world in ways that are not always in our best interests.

Look at the potential audience for the open house messages in the light of these ideas. Every member of that audience was different from every other member. Each was reading the newspapers, listening to radio, and watching television from his own unique point of view—seeing the content of these media through the filtering rose-colored glasses of his own individual meaning system. What he saw was consistent with his past experiences—what he expected to see and what he needed to see to deal with his particular needs and interests and concerns.

We do not know, of course, exactly why the members of the audience behaved as they did. We can only make some guesses, based on the theories of human behavior we have considered. Consider, for example, the person who thought the open house was just for employees and families. He may have assumed that no one but a relative could possibly have been interested in the place where *he* works, so why should it be any different with the company holding the open house? His experience with working for various organizations left him no basis for interpreting the open house as relevant in any way to him. And it is difficult to do anything about such a situation. What could you possibly say in the first sentence or two of a story that would give him the idea that somehow this was different?

The man who thought the stories were just propaganda

was also probably a victim of his own individual experiences. He may, for example, have attended such events before and found them thinly veiled excuses for high-pressure sales attempts. Or, he may have implicitly assumed that he would certainly be propagandizing if he were to run such an affair; hence, almost certainly that is what the people in our example would be doing. And, fearing the power of propaganda a bit (and our culture says it *is* powerful—and bad) he surely was not going to expose himself to such if he could avoid it.

The man who did not understand the words about electronic data processing equipment and the like could have failed to do so for several reasons. Recall the idea that people do not like unpredictable situations, especially those which suggest to them that they are not fully adequate to deal with the world. Such a person tends to avoid getting into situations where he is not sure what is going to be expected of him, and that he is not certain he will be able to handle. He may have considered the new equipment so proudly described in the stories as further instances of automation, a dangerous and unexplainable pestilence imposed on an unwanting world of laboring people. It is also possible that this gentlemen had learned vaguely to fear sophisticated electronic equipment—machines that seem to have the power to think and which some day might take over the world.

We could generate similar explanations for the other people who did not respond as we had hoped. The point of all this is simply that words and events do not mean the same to all people. When we read, we usually make a guess early in the story as to what it is all about and then proceed to read our expectations into the story, whether that is what the writer intended or not. The conclusion has to be that communication proceeds in terms of both the receiver's and sender's meanings, not the sender's alone. Both sender and receiver have to work at the process; both are obliged to be concerned about what the other may mean.

You never can assume that the person to whom you are talking or listening knows what you know, feels about events as you feel, is subject to the same kinds of pressures from the same kinds of people that you are, means by your words and sentences what you mean. He has his own peculiarly individualistic set of meanings and expectations, and all you can ever do is try to arouse in him the ones you want. You cannot "give" him your meanings; you can only stimulate him in some way, arousing meanings he already has, sometimes helping him to acquire meanings for events he does not know much about, and perhaps getting him to relate his meanings in ways he has not done before. *He can do no more for you—or to you.*

ANALYSIS OF COMMUNICATION SITUATIONS

When we attempt to analyze a communication situation, we often think of one person as a sender or source and the other person or persons as receivers. The sender has his own purposes in the situation and encodes messages to achieve those purposes. Because we think this way, we find it easy to think of the communication process essentially as a one-way operation with some amount of attention paid to returning cues that tell the source something about how well he has done.

For many of the situations in which we find ourselves each day, this concept of communication is probably sufficient to let us do what we want to do. There is, however, another point of view that may be more useful, that will better let us plan our own communication activities and better let us understand why sometimes things we want to have happen do not, or things we do not want to have happen do.

Let us take as a basic situation two persons speaking together. In each of them there are meanings, many similar and many different but all uniquely individual. Each has meanings—expectations—about himself, about the other in the situation, about the events of concern both in the situation and out of it, and about the symbols that each knows and has available for his use. They each, furthermore, possess various abilities for communication—abilities to speak and to hear, to write and to read, to analyze and to synthesize. And, no less important, each comes to the communication situation with purposes of his own, responses of some kind that he wants from the other.

**INDIVIDUAL
MEANINGS**

**INDIVIDUAL
MEANINGS**

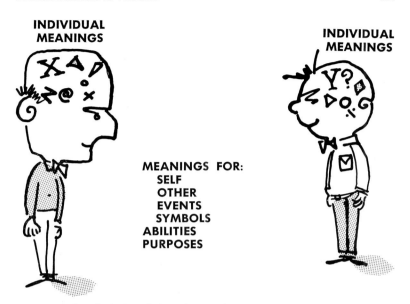

MEANINGS FOR:
   SELF
   OTHER
   EVENTS
   SYMBOLS
ABILITIES
PURPOSES

People bring their unique selves to communication.

Now one of our friends encodes a "message" in line with his intentions toward the other and "sends" this message out into the environment surrounding the two. He decides what symbols to use, and he uses them by making noises with his mouth, or squiggles on paper, or by smiling or frowning, or by laying his hand on the other's arm. These do not have meaning by themselves, but they *stimulate the receiver,* arousing in him the meanings he has for them as related to this source in this time and this place. He responds, and this is a message of his own, framed in terms of his own purposes. Each, then, is encoding messages designed to achieve his own purposes; each is responding to messages from the other and observing the responses of the other; each is checking up to see how well he is doing and trying to assess the intentions of the other. And, because messages designed to stimulate others also stimulate the sender to some extent, the sender has this as an additional source of feedback or check on what he is doing.

It is worth noting that communication does not occur in a vacuum. The world is a mass of stimuli, constantly impinging on the senses of people. In any conversation we

Communication is multiway stimulation and response.

have to contend with noise, literally and figuratively. Telephones ring, dogs bark, children shout, and radios play. Lights flash, shadows move, the wind blows, and mosquitoes bite. Air temperatures go up and down, and the gentle breezes waft odors of varying strength and delightfulness. These stimuli, too, arouse meanings, sometimes aiding and sometimes interfering with our conversation. (Think how a telephone call could interfere with our open house message on radio.)

Now let us take our two persons and separate them so that they must try to communicate over distance, or time, or both. They must now resort to various mechanical and artistic devices to overcome the separation, that is, by making phone calls, drawing pictures, appearing on television, or leaving notes in the trunk of a hollow tree. Essentially, this is what the mass media are designed to do—*to overcome the separation in time and space between people who want to communicate.*

FACTORS LIMITING COMMUNICATION

The mass media—books, magazines, newspapers, television, radio—can be analyzed in terms of how well they

bridge this separation. Some immediate limitations will
occur to you; for example, the limited capacity of the media
to stimulate more than one of the senses. Radio appeals
only to the sense of hearing, the print media mostly to the
sense of sight, with occasional appeals, through perfumed
inks and paper texture, to the senses of smell and touch.
Television stimulates both sight and hearing, with the added
value of providing a view of movement which means that
some of the supporting nonverbal codes can be used by the
the sender.

There are other limitations. For one thing, the mass
media communicator is mostly cut off from immediate feedback from his receivers. He cannot watch them respond as
a platform speaker can and use this as a basis for modifying
his message as he goes along. Furthermore, by virtue of the
numbers of receivers involved, he cannot very well pitch his
message at any one of them to the exclusion of the others.

Part of the stimulation comes from the environment.

People become separated by time and space.

He cannot choose his words in terms of what he knows of a single receiver, as he might do in a face-to-face situation, but must reach for some sort of average individual among his readers or hearers or viewers.

There is still another element that must be taken into

Media bridge the separation.

account—the man making decisions for the mass medium being used, the editor, news director, publisher, or program director, as the case may be. These people are sometimes called gatekeepers because they control the message channels between sources and receivers and decide which messages will move along the channels and which will not and whether those that do will do so in original or in edited form. They, like the rest of us, have ideas about what they want to do; and they, like us, bring their own stock of meanings to the communication situation. They, like us, have various groups to which they respond. Basically, if they are to aid us in our goals, they have to see our messages and our intended receivers as consistent with their own goals. When they do not, the "gates" are closed to our materials and we are left to look for other means of reaching our intended receivers.

Consider once again our open house problem. It is possible that the editors who did not use the stories did not know much about the company and, hence, did not see the stories as having any interest or value for their readers. If the editors did not know about the company, they had no basis to expect that their readers would either. Or, like a reader mentioned earlier, they might have construed the stories as commercial propaganda and an attempt to get free advertising space in the newspapers.

Obviously, if we want to transmit a message to some audience via the mass media, we need to know the mass media gatekeepers just as much as we need to know our intended receivers. Although there is a great deal of variation between individual gatekeepers and between the media they work for, there are many commonly defined purposes in the mass communication field. Most journalists agree that the mass media should inform people; explain for them what is going on in the world, and what it means or may mean; look after government and crime and sin and the state of society; confer status on persons and ideas deemed important and worthwhile; transmit the standards and values of the society; and advocate change as well as advocate against it. Messages consistent with these purposes ordinarily are welcomed by the mass media; inconsistent messages are not.

ROLE OF "OTHER PEOPLE"

Up to this point, the crucial role of "other people" in communication has only been hinted at. Man is a member of many groups throughout his life, groups which are more or less important to him because they affect his ability to secure the things he wants. Such groups are sometimes referred to as "reference groups," or the people in them as "significant others." The point is that for each of us there are other people and groups whose opinions are valued and whose ideas about what is good and bad and true and false in the world we take into account in deciding what events and messages mean and how we will respond to them.

We want to be right in our judgments about things and, because we are often unsure in our own thinking about what is best, we come to rely on certain others in whose judgment we have learned to have faith. And we also want

MEANINGS   MEANINGS   MEANIN
ABILITIES   ABILITIES   ABILITI
PURPOSES   PURPOSES   PURPOS

The media add other communicators to the process

the approval of other persons who have for various reasons come to be important to us. We want them to like us, to think well of what we do, to accept our ideas and opinions, and to respond to us in ways consistent with what we think we are and are worth.

The more we value our membership in some formal or informal group or value our association with some other person, the more we are likely to take that group's or person's ideas and attitudes into account in formulating and expressing our own. This does not necessarily mean that we adopt the other person's views as our own—only that we are very likely to be influenced in some way by them. It also follows that these associations support and reinforce some of our existing ideas and opinions, making them much more resistant to change.

Man forms hundreds of associations throughout his life, for in our society, at least, to live in isolation is practically impossible. We associate with some persons and groups just because they are physically close to us as members of our families, neighbors, and work colleagues. Aside from this, however, we tend to like persons and join groups that like us and to like those we see as sharing some of our own attitudes and interests and who possess characteristics we have come to admire. For these reasons, the persons in a group tend to have similar opinions about many issues and similar ideas about who is and who is not qualified to speak on those issues.

EFFECTS OF GROUP INTERACTION

Furthermore, interaction within groups tends to affect the form and content of messages coming in from the outside—through the mass media, for example. As mass media messages are passed along within the group on a person-to-person basis, discrepant information is often filtered out and ideas are shaped to fit the attitudes and desires of the group. Performing this function in many groups is the informal *opinion leader*, the person in the group to whom the other members most often look for guidance. Like the mass media editor, he acts as a gatekeeper

People bring their group

for some kinds of messages and, in passing parts of them and some of them along, adds his own opinions as to what they mean and how they should be taken. Such a situation may seem odd where mass media operate as extensively as they do in the United States. But we know that many people in our society do not read or listen extensively to news, and we know that opinion leaders have much higher exposure to the media than do most other members of the group.

From this we can see that each person in a communication situation brings to it—in addition to his meanings, abilities, and purposes—a set of past and present associations and relationships with various people and groups. These associations have been profoundly instrumental in

associations to communication.

making the person what he is and continue to be instrumental in determining his responses. Consider only one instance from the open house example discussed previously—the man who may have considered electronic data processing equipment another example of dangerous automation. Again we can only speculate, but it is possible that this man is a member of a laboring group all of whose members are worried about automation, or a member of a social group whose other members work at similar jobs and who share his concern about losing their jobs to a modern and sophisticated machine.

In conversation the members of these groups may share their fears and worries and reinforce each other's feelings that automation is an unfortunate and unreasonable thing. They may look for information to support their feelings and tend to avoid that which does not. They may look to one or two of their number to interpret news of automation to them. They may even feel somehow that people who hold different ideas are enemies and are not under any circumstances to be trusted.

All communication seems to proceed under the conditions described here. In the two-person, face-to-face situation the problem is relatively simple but still enormously complex. Here we can take specific account of what we know about just one person, and our chances of successfully communicating improve. (But even a loved one we have known intimately for years distresses us occasionally by responding in unexpected ways!) When we move away from our single respondent, when we increase him to a large and faceless number, problems of communication multiply greatly. And when we move to the level of trying to introduce change into a major social system, we have taken on what often seems—and sometimes is—an impossible task.

Past and present associations figure in a communication situation.

MEANINGS   **MEANINGS**
ABILITIES   **ABILITIES**
PURPOSES   **PURPOSES**
ASSOCIATIONS   **ASSOCIATIONS**

For here, as sociologist George Beal suggests, one must not only take account of a people's psychological, sociological, and cultural backgrounds but he must also consider such things as the organizational structure of society, the power relationships between and among groups and persons, the expected behaviors of persons who occupy various positions in organizations and government and various other groups, the conflicting desires of various groups, and even the history of the social system that has led up to the present state of affairs.[5]

COMMUNICATION AND SUCCESS

If it sounds like an enormous undertaking, it is. If it sounds impossible, it is not. Change does take place, sometimes because of the efforts of men, sometimes in spite of them. The important point is that successful planned change is usually no accident. It is promoted by skilled communicators who are sensitive to people, to situations, to organizations, to social and political movements. They are men who know enough about human communication to have a sense of what cannot be done, and who do not waste their time trying to do it. They are also men who have a highly developed ability to put themselves in their receivers' shoes, to anticipate how they will respond, and to see themselves as sources in the same way their receivers see them.

Man uses language to express himself—his feelings and ideas about events—and to affect the behavior of other people. He does not communicate randomly. He encodes and transmits messages with the object of securing a desired response—attention, understanding, acceptance, and sometimes action. All attempts at communication are persuasive in intent. This imposes on human beings both a responsibility and a necessity—responsibility for the effects achieved and the necessity of knowing what they are.

To be successful, to live with our successes and failures, and to know when we are or are not successful, we

[5] George M. Beal, "Social Action: Instigated Social Change in Large Social Systems," in: J. H. Copp (ed.), *Our Changing Rural Society: Perspectives and Trends* (Ames, Iowa State University Press, 1964).

need to be quite clear about what we try to do as communicators. We have to be honest with ourselves, and we have to express our intentions in terms of some kind of behavior that our receivers can perform, and we can observe. If we cannot observe responses, we cannot know if we achieved what we set out to do—or achieved some things we would rather not. The process works both ways. To live as free men, to be responsible for the things that we do, to feel that we are in fact masters of our own destinies, we also have to be quite clear about what others try to do to us. They are persuasive in their communication attempts no less than we are.

To communicate successfully, we have to think in terms of change—the changes we want to have occur in other people, both the gatekeepers and our ultimate receivers. The purpose of communication is response. When we communicate, we are not solely in the news release or reporting business, the tape recording business, or the annual report or the meeting business. We are in the *people* business. And we have to know what they are like and what we want them to do if they are to accept our ideas and suggestions.

There is no foolproof formula for success—only direction signs that suggest some ways of attacking a communication problem. There are many variables to take into account, not the least of which is yourself. As you approach your communication tasks, before you begin to build and send your messages, you might find it fruitful to ask and realistically answer these six questions:

Who am I? What kind of person am I? How do I deal with people? How do they see me? What do I really know and how do I really feel about things? With whom do I associate and whose approval do I seek?

What am I trying to achieve? What are my goals in life? What is important to me? What am I willing to do to get what I want? What must I gain to be happy? What do I want to be remembered for?

Who are they? What people have to do certain things in order for me to accomplish my goals? What kind of people are they? How do they deal with others? How do they see themselves? What do they know and how do they feel about things? With whom do they associate and whose approval do they seek?

What are they trying to achieve? What are their goals in life? What is important to them? What are they willing to do to get what they want? What do they need to be happy and what do they want to be remembered for?

What do they have to do for me to be successful? How must they think, feel, and act if I am to achieve my goals? What must they know? How must they respond, and when must they do it?

And, what are the consequences, to them and to me, if they do what I want them to do?

SUGGESTED READING

BERLO, DAVID K. *The Process of Communication.* New York: Holt, Rinehart and Winston, 1960.

SECORD, PAUL F., AND BACKMAN, CARL W. *Social Psychology.* New York: McGraw, 1964.

HARTLEY, E. L. AND R. E. *Fundamentals of Social Psychology.* New York: Knopf, 1955.

HAYAKAWA, S. I. *Language in Thought and Action.* New York: Harcourt, Brace & World, 1949.

SCHRAMM, WILBUR. *The Process and Effects of Mass Communication.* Urbana: Univ. of Ill., 1960.

SCHRAMM, WILBUR. *Mass Communications* (2nd ed.). Urbana: Univ. of Ill., 1960.

CARROLL, JOHN B. *Language and Thought.* Englewood Cliffs, N.J.: Prentice-Hall, 1964.

KLAPPER, JOSEPH. *The Effects of Mass Communication.* Glencoe: The Free Press, 1960.

★ *Only a demanding, aggressive, interested society can create an intelligent, viable press system.*

★ 11 ★ The Press and Society Are Interdependent

SEVERAL YEARS AGO police in a Minnesota college town arrested a pair of students at the college and charged them with selling narcotics. The Minneapolis *Star* and *Tribune* ran a story through several editions under a front-page streamer headline. A day or so later the *Tribune* received a letter signed by students at the institution involved complaining that the newspaper had overplayed the story and was guilty of "yellow journalism." The letter writers were concerned with the image of the college they attended and with their own images as students enrolled there. They pointed out that they had not sold or purchased narcotics and that only two students had been arrested. Therefore, they said, the banner headlines represented distorted values on the part of the editors. They charged the newspaper with "irresponsibility."

These Minnesota college students were not unique in their anguish nor in their charges. Every day some persons are wounded directly or indirectly as a consequence of stories in newspapers and magazines or on radio and television, and every day wounded persons react in anger to such stories.

It is easy to sympathize with many of them and to understand why they respond as they do. But to accept such charges as valid without examination is to seriously undermine the public information role performed by the nation's press. Critics, and especially wounded critics, need a clear understanding of the press in its interrelationship with society—that is, with all of us.

THE PRESS REFLECTS SOCIETY

As the late U.S. Supreme Court Justice Felix Frankfurter wrote:[1]

"A free press is indispensable to the workings of our democratic society. The business of the press . . . is the promotion of truth regarding public matters by furnishing the basis for an understanding of them. Truth and understanding are not wares like peanuts or potatoes. . . . I find myself entirely in agreement with Judge Learned Hand that neither exclusively, nor even primarily, are the interests of the newspaper industry conclusive; for the industry serves one of the most vital of all general interests: the dissemination of news from as many different sources, and with as many different facets and colors as possible. That interest is closely akin to, if indeed not the same as, the interest protected by the First Amendment; it presupposes that right conclusions are more likely to be gathered out of a multitude of tongues, than through any kind of authoritative selection. To many this is, and always will be, folly; but we have staked upon it our all."

We tend to regard the press, as we might a parent, as merely being present. Yet both are indispensable. Like our parents, the press is part of each of us. We turn to it for the information we need in order to perform the tasks of our own lives and of the society in which we exist. And those persons who operate the press try to give us what we must have and what we desire by way of information.

In this vital relationship your role as a reader, listener, or viewer is as important as the part played by the journalist. For if you demand entertainment only, the press will not, in the long run, offer enlightenment. Only a demanding, aggressive, interested society can create an intelligent, viable press system.

The building of a constantly improving mass society and its press requires of press and society that they criticize

---

[1] *A.P.* v. *U.S.*, 326 U.S. 1.

each other. The press carries out its duties daily in this regard through its editorial pages, critical columns, searching articles, and special radio and television programs. The public performs its critical function through howls of personal rage, complaining letters to editors, cancelled subscriptions, threatening telephone calls, and through the words of self-apponted, more visible critics of the press in government, institutions of higher learning, politics, and neighborhood saloons. Such criticism may be formal or informal, knowledgeable or ignorant, mean or constructive. All of it is important and needed.

The press, of course, is society in miniature. It is efficient or inefficient, venal or honorable, stagnant or growing, sensitive or insensitive, liberal or conservative, contemptible or praiseworthy, depending upon the person sitting in judgment and the unit of the press being examined. Yet it is possible to formulate a list of its presumed responsibilities as well as a list of the major criticisms commonly directed at it.

RESPONSIBILITIES OF THE PRESS

As is true of most persons, the press accepts criticism reluctantly. In 1946 a Commission on Freedom of the Press, formed to inquire into and report on the "present state and future prospects of the press," issued its mainly critical findings. The report became the subject of immediate debate, with much of the press taking the negative position. Over the years, however, there has been little disagreement with the Commission's listing of what it regarded as the responsibilities of the press (the Commission used the term "requirements"). The Commission said society required of the mass media:[2]

1. A truthful, comprehensive, and intelligent account of the day's events in a context which gives them meaning.
2. A forum for the exchange of comment and criticism.

---

[2] The Commission on Freedom of the Press, *A Free and Responsible Press: A General Report on Mass Communication: Newspapers, Radio, Motion Pictures, Magazines, and Books* (Chicago: Univ. of Chicago Press, 1947) pp. 20–21.

3. The projection of a representative picture of the con-
   stituent groups in the society.
4. The presentation and clarification of the goals and
   values of the society.
5. Full access to the day's intelligence.

   There have been many other discussions of press responsibility, of course, but most if not all of them turn upon
the principles enumerated in the Commission report:
Society must have a press that will supply facts (information) as the basis for rational discussion and debate so
that it can make intelligent decisions on issues that affect
its well-being.

WHO REALLY CONTROLS THE PRESS?

   Within this context, then, let us identify and evaluate
the criticisms most commonly directed at the press. Fore-
most among them is the charge that, where content is concerned, the press is overly susceptible to audience and advertiser pressure. The effect of this force, say the critics,
is that the press sensationalizes the news in order to attract
larger and larger audiences and declines to discuss issues or
report information that advertisers want suppressed or
ignored. These criticisms are not new. When it became
apparent that men could become wealthy as mass communication entrepreneurs and that advertising was big business,
the raw material was there for the critics to examine and
denounce.

   But the rapid changes taking place in twentieth century
society are bringing along with them corresponding modifications in our press system—modifications that make the
criticisms less pertinent now than they once were. Two of
the most noticeable changes in mass media operations are
(1) the rise of monopoly ownership and (2) revised methods
of distribution. These new conditions have substantially
reduced (but not altogether eliminated) the practical necessity for sensational treatment of the news by alleviating
much of the press' one-time sensitivity to pressures on content by audience and advertiser.

   Although there are certain, if not altogether effective,

economic and governmental obstacles to monopoly ownership of magazine, radio-television, and book publishing enterprises, monopoly ownership of the newspaper press
throughout the nation has become a visible fact of our lives.
Competing newspapers exist in only a few of our major
cities and in even fewer of our small towns. In 1960 only 89
of the 1,452 cities in the United States with daily newspapers had more than one independently owned newspaper.

Almost all Americans read a newspaper every day.
Most of them read their home-town newspapers, almost all
of which operate without direct newspaper competition.
There is, obviously, a certain amount of rivalry among the
various media for audience attention and for the advertiser's dollar. But it has become less necessary for the
monopoly publication to bow to pressures on the part of anyone, even the largest of advertising-space buyers. If newspaper space is important to the seller of goods, and there is
abundant evidence that it is, then it is sufficiently valuable
in the competitive business world to make that seller unwilling to withdraw his advertising for any reason.

As our systems of transportation have improved and
our urban society becomes more concentrated and affluent,
newspapers have developed home-delivery systems for most
of their sales. The great majority of readers today purchase
newspapers on a weekly, monthly, or even yearly basis. The
foundation for circulation claims rests on these stable and
virtually guaranteed sales—sales that fluctuate but little because of individual, exclusive, or sensationalized stories.
Only in the largest of our cities, where competitive situations still exist, do newsstand sales depend in any important way on aggressively exciting front pages.

EFFECTS OF MONOPOLY OWNERSHIP

But even as improved transportation and the rise of
monopoly were making the press less vulnerable to some
criticisms, they were creating situations which many responsible persons now view with mounting concern. These
critics see the increase in monopoly ownership of communication media as a threat to what Judge Learned Hand

called "right conclusions" which, he said, are "more likely to be gathered from out of a multitude of tongues." This necessary diversity of voices is not encouraged by monopoly, the critics point out. Intensifying the problem, they claim, is the fact that newspaper publishers and the proprietors of radio and television stations, as well as the owners of book and magazine publishing concerns, are largely alike in their social, educational, and economic backgrounds and thus in their interests and beliefs.

A prime critic, the Commission on Freedom of the Press said in its report that "the agencies of mass communication are big business, and their owners are big businessmen." The Commission quotes William Allen White, the late famous editor of the Emporia (Kansas) *Gazette*, as saying, "Too often the publisher of an American newspaper has made his money in some other calling than journalism. He is a rich man seeking power and prestige . . . it is hard to get a modern American newspaper to go the distance necessary to print all the news about many topics. . . ."[3]

More recently, Dan Lacy of the American Book Publishers Council has pointed to what he felt was the same narrowing effect in another area of mass communication, that of the news magazines. He says:[4]

The difficulties of starting and sustaining a magazine in this field have brought it about that there are only three news magazines of large national circulation—*Time, Newsweek,* and *U.S. News & World Report*—and a few others—like *Life* and the *Saturday Evening Post*—that editorialize a great deal. All of these, despite some minor differences among them, reflect substantially a uniform point of view, that of the dominant business community to which their owners and advertisers and no doubt the majority of their subscribers belong.

The view that limiting the number of voices in communication necessarily narrows one's range of information has not gone unchallenged. It has been argued, for example, that the competing publication is not, per se, the better publication. Carl E. Lindstrom, at one time a managing editor in a competitive newspaper situation, cites two

[3] *Ibid.,* pp. 59–60.
[4] Dan Lacy, *Freedom and Communication* (Urbana: Univ. of Ill. Press, 1961), pp. 51–52.

monopoly newspapers—the Des Moines *Register* and *Tribune* and the Minneapolis *Star* and *Tribune*—as serving their areas in "distinguished" fashion. He adds: "It is worth noting that where monopoly is associated with enterprise and imagination, as in Des Moines and Minneapolis, there exists also the will and incentive for research and experimentation, both of which are usually the liveliest where there is vigorous competition."[5]

As the critics in general have observed, the problem of monopoly is intensified by the decline in the number of domestic wire services and by the growth of newspaper chains. The 1958 sale of the International News Service to United Press (now United Press International) has reduced the number of major American services to just two—UPI and The Associated Press. Most American daily newspapers, the news magazines, and the broadcasting industry are served by one or the other or both. Thus, most of the national and international news distributed to the American citizen comes from one or two sources alone.

NEWSPAPER CHAINS AND AUTOMATION

Newspaper chains or groups, it is claimed, also do their part to narrow the range of information and opinion and to broaden the dulling effect of standardization. Chain newspapers are those published in more than a single community under one ownership. One of the most widely known is the Hearst chain, but there are dozens of others throughout the country.

Lindstrom has this to say about newspaper chains:[6]

As to chain ownership, one insoluble problem is the distinction in character between cities. A single owner or editor can, if he is diligent, succeed in attuning himself to a community. He must do so if he is to be successful and if he is to serve the news needs of the city understandingly. But to presume to own many newspapers in widely scattered and differentiated cities is perforce to adopt a pattern sufficiently neutral and nondescript

[5] Carl E. Lindstrom, *The Fading American Newspaper* (Garden City, N.Y.: Doubleday & Co., 1960), p. 119.
[6] *Ibid.*, pp. 106–7.

to somehow suit all of them. This is the policy of the average; these communities cannot be averaged, but the publisher will reckon they can be and then see to it that they become so according to his own lights.

One additional influence that tends to rob the news of individuality is widespread newspaper adoption of the mechanical device known as the Teletypesetter. By automating type composing machines, the Teletypesetter has converted copy editing from an important and needful task to an annoying expense. Wire service copy (from AP and UPI) comes to the automated newspapers on punched tape, ready to be run through the typesetting machines. Any copy changes that would add missing facts, localize the story, or broaden perspective would slow production and add to costs. As a consequence, many publishers of automated newspapers frown on anything but having proof read for typographical errors. On many an American newspaper today the copy desk does little but produce headlines, and some newspapers have even experimented with having their reporters write local stories on typewriters that punch tape for the automated typesetting machine as the story is being written. So whether you live in Hyannisport, Mass., or in Hibbing, Minn., your national and international news diet is likely to be largely identical.

THE PROBLEM OF TASTE LEVELING

Still another severe criticism is that mass media are guilty of purveying a calculated and consistent mediocrity that degrades rather than uplifts mass tastes. The criticism is likely to be more urgent, scathing, and frequent as an affluent society shifts its attention from purely material matters to more esthetic concerns. At issue is what the social critic refers to as the tastelessness of what he reads in magazines and newspapers and sees and hears on radio and television.

Newton Minow, former chairman of the Federal Communications Commission, shocked the broadcasting industry by charging that television programming was a "vast wasteland." Although Minow's voice was only one of the many that have been raised in criticism of mass media performance, such complaints tend to ignore the fact that the question is not one-sided. Two opposing forces are involved: (1) the social critic's laudable desire for a constantly more enlightened and edified populace, and (2) the grinding economic necessities of the business of mass communication. The conflict's basic query is this: Is it possible to raise the level of popular taste without risking economic ruin through loss of the mass audience?

In discussing the problem of taste leveling, two well-known sociologists, Paul F. Lazarsfeld and Robert K. Merton, commented:[7]

It is misleading to speak simply of the decline of esthetic tastes. Mass audiences probably include a larger number of persons with cultivated esthetic standards, but these are swallowed up by the large masses who constitute the new and untutored audience for the arts. Whereas yesterday the elite constituted virtually the whole of the audience, they are today a minute fraction of the whole. In consequence, the average level of esthetic standards and tastes of audiences has been depressed, although the tastes of some sectors of the population have undoubtedly been raised and the total number of people exposed to communications content has vastly increased.

These men were writing in 1948, and the drive of technological change and the accompanying, if less savage, drive for social change may well have altered even cultural levels to at least a slight degree. In that year, as the authors noted, "About half the population . . . have halted their formal education upon leaving grammar school."[8] Some persons are predicting now that within another generation or two, about half of this country's population will be college trained. It is reasonable to assume that general esthetic levels will rise with the educational level, and there is impressive evidence that the dual process is already well under way. Consider these facts:[9]

---

[7] Paul F. Lazarsfeld and Robert K. Merton, "Mass Communication, Popular Taste and Organized Social Action," in: Wilbur Schramm, ed., *Mass Communications* (Urbana: Univ. of Ill. Press, 2nd ed., 1960), p. 475.

[8] *Ibid.*, p. 472.

[9] Frank Stanton, *Mass Media and Mass Culture* (New York: Columbia Broadcasting System, Inc., 1963), p. 9.

By 1962 the number of symphony orchestras in the nation had risen from 800 in 1952 to 1,252; more Americans were attending concerts than were going to all major and minor league baseball games; 780 opera groups were performing in the United States, compared with 300 ten years previous; recordings of serious music sales had increased 80 per cent in three years; attendance at the Metropolitan Museum of Art in New York City had increased 200 per cent since 1950, and more than a billion books were being purchased and 800 million borrowed from public libraries annually (libraries circulated 500 million in 1956).

A noted representative of the mass media, Frank Stanton of the Columbia Broadcasting System, says that this great increase in American cultural activities can, indeed, be attributed in some degree to the media. Radio and television, he says, "have brought an awareness of fine music into millions of homes." And he believes that, "If millions of people see a painting in *Life,* hundreds are going to seek out originals in museums and galleries." In support of his general contentions, Stanton cites the specific example of the 25.6 million television viewers who saw and heard the two-hour concert celebrating the opening of the Lincoln Center for the Performing Arts in 1962 as contrasted to the 2,600 who attended the concert that night in Philharmonic Hall.[10]

Criticisms of any public or semipublic institution tend to abet desirable change. Mass media, since they are called upon to report the criticisms being leveled against them, are by no means unaware of their existence. And it can be conjectured that the media are at least as responsive to criticism as other institutions which have public responsibilities and private economic concerns. At this point in time, however, the press has a long way to go to wipe out current inadequacies. Monopoly remains, as do vestiges of subservience to economic pressures. Certainly, much that is printed, broadcast, and filmed will not survive to the credit cf our civilization.

VULNERABILITY OF THE PRESS

Because of its very nature, the press is particularly vulnerable to criticism. It offers itself regularly to intense

---

[10] *Ibid.,* pp. 19–27.

public scrutiny in a manner unique among the many and diverse units of an industrialized society. The aeronautical engineer, for example, operates in comparative privacy; even the legislator is relatively anonymous. By way of contrast, the newspaper reporter, the magazine writer, and the radio and television broadcaster offer their work for daily examination and evaluation by the consuming public. Moreover, the journalist's work must be performed under the pressure of imminent deadlines—an unfortunate but inherent factor that must be weighed in judging press performance.

STRENGTHS OF THE PRESS

As you are exposed to the output of mass media, you may find many grounds for disagreement—stories that are disturbing or factually inaccurate or evidence of prejudiced writing. The Commission on Freedom of the Press found many of these disorders during its inquiry. But in finding faults, the Commission also discovered strengths. Said the Commission:[11]

Private enterprise in the field of communications has achievements to its credit. The American press probably reaches as high a percentage of the population as that of any other country. Its technical equipment is certainly the best in the world. It has taken the lead in the introduction of many new techniques which have enormously increased the speed and variety of communications. Whatever its shortcomings, the American press is less venal and less subservient to political and economic pressure than that of many other countries. The leading organs of the American press have achieved a standard of excellence unsurpassed anywhere in the world. It is necessary to keep these general comments in mind in order to see the criticisms in proper perspective.

It is noteworthy that none of the serious critics have suggested, even in their more agonized moments, that the basic structure of the American press system be altered. A free press is so much the foundation of our political orientation that, even as we object to the observed inadequacies of the media in operation, we cannot bring ourselves to suggest

[11] Commission on Freedom of the Press, *A Free and Responsible Press*, p. 52.

the only apparent alternative—government-enforced standards. The dangers of such control are all too obvious. In discussing the possibility of a government-owned network in the British tradition, Dan Lacy commented:[12]

Nothing in our experience with other government adventures into mass communications suggests that creative independence could be maintained. Diversity and novelty would be far harder to achieve than under almost any form of private operation. And in any event, it is of the utmost importance to separate the communications system as far as possible from the other seats of power in our society.

Freedom of the press, in its position as an almost sacred American principle, receives our support insofar as we understand its meaning. It is unfortunate, and the cause of constant social tension, that many fail to grasp the concept in breadth and depth. A 1955 study found that 64.3 per cent of a sample of Texas students preparing for the teaching profession would approve of Congress passing a law prohibiting the Socialist Party from publishing newspapers in the United States. Fifty-three per cent said they would approve establishment of a state board to examine and censor all magazine items dealing with crime and sex and approve such a board's examining each issue of a magazine before it could be offered for sale in the state.[13]

The results of this Texas study could not help but be a source of worry for those concerned most directly with enforcing our basic freedoms, particularly when these results are substantially supported in other studies. These concerned persons point out that democracy as we profess it has no meaning without the freedoms of speech and of the press. The Supreme Court, in our time, has validated this standard by extending a "preferred position" to First Amendment freedoms when they are competitive with other rights—economic freedoms most specifically of late years. The late U.S. Supreme Court Justice Cardozo wrote of freedom to think and communicate that "one may say it is the

---

[12] Lacy, *Freedom and Communication*, p. 81.
[13] James L. Rogers, "Prospective Teachers' Attitudes Toward Freedom of Information," *Journalism Quarterly*, Vol. 32, No. 2, p. 172.

matrix, the indispensable condition, of nearly every other form of freedom."[14]

THE SOCIAL RESPONSIBILITY THEORY

The men who wrote the American Constitution and its Bill of Rights (the first ten amendments to the original document) believed in the "self-righting" theory of political organization. That is, they believed that if the people are given access to all shadings of opinion they will eventually ascertain truth. The press was conceived to be, with you, a "partner in the search for truth." In recent decades, however, a somewhat newer theory of the press's role in society has begun to emerge in answer to the problems posed by modern conditions, most specifically press monopoly. Terming this new concept the Social Responsibility Theory, the authors of *Four Theories of the Press* say that as a result of monopoly conditions:[15]

No longer is it easy for the press to be a free market place of ideas. . . . As the Commission on Freedom of the Press said, "protection against government is not now enough to guarantee that a man who has something to say shall have a chance to say it. The owners and managers of the press determine which persons, which facts, which versions of these facts, shall reach the public." This uneasiness is the basis of the developing Social Responsibility theory: that the power and near monopoly position of the media impose on them an obligation to be socially responsible, to see that all sides are fairly presented and that the public has enough information to decide; and that if the media do not take on themselves such responsibility it may be necessary for some other agency of the public to enforce it.

The question, of course, remains as to how the more irresponsible mass communicators may be forced or encouraged to accept their responsibilities to the community. The professors who wrote *Four Theories* are less than specific on this matter, as was the Commission on Freedom

---

[14] *Palko* v. *Connecticut*, 302 U.S. at 327.
[15] Fred S. Siebert, Theodore Peterson and Wilbur Schramm, *Four Theories of the Press* (Urbana: Univ. of Ill. Press, 1956), p. 5.

of the Press. At least two other theorists, however, advance ideas which may be, in the long run, somewhat fruitful.

One of these theorists, Dan Lacy, rejects the notion of direct government control but advocates expanded federal or foundation support in the areas of television, radio, and books and, to a lesser extent, for movies and magazines. Of newspapers, however, he says:[16]

I believe it is the part of wisdom to accept as inevitable the trend toward monopoly of newspaper ownership in all but the largest cities, and to attempt to offset its disadvantages in part by enlarging the distribution of information and views through other media and in part by encouraging in the press a professional sense of serving as a common carrier of news and opinion.

PROFESSIONALISM IN JOURNALISM

The other theorist, Professor J. Edward Gerald of the University of Minnesota, discusses professionalism in journalism at length. He observes that, under present conditions, the practice of journalism is not regarded as a profession. He points out, however, that First Amendment guarantees probably forbid formal professional status for journalists by prohibiting any attempt to restrict entrance to the field or to punish for unprofessional performance. He contends that professional standards could nonetheless be enforced through industry agreement on those standards and through education for the field. He says that professional status could be achieved if journalistic organizations:[17]

(1) Unify that part of their effort concerned with professionalism. (2) Provide central facilities for hearing, analyzing, and answering public complaints about journalistic performance. (3) Represent most journalists concerned primarily with daily news reports important to self government. (4) Provide a representative regional and national structure so that relations with the public could be dealt with uniformly in a local context. (5) Form a national council and provide it with financial support. (6) Accept responsibility, with the schools, for the imple-

---

[16] Lacy, *Freedom and Communication*, p. 87.
[17] J. Edward Gerald, *The Social Responsibility of the Press* (Minneapolis: Univ. of Minn. Press, 1963), p. 195.

mentation of a program of professional education. (7) Undertake comparative studies of professional employment standards.

It is obvious that although we insist that freedom of the press, as we know and value it, continue, we are seriously concerned that press performance improve to meet our pressing needs. One scholar cites the reasons for the search for quicker solutions: ". . . . the body of knowledge with which our communications system must cope is not only almost incomparably larger than ever before and must be conveyed to a very much wider audience than ever before, but it is changing very much more rapidly than ever before."[18]

It can be said that the schools of journalism are of high significance to the continued development of a sense of professionalism, of social responsibility, in our press system. In their more than half-century of existence, the schools have matured from primary concern with journalistic techniques to sophisticated institutions offering an understanding of the communication process and its importance. Contemporary graduates are likely to have a firm sense of profession.

The core of the professional sense in the newsman is his sense of news judgment, which is akin to the physician's diagnostic function. In both are centered the true professional's use of knowledge and experience and his moral and ethical standards. And while their diagnoses may be, and frequently are, questioned, the odds must be much better than even that the physician and the newsman are correct in their own fields on any specific occasion. As the medical school attempts, in essence, to produce a better medical diagnostician, so the journalism school strives to graduate a better news diagnostician.

CONSUMER RESPONSIBILITY

The chances are, therefore, that the Minneapolis newspapers were correct when they gave front-page, banner treatment to the story of narcotics selling by college

---

[18] Lacy, *Freedom and Communication*, p. 14.

students. Certainly, the story was news, and big news, if
we consider, first, the importance of our institutions of
higher learning and, second, the comparative unusualness
of narcotics peddling by midwestern college students. It is
not the job of the newspaper to worry about the image of
institutions or individuals; it is the newspaper's job to report
the news as judged by it. In any case, what change of image
took place resulted from the illegal actions of two students.

The ultimate decisions which must be made concerning the press in a free-enterprise society are in the hands of
you, the consumer. Your responsibility should be clear.
Since an adequate system of mass communication is vital
to the welfare of the society in which you exist, your understanding of the manner in which that system operates and
your judgments concerning its performance are crucial.
You must make your decisions from knowledge gained out
of interest.

SUGGESTED READING

The Commission on Freedom of the Press. *A Free and Respon-
    sible Press: A General Report on Mass Communication:
    Newspapers, Radio, Motion Pictures, Magazines, and Books.*
    Chicago: Univ. of Chicago, 1947.
LACY, DAN. *Freedom and Communications*, 2nd ed. Urbana, Ill.:
    Univ. of Ill., 1965.
LINDSTROM, CARL E. *The Fading American Newspaper.* Garden
    City, N.Y.: Doubleday & Co., 1960.
SCHRAMM, WILBUR, ed., *Mass Communications*, 2nd ed.
    Urbana, Ill.: Univ. of Ill., 1960.
SIEBERT, FRED S., PETERSON, THEODORE, AND SCHRAMM, WIL-
    BUR. *Four Theories of the Press.* Urbana, Ill.: Univ. of Ill.,
    1956.
STANTON, FRANK. *Mass Media and Mass Culture.* New York:
    Columbia Broadcasting System, Inc., 1963.
GERALD, J. EDWARD. *The Social Responsibility of the Press.*
    Minneapolis, Minn.: Univ. of Minn., 1963.

★ *Invention, lessening of censorship, and pressures to achieve a responsible press have made communication media a powerful force in today's world.*

★ 12 ★ Three Revolutions Shape Journalism History

WHEN YOU READ OR HEAR of violent political change in some far-off land, look for a report that "the rebels seized the capital city's radio stations." The strategic patterns of recurrent rebellions throughout the world testify again and again to the respect men have for the influence of the mass media of communication. Those who would lead revolts deal in basics—control of the armed forces and control of the mass media.

A bloody coup d'état, however, is not needed as testimony to the power of modern communication systems. In America, the virtually instantaneous spread of the latest joke, fad, or fashion—to say nothing of news—binds this nation together as surely as do the federal and state governments. The reader, the viewer, the listener—all are at the focal point of three converging and interwoven revolutions in communication which have come about since this continent was colonized: (1) invention, innovation, and technological change, (2) lessening of controls over the media as a social force, and (3) strengthening of controls over the media as a business.

Aspects of these three revolutions may be found in tracing the lives of both the great men and the rascals who participated in the development of American journalism. These revolutions may also be seen in the time periods which historians have identified as eras in the history of communication in this nation.

MOVABLE TYPE OPENS WAY

About the year 1440 Germany's Johannes Gutenberg introduced movable type to the European continent. This was to prove a world-shattering innovation, for it meant that books would no longer have to be hand-lettered or printed from laboriously carved plates and could be produced fairly rapidly and in quantity. The ability to print with movable type, however, did not bring with it a corollary right to print.

Rulers, fearful over what they saw as a mounting threat to their authority, took precautions to see that printed material did not contain information that would stir up discontent among the people. As a result presses were licensed, and only printers who were approved by a king or government could legally publish anything. Even then censors appointed by the government would scrutinize the printed material to make sure that no derogatory comments about the king or government or established religion would be made available to the public.

PRINTERS NOT FREE TO CRITICIZE

In time this censorship bureaucracy broke down in Europe, because there came to be more printed matter than the censors could read before it was offered to the public. But printers still were not free to do as they wished. Those who dared to criticize government officials could lose their property, or even their lives, if they published what was then called "seditious libel." Almost any criticism of the king or government or the laws of a nation might be termed seditious libel, and could lead to horrifying penalties.

In England in 1663, for example, a court found John Twyn guilty of taking part in the publication of a writing which "imagined" that King Charles II was dead. The judge ordered that Twyn "be hanged by the neck, and being alive, shall be cut down, and your privy members shall be cut off, your entrails be taken out of your body . . . your body to be divided into four quarters and your head and your quarters to be disposed of at the pleasure of the king's majesty. And the Lord have mercy upon your soul."

This cruelty masquerading as law, as well as the notion that government should control printing, furnished at least a part of the background for the adverse attitude toward printers the king's agents brought with them to Colonial America. It is not surprising that the revolutionary idea of freedom of speech and press experienced a slow, uncertain growth on this continent.

"TREASON" IN THE COLONIAL PRESS

For many years after 1638, the date the first press in America was set up at Harvard College, presses were operated by "public printers." These men, dependent upon government support for much of their income, were paid for publishing laws passed by colonial legislatures and proclamations issued by colonial governors. For more than 135 years after the first printing press in America slapped out its tiny 10 x 15-inch sheets, printers continued to be regarded as instruments of a ruling elite.

Small wonder that many colonial aristocrats agreed with the idea expressed by Governor Sir William Berkeley of Virginia, who said in 1671, "I thank God, there are neither free schools nor *printing,* and I hope that we shall not have them these hundred years; for *learning* has brought disobedience, and heresy, and sects into the world, and printing has divulged them, and libels against the best government. God keep us from both!"

But in spite of the attempts at control the role of the press changed. Aggravations such as the Stamp Act and the Tea Act during the 1760's and 1770's brought angry protests by America's colonial legislatures, some of which viewed themselves as miniature parliaments. After 1765, when many powerful American politicians opposed the colonial policies of the British Parliament, printers published the legislators' protests in newspapers and pamphlets. And it was during these early stirrings of the American Revolution that printers seized the opportunity to comment almost without restraint on rulers—some far away in England and some close at hand in America. They also freely criticized government actions and laws which rebellious Americans considered unjust.

From the British point of view, the 37 tiny American weekly newspapers published in 1775 were full of treasonable writings. One New York aristocrat who favored continued British rule of America said of the revolutionists; "Poor reptiles . . . ere noon they will bite." While supporters of British authority may have despised the American newspapers, they also recognized their influence. The Tories who tried to prevent the American Revolution knew that the newspapers had great power to mobilize public opinion.

NEWSPAPERS MOVE WEST

The *Pennsylvania Journal*, published in Philadelphia by Colonel William Bradford, was one of the most important newspapers of the Revolution. In 1775 it appeared only once a week and had a circulation of little more than 2,000. Even so, this newspaper was known and read and quoted throughout the American colonies. Although only eight copies of the *Pennsylvania Journal* were sent to Connecticut, the little newspaper clearly reached opinion leaders with its arguments. Copies went to the postmaster at Hartford; to two printers in New London; to the publishers of a newspaper at Norwich; and to Silas Deane, an important Connecticut merchant-politician. Once the *Journal* arrived at its destination, other printers republished excerpts from it in their own newspapers. A sarcastically worded political item placed in the newspapers of Philadelphia or Boston or New York might still be appearing months later in newspapers published from New Hampshire to Georgia. Tiny weekly newspapers, then, had an important impact all up and down the Atlantic Coast. The product of the presses, in the words of revolutionists, was the raw material for change—political, social, and industrial.

The hand-fed, hand-cranked presses in use before 1800 were slow and cumbersome devices, and newspapers were too expensive for most families to buy. Two men laboring ten hours at a press could print only 1,000 four-page newspapers. Once this arduous job was done, the task of distribution remained. By stagecoach and postriders, these newspapers circulated up and down the coast to eager subscribers. Since many persons could not read, these newspapers were read aloud in taverns and coffeehouses, line by line, including news items, anecdotes, and advertisements. Postriders who did not keep a close watch on their saddlebags learned that nonsubscribers would often steal tiny but expensive sheets. From Revolutionary times until long after 1800 the great majority of Americans lived on farms far from major population centers. Small wonder that the hunger for news made newspapers—even old ones—greatly welcome on the frontier.

News traveled slowly until after the successful demonstration of the telegraph in 1844. Prior to the telegraph and the simultaneous rise of the railroads, news could move no faster than the coastal winds, the often muddy and always rutted roads, or the river steamboats would permit. Back in 1775 news of the battles of Lexington and Concord, which began the actual armed conflict of the American Revolution, took four days to reach Philadelphia from Boston—about 300 miles. Thirty years later the great journey made by Captain William Clark and Meriwether Lewis from Missouri to the Pacific Coast was inadequately reported because of the difficulty of communication. The explorers had left the area near what is now Bismarck, North Dakota, early in 1805. The Indians of North Dakota knew in 1806, by their own mysterious way of transmitting rumors across the prairies, that the party had reached the Pacific. Before the Indian rumor could reach the white settlements, the explorers were safely back at St. Louis, Missouri, where they learned that most Americans—with the exception of an optimistic President Thomas Jefferson—had long since given them up for dead.

FREEDOM TO CRITICIZE UPHELD

During this nation's first 50 years the steady growth of the press was for the most part a reflection of the public's hunger for news. Most newspapers printed in 1825 were produced in much the same laborious fashion as those of 1775 had been. No great technological advances had spurred printing speeds, and improvements in transportation were appearing only slowly. But the new nation did undergo political battles which helped put meaning into the quicksilver phrase "freedom of the press." During the first half-century a basic ground rule was laid: In America the press was to have the freedom to criticize the government.

The First Amendment to the Constitution of the United States provided that "Congress shall make no law . . . abridging the freedom of speech, or of the press." This clear statement of a right we now regard as basic was adopted in 1791 along with the other nine sections of our Bill of Rights. In spite of the guarantee, however, most Americans still assumed that criticism of the government might be punished as a crime, as it had been in England and in Colonial America. In 1798 a Federalist-controlled Congress enacted the now infamous Alien and Sedition Acts. These measures pronounced it a crime to criticize the government, government officials, the Constitution, or the laws of the United States. Some 20 Republican (Jeffersonian) editors were prosecuted and served jail terms.

Such drastically repressive measures, however, quickly revealed themselves to be a huge political mistake. They contributed mightily to the Jeffersonian success in toppling the brilliant but unpopular President John Adams in the elections of 1800. The lesson was not lost on the politicians. Eminently practical men, they had learned that it was risking political suicide to try to muffle the voice of an opposition party. To their credit, the victorious Jeffersonians allowed the Alien and Sedition Acts to expire in 1801.

PUBLISHERS AND POLITICIANS

The death of the hated acts, however, did not altogether free the press, which remained a victim of its own eagerness to tie itself to government. The printing of laws and proceedings of legislative bodies plus such auxiliary services as providing official stationery were for many years important forms of revenue for the printers of American newspapers.

Today if you hear that a certain newspaper or journalist is "in the pocket" of a governor or a legislator, you know that is a term of derision. In the early years of the United States, however, printers and journalists competed openly for the privilege of getting into governments' pockets.

What happened during the scramble among five candidates for the Presidency of the United States in 1824 was all too typical of that era. The major candidates—Secretary of State John Quincy Adams, Secretary of War John C. Calhoun, Secretary of the Treasury John H. Crawford, Henry Clay, and Andrew Jackson—all sought newspaper support. This campaign was instrumental in the founding of a number of newspapers around the nation, and two new papers were started in Washington, D.C., especially to further the candidacies of Calhoun and Adams. Washington's other two newspapers supported Crawford. Henry Clay's adherents tried to set up a paper but failed.

Similar shenanigans in behalf of politicians continued for many years. Politicians often set up special campaign newspapers to boost their chances, and established newspapers would lend editorial support to the candidate of their choice. The latter often turned out to be men who had offered a political favor or a lucrative government printing contract if elected.

ADVERTISING AND TECHNOLOGY OPEN DOORS

The American economy, however, was moving toward something new—mass production and mass distribution. The growth of mass markets gradually provided the force—advertising—which helped free newspapers from dependence on political connections. The growth of advertising's importance coincided in large measure with the development of technological devices which sharply reduced distances. The telegraph, the railroad, and the steamboat all made possible the transmission of news at speeds which would have pleased (if not surprised) Colonial printer-inventor Benjamin Franklin. Printing facilitated the storage and transmission of knowledge, and the results of many centuries of invention and discovery began to be focused in America.

Advertising had helped fill the columns of the 37 weekly newspapers published in America in 1775. But advertising remained of only limited importance while newspapers and magazines had to be produced on creaking, balky, inefficient presses. Not until around 1800 did the first iron press come to this country—a machine more than twice as fast as its wooden ancestor. It was an improvement, to be sure, but still hand operated and far too slow for anything like mass production and its accompanying economies.

Change, however, was in the making—stimulated by the currents of invention (discovery) and innovation (adaptation of old knowledge in new ways). By 1830 Isaac Adams of Boston had produced a steam-driven press that could turn out 4,000 copies of a newspaper in an hour, a production rate that was about 20 times faster than that of a hand-operated press, although still far below the 50,000-plus copies per hour printed by high-speed presses today. In that year of 1830 America had 64 daily newspapers. Forty years later, in 1870, America had 489 English-language daily newspapers. This linking of steam power with the printing press made possible what historians now call a "press for the masses."

PENNY PRESS BRINGS NEWS TO ALL

From 1830 on, as newspapers and magazines were circulated more widely, businessmen began to place greater value on the advertising space they were buying. Moreover, the additional emphasis on advertising aided the economy by assisting in the mass distribution of goods. In turn, increased advertising revenue enabled more and more newspapers to avoid dependence on funds of political parties or branches of government. One consequence was the era of the penny press.

In 1833 Benjamin Day brought out his New York *Sun* and sold it for only a penny a copy instead of the 6 cents charged by other papers. The low-priced *Sun* ("It Shines for All") printed sensational crime or human interest stories and became an immediate circulation success, attracting thousands of readers from the middle and lower classes. Another successful publisher of penny newspapers was James Gordon Bennett of the New York *Herald*. The *Herald*, like the *Sun*, offered gaudy coverage of crime news. But the *Herald* also provided detailed news of politics and foreign affairs and operated a pony express to bring back news dispatches from Washington. In effect, the *Sun* and the *Herald* were the first of America's mass circulation newspapers.

CIVIL WAR TESTS RIGHT TO PRINT

As mass circulation newspapers were born, the North-South tensions that eventually erupted into Civil War were being reflected in the press with increasing urgency. Advocates of sectionalism and of slavery and antislavery philosophies used national newspapers such as *The National Intelligencer* to carry their beliefs to the public. As feelings grew ever more heated, press freedom was often endangered. A publisher whose career summed up the troubled times before the Civil War was Elijah P. Lovejoy, editor of the violently antislavery St. Louis, Missouri, *Observer*.

Lovejoy's outspoken editorials led to the gathering of a mob in St. Louis determined to prove that the constitutional guarantee of freedom did not include such newspapers as the *Observer*. Lovejoy eventually moved his newspaper across the Mississippi River to Alton, Ill. But violence followed him. Twice he tried to set up a press in Alton, and twice his press was destroyed. When Lovejoy made a third try late in 1837, he was killed by a mob. He was neither the first nor the last American journalist who died defending his right to free expression. The next time you see a televised news film showing a reporter or news photographer being beaten by a mob, perhaps you will know why honors for courageous journalism are given in the name of Elijah P. Lovejoy.

When the Civil War began in 1860, publishers learned

anew what printers had experienced during the War for Independence 85 years before: Unpopular presses see uneasy times when a nation is at war. President Abraham Lincoln was greatly concerned about newspaper influence. He worried, for example, about the effects that the gloomy war dispatches printed by the flamboyant James Gordon Bennett's New York *Herald* might have on European and British opinion. Even so, the President came to the defense of editors who were imprisoned for printing "Copperhead" (pro-Confederate) views. But Lincoln, who had a much greater regard for a free press than many Presidents, was not able to halt all suppressive acts toward newspapers. He did not feel, for example, that he could cancel closings of newspapers ordered by military commanders. Although a few newspapers were closed by military orders, many more were threatened—and damaged—by mobs.

THE AGE OF COMMUNICATION

The Civil War drained much of the nation's energy. Nonetheless, signs of recovery and growth coexisted during the darkest days of the war and during the troubled Reconstruction Era that followed. By 1860 the railroad had pushed through to California. This coast-to-coast link, more than any other single accomplishment, signaled the beginning of the Age of Communication: the revolution of innovation, invention, and technological development. The railroad's growth, accompanied by the constantly expanding telegraph service, represented only a part of the story. Perhaps most important, American cities were reaching the years of their greatest growth. Immigrants by the hundreds of thousands soon made the strange cadences of European languages familiar in America's large cities.

Between 1870 and 1900—in only 30 years—the United States doubled its population, and tripled the number of urban residents—persons who lived in communities of more than 8,000. Even more startling was the quadrupling of the number of daily English-language newspapers, from 489 in 1870 to 1,907 in 1900. And in that same 30 years daily newspaper circulation increased more than five times—

from 2.6 million copies each day in 1870 to over 15 million copies each day in 1900.

All this yeasty growth was not without price. John Steinbeck has written of "our wolfish financiers who spend two-thirds of their lives clawing fortunes out of the guts of society and the latter third pushing it back." The press was expanding in a booming economy that depended upon constantly improving national distribution of products and upon a large foundation of low-priced, often foreign-born labor.

THE PRESS DEVELOPS A CONSCIENCE

As time passed, and especially after the Civil War, the press began to recognize the presentation of straight, factual news as its greatest obligation. Gradually, publishers realized that readers wanted factual and complete information in addition to the personalized, opinionated journalism of such men as James Gordon Bennett, Sr., of the New York *Herald* and Horace Greeley of the New York *Tribune*. In the 1870's and 1880's the big names in newspapering are names which are still remembered: Edward Wyllis Scripps of the Cleveland *Press* (parent paper of what became the Scripps-Howard organization), Joseph Pulitzer of the St. Louis *Post-Dispatch* and William Randolph Hearst of the San Francisco *Examiner* (parent paper of the Hearst chain).

While the newspapers were increasing in size, number, and importance during the closing years of the nineteenth century, the more responsible among them were beginning to separate editorial opinion from the news. Many newspapers also tried to correct ills that they found in society. One of the most glorious stories of American journalism is the way in which the New York *Times* and *Harper's Weekly* managed to find and publish indisputable evidence of thefts by the infamous Tweed Ring. Tammany boss William M. Tweed was so sure that his crooked empire was invulnerable that he even listed a plasterer's pay, on construction of a New York courthouse in 1870, at $50,000 a day. Thomas Nast, a cartoonist for *Harper's Weekly* magazine, turned his artistic talents against "Boss" Tweed and was even offered

a bribe to stop his barbed attacks on Tammany. Nast de-
clined the offer and continued to snipe away at his favorite
targets. Today the cartoonist is best remembered for invent-
ing the cartoon symbols for political parties so familiar to
everyone—the Democrats' donkey and the Republicans'
elephant.

MAGAZINES AND POSTAL RATES

Meanwhile, magazines such as *Harper's Weekly,* the
Nation, the *Century, Scribner's,* and the *Atlantic Monthly*
were becoming solid successes. By the 1880's these magazines, plus others featuring humor and cartoons—such as
Judge and *Puck*—were increasingly important in American
life. In 1879 Congress established an important policy decision with the act which provided "Second Class" mailing
rates. The law not only offered low postal rates; it made it
as inexpensive to mail a magazine or a newspaper across
the continent as to mail it across a small town. Without
question, these favorable mailing rates have had an incalcu-
lable effect on the nation's political, economic, and social
character. When persons in San Francisco became accus-
tomed to reading the very same magazines that were being
read by New Yorkers or Iowans, it could hardly have been
otherwise.

PULITZER PUBLISHED FOR MASSES

While magazines became more important nationally,
newspapers of New York City were being revolutionized in
the 1880's by the influence of a young phenomenon from St.
Louis named Joseph Pulitzer. Pulitzer had come to this
country from Hungary in 1864 as a youth of 17. The Union
Army was desperate for Civil War volunteers, and young
Pulitzer signed up with an American agent and was shipped
to the United States for military duty. When the war ended,
Pulitzer was a penniless immigrant adrift in New York, able
to speak only a few words of English. But within the next
15 years Pulitzer made his way to the Midwest where he
bought the St. Louis *Post-Dispatch.* In 1883 Pulitzer was

back in New York, but this time he made a down payment on a then dying newspaper, the New York *World*.

An immigrant himself, Pulitzer saw his potential audience clearly. New York increased its population by 50 per cent during the 1880's, and many of these people were new to the English language. Pulitzer determined to give the *World*'s struggling readers news and entertainment. The new publisher tried to serve two masters with his newspaper; he wanted to offer solid, worthwhile news to the public and to provide that news in a sensationalized form they would enjoy reading. Headlines such as "Little Lotta's Lovers" and "Burning Bloodbath" often spiced the *World*'s pages, and the sensationalism paid off in readership. The newspaper's circulation rose from 15,000 in 1883 to 250,000 in 1887.

Sensational or not, the *World* performed useful services. The newspaper carried on noisy crusades against crime, poor housing, and bribe-taking city officials. Calling itself "the people's paper," the *World* offered, among other things, dinners for the poor. Pulitzer's newspaper also campaigned successfully for over $100,000 in donations which were used to construct a pedestal for the Statue of Liberty.

"YELLOW JOURNALISM"

If Pulitzer's newspapers merited being described as representatives of the "new journalism," the newspaper tactics which William Randolph Hearst brought to New York City in 1895 deserved their label of "yellow journalism." Hearst, backed by his late father's money and his successful operation of the San Francisco *Examiner,* purchased the New York *Journal* in 1895. Where the *World*'s reporting had been somewhat flashy, the *Journal*'s news coverage under Hearst became downright lurid. Yellow journalism was summed up in words said to have been uttered by Hearst himself: "Don't wait for things to turn up. Turn them up!" Another New York editor, enraged by Hearst's tactics, declared that the yellow-journal newsrooms were the perfect places to prepare a young man for perdition.

Hearst liked to flatter himself that he had played a large role in driving America into the Spanish-American War, and at least some historical opinion has perpetuated the myth. In all fairness it should be noted that the irrepressible Hearst did once tell an artist he paid to depict the Cubans' struggles against their Spanish rulers, "You furnish the pictures and I'll furnish the war." Critics of the press have never forgiven Hearst for his foibles, perhaps because they believe he was the natural father of all that is undesirable in latter-day journalism. Whether that is true is open to debate, but there is little doubt that Hearst dramatically influenced the shape of journalism at a particular point in the nation's history.

MUCKRAKERS WORK FOR REFORM

In a nation where a Hearst could believe that he had played a major role in starting a war—or could even want to run for President—the counterreaction eventually set in. Soon after 1900 a journalistic reform movement developed that was labeled "muckraking" by a scornful President Theodore Roosevelt. When he uttered the word, Roosevelt was angered over a tough reporting performance that he regarded as being unfavorable to him. But the term muckraking stuck and, in time, became a label of approval for journalism which exposed corruption in American government and business.

These muckraking exposés were symbolized by reporter Lincoln Steffens' distrust of government. Steffens developed the theory that corruption is an inevitable part of any form of government or society. And he set out to lay bare the rot. Inevitably, the crusading spirit spread to other areas. While Steffens attacked corruption in city governments, Ida M. Tarbell exposed dishonest practices by the Standard Oil Company. And Upton Sinclair's book, *The Jungle*, horrified readers with its description of filth in Chicago meat packing plants.

Sinclair's book and other exposés led to the beginnings of responsible controls over advertising in the newspapers and magazines. In the 1890's and for at least 100 years before, leading advertisers in the press had been the patent medicine manufacturers, salesmen, and quack physicians. Much of the advertising hawked cure-all preparations and echoed the medical quack's pitch that had been heard in this nation from its beginning. Most of these claims were greatly exaggerated and in tune with druggist Samuel Dellap's advertisements which appeared in the Philadelphia newspapers before 1800. Dellap, for example, would advertise "Doctor Hill's genuine invented MEDICINES," including "ELIXIR of BARDANA for the gout and rheumatism. . . ." and "ESSENSE OF WATER DOCK, excellent for the scurvy, leprosy, and all obstinate cutaneous disorders. . . ." A century later the press of America was filled with ads for compounds such as "Dr. Williams' Pink Pills for Pale People."

ENFORCE TRUTH IN ADVERTISING

Spurred by the muckrakers' revelations, Congress in 1906 passed the Pure Food and Drug Act, which clamped down on the manufacturers of harmful or polluted goods. The 1906 law, however, did nothing to insure truth in advertising. Nevertheless after 1911 many states adopted laws to make deceptive or misleading advertisements punishable as a misdemeanor. To prevent publishers from sneaking in hidden advertisements to fool gullible members of the public, Congress passed the Newspaper Publicity Law of 1912. This statute requires that all items resembling editorial matter that are published for money or other payment must be clearly labeled "advertisement."

By 1910 daily newspapers had reached the peak of their influence—if we measure influence in terms of numbers. In that year, there were 2,600 daily newspapers, with 2,200 of these being English-language, general circulation publications. Only the strong, however, were destined to survive. Weaker newspapers succumbed to competitors, a trend that was hastened by the disruptive forces of two world wars and the economic realignments that followed. By the mid-1960's, only a handful of America's major cities had competitive newspapers and the total number of daily newspapers published was around 1,750.

WORLD WAR I UPSETS PRESS FREEDOMS

The tumultuous years of World War I again saw the passage of laws similar to the Alien and Sedition Acts of 1798. The new wartime sedition laws were used by frightened courts—even the Supreme Court of the United States—to apply punishment to utterances which now appear to have been perfectly harmless. As U.S. Supreme Court Justice Oliver Wendell Holmes wrote in objecting to a jail term imposed on a pathetic immigrant, "sentences of twenty years imprisonment have been imposed for the publishing of two leaflets that I believe the defendants had as much right to publish as the Government has to publish the Constitution of the United States now vainly invoked by them."

With the end of World War I the most repressive features of the new sedition laws were taken off the books. Some men perhaps dared to assume that the press would then simply swing back to its prewar freedom. Unfortunately, the war had upset our society too much. After the shooting stopped, there arose a kind of superpatriotism which helped to keep the nation in turmoil. The chief bugaboos were "anarchists" and the "Red Menace." U.S. Attorney General A. Mitchell Palmer and his men made repeated searches for Communist arms caches which always eluded discovery. Fearing that disloyal aliens might be planning to overthrow the government, Palmer's Secret Service men conducted raids—often without warrants— and invaded the rights of many native-born citizens in their zeal to find dangerous aliens.

The Red-scare activities of the overzealous G-Men of the 1920's provided an appropriate counterpoint for the style of journalism which evolved after World War I. Known as "jazz journalism," it was a revival of the gusty Hearstian sensationalism of the 1890's. Typical of the era was the New York *Daily News* of Captain Joseph Medill Patterson, a small-sized or "tabloid" newspaper that specialized in stories featuring crime, sports, and sex. And physical culture enthusiast Bernarr Macfadden brought out an even more ribald, and very successful, tabloid, the *Daily Graphic*. These tabloids' successes were appropriate to the twenties, when politicians tended to be corrupt and when gin, jazz, and jalopies were occupying the public's attention.

With the advent of the 1930's, the Great Depression settled over a sobering America. Publishers soon found that economic recovery legislation passed by Congress during the depression had widespread effects on all business, including the press. Such laws and regulations were numerous—labor relations, social security, taxes, wage and hour provisions, advertising regulation, rulings of such agencies as the Federal Trade Commission and the Interstate Commerce Commission.

ELECTRONICS ADD NEW DIMENSION

As the print media wrestled with new regulations piled atop the old, a much newer medium developed by the technological revolution—radio—was experiencing severe growing pains. In the beginning radio's main possibilities had seemed to lie in such uses as wireless ship-to-shore telegraphy. At the outset of World War I, broadcasting was almost entirely experimental. The Department of the Navy took charge of radio communications for the war's duration and then reluctantly gave up its authority over broadcast bands several years after the shooting stopped.

During the 1920's, commercial broadcasting got underway. Regulation of broadcast frequencies, since there were not enough wavelengths to go around, had been placed by Congress in the hands of the Department of Commerce. Secretary of Commerce Herbert Hoover parceled out broadcast frequencies to various stations in order to cut down on interference among broadcasters. But Hoover's attempts to create order were defeated by the courts, which ruled that the Secretary had no legal right to "legislate" the broadcast frequencies.

But by 1927 there were over 700 radio stations in the

United States. Because they were unregulated, these
stations moved about on the broadcast band, attempting to
avoid interference from other broadcasters. Naturally, the
result was utter chaos. In 1927 Congress passed the Federal
Radio Act in an attempt to create order. This act gave the
Commission power to issue broadcast licenses, assign wavelengths, and determine the power of transmitters. In 1934
the Federal Communications Act set up a seven-member
Commission with authority to regulate all telecommuni-
cations, not just radio.

Years before, licensing had prevented press freedom in
England. But in the twentieth century, the licensing of
radio and television stations was not done to diminish the
public's freedom. Regulation of the electronic media recognized that the airwaves are the public's property, to be used
"in the public interest, convenience, or necessity." The Federal Communications Commission has the power to revoke
stations' licenses for irresponsible broadcasting, but this
power has rarely been used.

SUMMARY

There are now something over 4,000 AM (standard
broadcast) commercial radio stations, plus some 670 commercial television stations. It is now estimated that there
are more television sets than bathtubs and showers in American homes, which once led comedian Johnny Carson to observe that this nation must have many dirty viewers. Americans, on the average, spend one-fifth of their waking hours
giving attention to one or more of the mass media—newspapers, magazines, motion pictures, radio, or television.
The media today are pervasive; transistor radios are carried
on buses, and portable television sets are taken to beaches.
First-run movies are shown on scheduled airliners. In an
age of communication satellites circling the world, instantaneous worldwide communication now offers possibilities for increased international understanding—or misunderstanding.

Some commentators fret that the media reach too
many of us with too many similar messages. Such critics

wonder if we may not all be too much exposed to a leveling influence bound up in the "communication of common values." Another worried commentator was a young Senator from Massachusetts named John Fitzgerald Kennedy who wrote in 1956 that "our everyday life is becoming so saturated with the tremendous power of mass communications that any unpopular or unorthodox course arouses a storm of protests. . . ."

Despite such worries, on balance it would seem that the media of the United States have done well enough to deserve the freedom promised them in the First Amendment to the Constitution. The American experiment has endured, and many persons believe that our free—if sometimes irresponsible—press has been important to the survival of our system of government. The press of America has spent more than 200 years trying to be free and less than 50 years trying to be responsible. A great historian, Charles Beard, has written that freedom of the press 100 years ago meant "the right to be just or unjust, partisan or non-partisan, true or false, in news columns and editorial columns." Over time, then, the press has improved.

Answers to unfriendly critics of the mass communication industry are inextricably bound up in the chicken-egg dilemma of what the media cause and what the media reflect. But even today, perhaps, the judgment of Thomas Jefferson could be justified: "Were it left to me to decide whether we should have a government without newspapers, or newspapers without a government, I should not hesitate a moment to prefer the latter." We can guess that Jefferson would have been willing to add the newer, nonprint media of motion pictures, radio, and television to his statement.

SUGGESTED READING

CHAFEE, ZECHARIAH. *Free Speech in the United States.* Cambridge, Mass.: Harvard, 1941.
EMERY, EDWIN. *The Press and America.* Englewood Cliffs, N.J.: Prentice-Hall, 1962.
EMERY, WALTER B. *Broadcasting and Government.* East Lansing, Mich.: Mich. State, 1961.

LEVY, LEONARD W. *Legacy of Suppression.* Cambridge, Mass.: Belknap Press (Harvard), 1960.

MOTT, FRANK LUTHER. *American Journalism.* New York: Macmillan, 1960.

SIEBERT, FREDRICK S. *Freedom of the Press in England, 1476–1776.* Urbana, Ill.: Univ. of Ill., 1952.

SMITH, JAMES MORTON. *Freedom's Fetters.* Ithaca, N.Y.: Cornell, 1956.

SWANBERG, W. A. *Citizen Hearst.* New York: Scribner, 1961.

★ Index